In this ground-breaking book, Joseph M. Bradley focuses on aspects of the story of the Irish in Scotland as seen through a number of cultural, social and political strands.

This is achieved by surveying the history of the Gaelic Athletic Association in Scotland. The G.A.A. is the biggest and most significant cultural and sporting organisation in Ireland. It has also been important wherever sizeable numbers of the Irish have settled and has been present in Scotland since the Irish in Glasgow founded the Red Hugh O'Neill Gaelic Athletic Club in 1897.

By looking at the G.A.A. and situating it within the larger story of the Irish in Scotland, Bradley adds to our knowledge and understanding of this community; a community that comprises Scotland's greatest single group of immigrant descent: a community that in the new millennium partly reflects Scotland's status as a multi-ethnic and multi-cultural society.

Joseph M. Bradley is lecturer in Sports Studies at the University of Stirling. He has published extensively about the links between sport and society, including books, academic papers and in the press.

previous books by the author

Ethnic and Religious Identity in Modern Scotland (Avebury, 1995)

Sport, Culture, Politics and Scottish Society (John Donald 1998)

Sport Worlds: A Sociological Perspective (Human Kinetics, 2002)

Celtic Minded: essays on religion, politics, society, identity and football (Argyll Publishing, 2004)

Celtic Minded 2: essays on Celtic Football Culture and Identity (Argyll Publishing, 2006)

The Gaelic Athletic Association and Irishness in Scotland

History, Ethnicity, Politics, Culture & Identity

Joseph M Bradley

Argyll Publishing

First Published by
Argyll Publishing
Glendaruel
Argyll PA22 3AE
Scotland
www.argyllpublishing.com

A previous version of this book was published under the title *Sport, Culture, Politics and Scottish Society – Irish Immigrants and the Gaelic Athletic Association* (John Donald, 1998)

British Library Cataloguing-in-Publication Data.
A catalogue record for this book is available from the British Library.

ISBN 978 1 908134 01 3

Printing & Binding Bell & Bain Ltd, Glasgow

Dedicated to those who perished as a consequence
of the Great Irish Famine of 1845-51
and the descendents of those who survived amidst the Irish diaspora.

Contents

ACKNOWLEDGEMENTS

The assistance of the many individuals who supplied information and photographic material, and in other ways contributed to this book, is gratefully acknowledged. Thanks to past and present players, managers, officials and supporters of Gaelic clubs and the Gaelic Athletic Association in Scotland, who by virtue of their voluntary efforts, activities, enthusiasm and passion, have made this work possible. In addition, the financial support of Alexander, Jubb and Taylor of Glasgow, solicitors to the G.A.A. in Scotland, has also contributed to the provision of the research that has made this project possible. Similarly, the support of former G.A.A. Uachtarán Séan Kelly and the Gaelic Athletic Association in Ireland is deeply acknowledged, as is that of Decent Suit Productions and RMG Chart Entertainment Ltd, Ireland.

Go raibh maith agaibh.

Introduction

The Gaelic Athletic Association (G.A.A.) is a remarkably significant sporting and cultural body in Ireland that has become an important symbol and expression of Irishness since the late nineteenth century. The G.A.A. has also had resonance for many Irish and their offspring abroad in the Irish diaspora. This book focuses on the history, culture, politics and identity of the Gaelic Athletic Association in Scotland. Although there are many parts to the story of the G.A.A. in Ireland and abroad that are comparable, accounts in Scotland also reflects the variations that exist in terms of the distinctiveness of the Irish diasporic experience.

Like any sporting body, the G.A.A. provides an environment to experience sport as an exhilarating fitness- and health-imparting pasttime that also offers an opportunity to socialise and compete in various ways and at numerous levels. However, although these are intrinsic to its attractions, the G.A.A. exists as much more than this. Reflecting the substantial and more wide-ranging features of the Association, as Professor John Hoberman states, 'sport has no intrinsic value structure, but it is a ready and flexible vehicle through which ideological associations can be reinforced'.[1]

With this perspective in mind, this book utilises sport generally, and the history of G.A.A. specifically, as a means to enhance our understanding of aspects of the experience of the Irish diaspora in Scotland. To this end it examines the G.A.A. as seen through the constellation of cultural, social and political circumstances that have shaped its development in Scotland since the first recorded founding of a G.A.A. club in 1897. Importantly, and constituting a substantial part of this book, this also enables us to look at features of the multi-generational Irish community that in the early twenty first century comprises Scotland's greatest single group of immigrant descent.

This book aspires to inform the Irish who live on the island of Ireland about a noteworthy part of their diaspora. It also seeks to assist in the pursuit of an understanding that facilitates progress towards a more knowledgeable and genuinely multi-cultural Scotland.

1. John Hoberman, 'Sport and Political Ideology', Heinemann, London, 1984, from Sugden and Bairner, 1993, p10.

Part 1
History

Chapter 1

The Significance of Sport

THE STUDY OF SPORT

In recent decades, sports history, sociology and general studies have undergone major transformation. Apart from a growth in studies and research in sports science, a growing literature on the links between politics, culture, nation, identity and sport is evident. It is widely recognised that sport provides both a window and a mirror for the study of society.

SPORT IN HISTORY

It is possible that prehistoric peoples engaged in organised sport. By the time sport was organised in Roman and Greek societies several features began to resemble sport as we recognise it today. By the Middle Ages sport had changed substantially and was organised mainly by the nobility or the peasant masses. Many of the events and competitions that dominate contemporary world sport have a peasant background, including soccer, rugby, baseball, cricket and Gaelic games. In a wider European sense, the Industrial Revolution finally helped shape much of the sport experienced in the western world today.

Sport has long served a number of different functions within societies although there have always been physically expressive, artistic and competitive roles involved in sporting activities. In Greece for example spiritual and supernatural beliefs appear to have been the main functions. Wealth was also an important prerequisite to sporting participation in ancient Greece and this stratification was added to by the dominance of male athletes as opposed to female ones. Eventually, sport in Greece gradually became more visible, popular, political and even commercial.

The sporting spectacles of early Rome were designed to entertain and occupy the masses. They functioned as symbols of power for political leaders while they also became avenues for the disposal of troublesome sections of the population like Christians, criminals or rebellious parties. They also functioned as occasions for training the military might of the Empire.

During the Middle Ages (AD 500 to 1300) 'sporting' tournaments were held by the ruling military classes primarily as ways to entertain but also to serve as a means of military training. These same classes viewed the more popular activities pursued by the peasants as often violent and brutal, functioning as safety valves for discontent. For Coakley, the warlike nature of many of these activities was gradually 'softened by colourful ceremonies and pageantry, and entertainment and chivalry took priority'.[1]

From the Ancient Greeks and Romans, from the Middle Ages through the Industrial Revolution and on to the globalised and capitalist world of today, sport has provided exercise, artistry, competition, organisation and entertainment. Nevertheless, some of sport's other important functions – namely, displaying national and ideological expression, resistance, dominance or superiority, asserting a form of control and bringing together an otherwise diverse group of people to display a sense of community – have also been themes throughout the history of sport.

SPORT AS MIRROR AND WINDOW

Apart from their artistic, competitive and physical attributes, sport has gained a profound influence on modern lifestyles, both in terms of active participation and spectating. For Coakley:

> sports have never been so pervasive and influential in the lives of people

> as they are in many societies today, and never before have physical activities and games been so closely linked to profit making, character building, patriotism, and personal health. Organised sports in the United States have become a combination of business, entertainment, education, moral training, masculinity rituals, technology transfer, declarations of identity, and endorsements of allegiance to countries and corporate sponsors.[2]

It is the capacity of sport to embody, actualise and express a multiplicity of identities; national, cultural, ethnic, religious, social, political, economic and community, that forms much of the underlying rationale for this book. Sport can be seen to achieve this in ways that few other social manifestations can. This has been recognised by sociologists of sport. Giulianotti for example states that:

> The sky-blue shirt was proof of the existence of the nation: Uruguay was not a mistake. Football pulled this little country out of the shadows of universal anonymity.[3]

Historian and social commentator, Eric Hobsbawm, expressed a similar sentiment regarding his recognition of soccer as a site for the construction, expression and imagining of national identity. Hobsbawm made the observation that the identity of a nation of millions 'seems more real as a team of eleven named people'.[4]

Hobsbawm's observation links to the work of Benedict Anderson who is amongst those who have debated questions of imagined communities, stressing that human identity is a social construct.[5] This means that little is inevitable concerning identity except that it is imagined in the context of time, circumstances and environment. Both notions have passed into the discourse of sports research and prove useful to our consideration of the identities involved in sport.

Notions of all communities are myths and the contradictions of the myth are lived through the description and language of the imagined community. Such communities, even the smallest ones, will never know most of their fellow members, meet them, or even hear of them, yet in the minds of each lives the image of their communion. They are connected though never acquainted. This is not to mean that they are false – that is not the meaning of the word myth in this context. But it does mean that communities are distinguished by the style in which they are imagined. This in turn means that social and cultural identities are taught, learned and experienced, consciously or unconsciously.

Communication and community construction come through the depth and range of symbols or practices that unite, effectively forming alliances. Usually, this originates with religion, ethnicity and civic or national identity. Originating from common features, this in turn leads to a sense of place, of belonging, or of difference vis a vis a constructed 'other'. One way this can become articulated and manifest is through sport. Sport has become one of the greatest indicators and symbols of not only identity but also of community.

Related to this, and further indicating the importance of sport in the modern world, is the fact that sport has the capacity to reflect and acquire political, cultural, religious, national, ethnic and civic characteristics. At a basic level these can be expressed through emblems, flags, supporter songs, t-shirts and music. These are all means of social communication, internally within the community and externally to those outside the community.

SPORT AS COMMUNITY, PASSION AND POLITICS

The idea of the imagined community allows us to begin to understand the construction of human togetherness as well as distinctiveness. Whether this is within nations, cities, towns, or with reference to religions, languages or cultures, is not important here. The essential point is that all communities are socially constructed using these characteristics as the basis and legitimacy for their making. They do not remain secret and indeed, seemingly require to be expressed in some form. One of the main forms of expression for the imagined community that has developed across the globe has been sport.

This need for expression means that not only is identity important to sport but so also is passion. It is difficult to see how many sports could survive the generations without their ability to stir countless passions. The crowds that flock to, or watch on television, the final of the Super-Bowl, the soccer World Cup and the Olympics, show that at the highest levels, sport can excite some of the greatest passions.

Religion, politics, economy, class, tradition, cultural practices and beliefs, all have a role to play in sport. All of these can evoke passion. Passion involves enthusiasm, emotion, hate, love, anger, intensity, affection, fanaticism, partiality, spirit, hunger and desire. In turn these can be witnessed in sport. They can be controlled and positive or they can be misplaced and negative. Passion has helped sustain sport into the twenty first century. It is the main factor in the creation of anticipation and atmosphere at sporting occasions. It can be a source of friendship or a site for confronting an enemy. It can be both of these simultaneously. It helps provide the very lifeblood of sporting dedication and involvement. Without passion, the cultural, political and social dimensions of sport would all disappear: Without passion, sport would be 'limited' to exercise and health and, essential as they are, would have little meaning beyond these.

An alternative view of sport might argue that with such an investment, it might be possible that sport can actually be a diversion from other things that have more substance and which are more fundamental to human life and progress. Sport might be seen to sap the thoughts and energies of people to an extent that it serves only those who retain economic, social, political and ideological power in societies.

An example of this might lie again with the former Soviet Union where repression and suffering were masked, as citizens believed the contrivances of the state machine. This was an existence where the state's ideology was a substitute for original thinking, an opiate of the people, and where as one worker explained, 'all we could do was chat over a beer, and we were far more interested in sport'.[6] Connecting soccer to politics Scottish National Party member Jim Sillars implied a similar link when he criticised the Scottish international team's followers as being 'ninety-minute patriots'. Other commentators think similarly and see sport as having a distracting or dysfunctional role in the serious business of life, particularly political and cultural aspects. For Sillars, and Marxist commentators like Miliband and Hobsbawm,[7] there is a belief that sport has a part to play in a culture of evasion, that is, a substitute for involvement or substantial concern with issues which may be more intrinsically fundamental to the economic, social and political orders.

Nonetheless, sport can also serve a positive and confidence building purpose even at the level of national and international politics and culture. The place of boxing in Cuba serves as an example of how sport can gain political and cultural significance. Since the Revolution of 1959, under Fidel Castro, Cuba has grown to be a world leader in amateur boxing. This has been achieved in the context of continued US involvement in the condition and affairs of the state of Cuba: historically a situation bitterly resented by many Cubans.

In the period after the revolution Castro began to influence Cuban sport. For a number of decades Cuba has invested heavily in its athletes. From the early 1960s Castro aimed to bring sport to the masses as well as produce champions. Professional boxing was outlawed but at an amateur level the sport became one of the key targets of the new regime and was viewed as having the capacity to increase Cuban achievement and produce Olympic champions.[8] This would serve the purpose of producing amateur victors who would participate purely for the love of country and people. In itself, this was an ideological foresight. The place of boxing in Cuba invoked visions of Cuba's new and 'successful' socialist identity. Nationalism and socialism have been carried on the back of Cuban boxing successes and the place of boxing in Cuban society has been invoked as a metaphor for the dominant ideology. Isolated, and under a perceived constant cultural and economic attack by the USA, continued boxing successes serve to raise the esteem of Cubans while showing the rest of the world that socialism can win in the face of hegemonic capitalism.

Although such ideological nuances can be drawn and constructed from many sporting occasions in other countries over hundreds of years, the ideological clash through sport between East and West during the years of the Cold War, serve as an apposite example of how intense and significant these struggles can become. Cuban socialism's conflict with capitalist USA has many theatres and the place of sport, particularly boxing, in this struggle, has become crucial for many Cubans.

Sugden and Bairner state, sport is 'an important bridge between the individual and society'.[9] Where a particular sport is deemed important, it is unlikely to remain detached and autonomous from the rest of society, including its politics. Indeed, histories of sporting institutions show that without social, communal or political emotion and definition, sport is unlikely to have gained its present status or importance in the modern world.

SPORT, SOCIAL IDENTITY, ETHNICITY AND DIASPORA

The concept of identity is crucial in the social sciences. Identity helps us understand the social world we construct. However, the term should not be seen as a rigid one: one that absolutely categorises people into one group or the other. In our quest to understand community, it can be used to identify common attributes or beliefs which mark out a group of people as having something quite significant in common with one another and equally, as being different from others.

As well as having physical and psychological significance sport functions as a provider and resource for an array of identities. A significant amount of investment in sport is linked with some of the chief cultural identities found within the human experience; ethnic, civic, national, regional, religious and cultural.

Self and group esteem can be gained through sporting participation and achievement. At an individual level, the identity that one can gain through sport clearly has the capacity to provide income, passage, fame and even fortune. In whatever shape or form, sport as winning, participation, representation, good health, sociability, improving, and as a site of resistance, involves identity. Identity lies at the heart of human fascination with sport, its modern development and its continued appeal.

The creation or appropriation of certain sports as vehicles for identity is symbolic of sports importance for many people. Humans feel a need to display togetherness as well as difference and distinction. Nations, communities and groups require to authenticate, demonstrate and perform identity. This is most obviously achieved through symbols, systems and widely held associations, beliefs and perceptions. The representation of identity through the medium of sport often seems just as important. In obvious but nonetheless sensational and dramatic fashion, the exhibiting of national symbols, music and talents at events like the Olympics and soccer World Cup reflects how sport is a means to achieve this.

Identity in sport can symbolise common ground or become a manifestation of distinctiveness as well as division. Sport has the capacity to provide an environment for people to come together and constitute or further contribute to the idea of community, especially regional, national, ethnic and civic. This coming together can also contribute to the construction of 'the other'. Sport offers a resource for the construction of markers of how people view themselves as well as of how others view them. It contains the potential to be an environment for the construction and the display of identity. Sport also constitutes a medium for self and group analysis as well as an opportunity to view whatever constitutes 'the other'. Sport can represent or identify the existence, presence, origin, authority, possession, loyalty, glory, beliefs, objectives and status of an imagined community.

The concept of ethnicity might be considered in terms of any group which is defined by shared cultural background, religion, or national origin, or some combination of these categories, and which results in a common social psychological referent. Schermerhorn defines an ethnic group as:

> a collectivity within a larger society having real or putative common ancestry: memories of a shared historical past, and a cultural focus on one or more symbolic elements defined as the epitome of their peoplehood. Examples of such symbolic elements are: kinship patterns, physical contiguity (as in localism or sectionalism), religious affiliation, language or dialect forms, tribal affiliation, nationality, phenotypical features, or any combination of these.[10]

This reflects that individual and collective identities are not exclusively defined by the nation-state or nationalism. Ethnicity and ethnic identities can be just as important. Sport provides an arena for observing features of ethnic identities. The linking of ethnicity and sport also provides us with an avenue to study societies that contain groups of people with varying origins as well as to how these distinctions are managed.

Parkes discusses Azoy's references to the significance of Buzkashi tournaments, a highly dramatized equestrian game in Northern Afghanistan. There, the minority Uzbeks. . .

> exploit these tournaments as one means to wrest a distinctive identity, to convey their own regional aspirations of rugged autonomy from the alien hegemony of Pashtun officials in the capital, Kabul.[11]

Ethnic identity is therefore forged within this context.

McPherson, Curtis and Loy, argue that in the USA, connections between sport and ethnicity often follow the patterns of immigration of the period in question.[12] So, apart from Scots and Anglo-Saxons, most of the early American football players were German, Irish or Jewish, to be followed by eastern and southern Europeans who immigrated in the late 1800s and early 1900s. Like boxing, once dominated by the Irish, many of those who now dominate football are Afro-Americans, this group being the latest to achieve in this arena of American life. As far as Hispanics in the USA are concerned, little attention has been given to their contribution to American sport while Native Americans or Indians have experienced their own struggles. For Coakley, the use of names like Washington Redskins for football teams has served. . .

> to perpetuate stereotypes that have contributed to the powerlessness, poverty, unemployment, alcoholism, and dependency of many native peoples in the United States.[13]

One of Europe's outstanding 'ethnic' problems is that which affects Spain. Amid the complexity of Spanish history and society exist a number of ethnic identities based significantly on a strong sense of culture, pro-centralist Spanish state or anti-centralist regionalism. In the Catalan region of Spain, Barcelona Football Club has traditionally been a vehicle for the display of Catalan symbols that contest centralist Spanishness in favour of a more meaningful regional ethnic identity. Likewise, in the northern part of the country Athletic Bilbao has become the quintessential Basque team, virtually being viewed as the region's 'national' representatives. Soccer in Spain is but one example of sport providing a site for the manifestation of distinctive ethnic characteristics as well as expressions of hegemonic state identities.

Experiences in other countries, amongst other diasporic communities, can be important to our knowledge and understanding of Irish cultural and sporting accounts in Scotland. This can be illustrated in the case of the many British-born Pakistanis for whom cricket provides an ethnic space and a source and a manifestation of their connections with the country of their forefathers and families. Cricket is part of popular culture and provides the British-born Pakistani diasporic community with a public arena to display distinctiveness and otherness. For many members of this community, cricket might also be considered a space for empowerment and public celebration where these may be otherwise lacking for many British-born Pakistanis in British society.

In April 1992 the Pakistan international cricket team, captained by Imran Khan, won the World Cup Limited Overs Cricket Competition in Sydney. A young Pakistani, born and bred in Britain, told his English friends, 'I'm proud to be British but when it comes down to the hard core, I'm really Pakistani'. Another celebrating young man told a Guardian reporter, 'if you cut my wrists green blood will come out'. The Pakistani flag is green, the colour of Islam. When young British-born Pakistanis go to see the Pakistan national team play cricket in Britain their cry is often, 'Pakistan zindabad, Islam zindabad, Pakistan forever, Islam forever'.[14]

A similar set of social constructions and meanings arises for the Croatian diaspora in Australia in relation to football. Jones and Moore state that for the Croatian community in Australia:

> The soccer ground becomes a focus for a dispersed ethnic community . . . For the normally residentially dispersed supporters, it is the soccer fixture that has become a major rationale for coming together as a group and publicly expressing their shared ethnicity.[15]

The importance of soccer for the community network was highlighted by one member who believed:

> In the Croatian community everything is tied together, church, family,

> social functions, football whether or not you're interested in football you're interested in Sydney Croatia's result.[16]

For those of the Croatian diaspora in Australia who build much of their social life around soccer and in particular Sydney United-Croatia, this environment provides and sustains a social setting based on kinship, friendship, shared experience and mutual understanding. Within Australian soccer people exercise their Croatian ethnicity as a central characteristic of the existence and nature of such clubs. In one sense the involvement of Croatians in Australian soccer allows them to enjoy a communal experience, a home from home as one fan put it.[17] As Bale might say, the Croatian sports centre based on soccer is a much-loved space that provides a sense of place where the person belongs as an individual and as a member of a community.[18] This is important given their existence as part of a diaspora. This is a primary manifestation of the Croatian diaspora in Australia and is further evidence of the way sport can become an expression and reflection of ethnicity and communal solidarity.

Sport is partly symptomatic of society. It might be argued that the connections and links between sport and culture, sport and nationalism, sport and economy, sport and the media, sport and religion, sport and youths, sport and politics, sport and race, sport and community and sport, identity and diaspora, all reflect that fact.

SPORT AND IRISHNESS

For hundreds of years conflict has significantly shaped and characterised relations between Ireland as colonised and Britain as coloniser. As a result many of the identities constructed in Ireland have been expressed within a context of a struggle to resist and expel British influences and hegemony. These struggles have also witnessed manifestations through sport.

Having knowledge of Ireland's conquest and domination by the British is crucial to understanding the position of the Irish and their offspring within British society. This arrangement has traditionally been one of subordination resulting from the imperialism of the English throne towards Ireland with a series of military and political invasions from the twelfth century onwards. Edward Said has stated that from this time a process began which engendered a persistent cultural attitude towards Ireland as a place whose inhabitants were perceived as a barbarian and degenerate race thus justifying invasion and subordination.[19] With the Union of the Scottish and English crowns in 1603 (and in 1707 the Union of the Scottish and English Parliaments), the English colonisation of Ireland became a British process. This resulted in a further more successful plantation of Ireland by British Protestant settlers who came mainly from Scotland and who were settled in Ulster under favourable terms:

> in exchange for swearing allegiance to the Crown and agreeing not to inter-marry or learn the language of the native Irish.[20]

For one sociologist, British colonisation in Ireland has been as imperialistic as anything the great powers have done anywhere in the world.[21] This imperialism can also be seen to represent the introduction of colonial, political and religiously inspired racism and prejudice into Ireland. Reference to the colonisation of Ireland is important to a contextual understanding of issues of racism and sectarianism within Scottish society. The descendents of the people who were colonised and subjugated are now either living on the island of Ireland or are part of the worldwide Irish diaspora that includes Scotland's community of Irish descent.

The study of sport can expose to us to knowledge of history as well as many aspects of people and society. Closer analysis, observation and research can enlighten us to the capacity of sport not only to be fulfilling in the sense of competition, artistic display or in terms of health, fitness and self and community esteem, but a sociological approach to the study of sport can also demonstrate to us the potential of sport to be significant for nation, economics, community, politics, culture and social identities.

This book uses sport to explore and illuminate aspects of Irishness on the island of Ireland as well as beyond in the Irish diaspora. It is also considers the survival and expression of Irish identity through sport.

For over one hundred years identity in much of Ireland has often been defined with a significant strain of passion for Gaelic sports. This passion has invoked nationalist, political, cultural, as well as purely sporting sensibilities. For Irish 'gaels' many of these passions came together with the formation of the Gaelic Athletic Association in 1884. The G.A.A. is part of the history, culture and political nature of modern Ireland. It forms part of the story of the people of Ireland, including its diaspora, and it reflects on activities that run deep in the Irish consciousness. The Gaelic sports body, the G.A.A., assumes a commanding presence in Irish life. In addition, the G.A.A. has seen its influence spread among the Irish in the USA and Britain, and its games have been played in almost every country that has experienced a sizeable Irish presence.

This book focuses on one part of the Irish diaspora, the Irish and those of Irish descent, and uses Gaelic sport to explore aspects of the story of the Irish in Scotland. Using the focus of Ireland's Gaelic sporting traditions, the aim of this work is to advance our knowledge and understanding of not only those sporting traditions but also of the Irish abroad, in particular, aspects of the Irish diaspora in Scotland: a multi-generational community extending from the mid-nineteenth century until the present day.

Conquest, colonisation and the resultant conflict in Ireland's history, has meant that culture and identity amongst the Irish has long been characterised by questions of a broadly political nature. For this reason, and particularly because of the roots and history of the Gaelic Athletic Association, politics has an important contribution in any account of the G.A.A. as well as of the Irish diaspora in general. This book uses sport to examine some of the social, cultural and political experiences and perspectives of the Irish in Scotland.

This work reflects on the origins, importance and character of the Gaelic Athletic Association in both Ireland and Scotland. Against this background of Irish and Scottish historical development, it examines the location and participants in Gaelic games in Scotland as well as registering who was present and who achieved what in Irish sporting, cultural and political contexts. This has as much to do with recording aspects of familial histories as it has with gaining further insight into the individuals and communities involved. This book is a contribution to an historical, social and political understanding of the Irish in Scotland, the country's largest multi-generational ethnic community.[22]

1. Coakley, 1998, p48.
2. Ibid, p85.
3. Giulianotti , 2000, p134.
4. Hobsbawm , 1990, p43.
5. Anderson, 1991.
6. BBC 1997.
7. See Jarvie and Walker, 1994, p1.
8. Sugden, 1996, pp131-171.
9. Sugden and Bairner, 1993, p9.
10. 1970, p12.
11. 1996, p43.
12. 1989, p208.
13. 1998, p272.
14. Werbner, 1996.
15. Jones and Moore, 1994.
16. Hughson, 1997.
17. Ibid.
18. Ibid.
19. Mac an Ghaill, 2001.
20. Audrey, 2000.
21. Jacobs 2005.
22. Devine, 1991.

Chapter 2

A history of Gaelic sport

ORIGINS AND EVOLUTION

In its varying forms and styles the Irish sport of hurling has a history going back at least two thousand years. The tribes and heroes of ancient Ireland's sagas – the Firbolgs, Tuatha de Danaan, the Red Branch Knights and Cuchulainn – have all made their mark in the story of hurling and this has engendered the game with a modern nationalist mystique. The Brehon laws, Ireland's first legal system, 'declared that there should be compensation in cases where people died as a result of hurling accidents', while,

> hurling is accorded a prominent place in Irish folklore and legend where it is depicted as an aristocratic or even royal game.[1]

There was an attempt to ban the game in the fourteenth century under the colonial administration's 'Statutes of Kilkenny'. Again in 1527 the 'Statute of Galway' ordered that no hurling should take place whilst the 1695 Sunday Observance Act enacted, 'that no person or persons whatsoever, shall play or exercise any hurling'.[2] Although acts like the Statutes of Kilkenny and of Galway were meant to dissuade early English colonists from adopting Irish ways and becoming 'more Irish than the Irish', in creating these laws the forces of conquest in Ireland also made clear their intention to subvert Irish pastimes. Thus, for many centuries, even before the birth of the Gaelic Athletic Association, sport in Ireland exhibited resonances that were linked to identity, culture and politics.

In terms of the development of Gaelic sport, by the eighteenth century it is clear there were two principal, and regionally distinct, versions of hurling in Ireland. The northern half of the country played the version called caman, anglicised as 'commons'. The southern half of the country played the game known as ioman or baire. The main difference in each version was that the latter was played during the summer with a soft ball or sliothar which could be handled. The version played in the northern part of the country was mainly a winter game in which the ball could not be handled.[3] Although the game today is unrecognisable from its unstructured and often violent antecedents, of all Gaelic sports it is hurling which owes its origins to the Gaelic world of the past.

Gaelic football and other Gaelic sports of camogie, handball and rounders, have a more recent history. In football, there are few references before the 1600s, but these are more frequent by the late 1700s.[4] Tipperary, Clare, Wexford, Wicklow, Monaghan, Armagh and Donegal are some of the counties from where there are reports of both hurling and football matches from the early modern period. In addition, by the time of the organisation of Irish sports in the late nineteenth century, it was probably football as opposed to hurling that was more in need of preservation and cultivation. Even though the Famine of the mid-nineteenth century killed over one million people, prompted the mass emigration of at least one million more, demoralised those who survived and almost destroyed the rural social system, in one form or another, Gaelic sport survived.

From the twelfth century, few comments regarding social or political developments in Ireland can be made without reference to the context of Ireland's relationship with England, and subsequently, Britain: Gaelic sports are no different. Ireland's link with Britain was of a complex colonial nature. Subject to rule from London, this relationship invariably had a vast number of economic, social, cultural and political consequences for the people of the island. One of the results of this domination was that by the late nineteenth century, as organised sport began to develop in much of Europe as a result of the extension of the recreational aspects of contemporary lifestyles, in Ireland regulated sport was largely the preserve of the upper and middle classes. These classes were invariably recognised by the rest of the population as British, Colonist and Unionist. Controlled by those who retained privilege and power, this meant that organised sport in Ireland also served as a vehicle for the promotion of British and Unionist identities and power. The rest of the population demoralised and lacking resources, were largely excluded from regulated sport.

Features of life in Ireland considered worthwhile and held in esteem were inevitably British influenced. Colonial Ireland was multi-faceted in its anglicisation. Sugden and Bairner emphasise that:

> While British domination had always been challenged by the indigenous population, only gradually did this resistance take an overtly nationalist form. Sensitive to the threat of emergent Irish nationalism, the British endeavoured to suppress expressions of Gaelic culture. Part of this programme included the discouragement or prohibition of Gaelic games. At the same time distinctively Anglophile sports, introduced into Ireland by settlers and the agents of the Crown, and encouraged by British landlords, grew in popularity. In addition to these factors the devastating effects of famine pushed Gaelic games nearer to extinction.[5]

As a cultural, sporting and political reaction to this state of affairs, the G.A.A. was founded in 1884.

> On All Saints' Day, 1 November 1884, a small group of men met in the billiard room of Miss Hayes Commercial Hotel, Thurles; they formally founded 'The Gaelic Athletic Association for the Preservation and Cultivation of National Pastimes', ever since known as the Gaelic Athletic Association or, more familiarly, the G.A.A. [6]

Michael Cusack, Pat Nally and Maurice Davin among others, became synonymous with the Association's beginnings. Its patrons, Michael Davitt (founder of the Land League), Charles Stewart Parnell (leader of the Irish Parliamentary Party) and Archbishop Croke (Archbishop of Cashel) became equally associated with the origins of the new organisation. A letter received at the founding of the Association from Archbishop Croke remains an important statement with regards to the G.A.A.

> . . . if we continue travelling for the next score years in the same direction that we have been going in for some time past, condemning

> the sports that were practised by our forefathers, effacing our national features as though we were ashamed of them. . . we had better at once, and publicly, abjure our nationality, clap hands for joy at sight of the Union Jack and place 'England's bloody red' exultantly above the green. . . [7]

Croke was also disturbed at the sight of 'youths and young men lolling by the roadside or sneaking about with their hands in their pockets, and with humps on them. . . '[8] Further, Croke made it known that although he supported Irish sports, especially at the expense of the growing British domination of the country, he felt sure that there was room for all recreation: he had no wish to deny other sports and pastimes simply because they were not national. Michael Davitt stressed that as far as he could interpret, the G.A.A. did not begin with any great political ideal though its aims were national.

> When the Gaelic Association movement was first projected. . . the idea was national and not political. It was intended to counteract to some extent the denationalising work and tendencies of systems specifically framed to destroy every remnant of our Celtic institutions.[9]

Davitt's involvement with the new Association not surprisingly drew vitriol from the London Daily Telegraph, the paper claiming that a taste for agrarian crime would not be a hindrance to anyone wishing to join the new body.[10]

The idea of political assertion aligning itself with any national project during these years in Ireland seems inevitable. Mullan writes that conflict between native and coloniser over scarce economic resources and occupational life chances. . .

> established a set of conditions that, by the 1880s, undermined any possibility for the peaceful integration of modern sports.[11]

For Tierney:

> the founding and consolidation of the G.A.A. was part of the social revolution, perhaps its most vital expression. Popular sports, it was said, should be open to all and should be organised by the people not by the ruling class. Here was democracy working its way into rural Ireland, asserting the rights of the Irish people to control their own pastimes. . . Working class people might watch while the gentry hunted, shot or played tennis, but they must not be allowed to compete. The same

> applied in athletics, where gentlemen could not imagine themselves having to compete against artisans or agricultural labourers. . . The G.A.A. hoped to provide a counterblast to the existing class distinction in sport.[12]

Holt states that 'the formation and early history of the GAA is arguably the most striking instance of politics shaping sport in modern history'.[13] Nonetheless, despite the accuracy of this statement, former Fenian Michael Cusack qualified this believing that though every social movement in Ireland was to some extent political, the Gaelic Athletic Association was not a political organisation.[14] In relation to the history and contemporary constitution of the Association the thinking of Cusack is important to understanding the political as well as non-political nature of the G.A.A.

Cusack's great friend and fellow founder of the G.A.A. was a political activist. Patrick Nally, a member of the Irish Republican Brotherhood, one time Connacht representative on the organisation's supreme council, was to die in 1891, incarcerated by the British in Mountjoy prison for his Republican activities. For Holmes, 'Irish nationalism in the nineteenth century revived Gaelic football', whilst the founding of the G.A.A. is seen as an important step in the assertion of an Irish national identity.[15] Cultural and political activists in Ireland demonstrated that they wished to reclaim cultural influence and authority, to begin the process of reviving confidence and pride in being Irish and end the ascendancy and hegemony of British Protestants over Irish Catholics. Likewise, the Association's founding allowed for the inclusion of the impoverished majority in Ireland in sporting activities. Therefore, the G.A.A. also had significance in challenging both the class and the religious domination of sport.

Apart from its objectives of celebrating and promoting Irishness through sport, its political consequences, and its aim of achieving the democratisation of sport in Ireland, the greatest immediate impact of the G.A.A. was the organisation and standardisation of games throughout the country. As a result of the nationalisation of Irish sport, Gaelic games were both saved and rejuvenated. The 'movement' took root rapidly throughout the country. Indeed, using the southern version of hurling as his measure, Michael Cusack codified hurling along the lines of which he had known himself as a child in County Clare. For one writer, 'the founding of the G.A.A. caused something of a social revolution'.[16]

It would be erroneous to see the revival of Gaelic games in simply nationalist or political terms for the movement and organisation of Gaelic games had many facets. Nevertheless, Cusack and his G.A.A. backers also wished to use the game as a nationalising idiom, a symbolic language of identity filling the void created by the speed of anglicisation. Cusack and others recognised that colonialism in Ireland meant that Ireland's was a politicised culture and any attempt to promote and defend Irishness in the context of a country ruled from London within the British Empire was bound to have political resonances, to a greater or lesser extent. To resist British colonialism in Ireland, or to labour to sever that dominance, political, economic, social, cultural or sporting, was a political act or aspiration.

Only a few years after its founding, the G.A.A. was already aligning itself with various groups of evicted tenants as well as in the building of nationalist monuments. Its principal backers were those already active in the nationalist political culture of the time, classically the IRB (Irish Republican Brotherhood). Its spread depended on the active support of an increasingly nationalist Catholic middle class and its social constituency especially included journalists, publicans, schoolteachers, clerks, artisans and clerics.[17]

The revival of Gaelic sports in Ireland also paralleled the success of the codification of games such as soccer and rugby in Britain. With the shortened working week, its associated concept of 'the weekend', rising spending power and a general organisation of society, conditions suited the development and expansion of sporting activity. It can be argued that precedents created and set in place for the development of sport in Britain also helped shape sporting developments and progress in Ireland. The sporting revival in Ireland also mirrored events in Australia and the USA. Indeed, Australian Football and American Football (which are much more recent inventions) can also be viewed partly as avenues for the construction of national identities.

The growth experienced by the G.A.A. was essentially imitative of the

> world-wide phenomena whereby various types of ball-games were becoming an integral part of the social fabric. In effect, the growth of Gaelic games as popular sports paralleled the growth of like organisations in North and South America, in Australia, New Zealand, South Africa, India and much of Europe.[18]

DEVELOPMENT OF THE G.A.A.

Despite the G.A.A.'s initial successes, many practical problems faced the organisation. Years of internal struggles (financial and personal) and the effects of the nationalist question (including Fenian against constitutionalist and Parnellites versus anti-Parnellites) had their negative effects, although the latter also had a positive influence. A patriotic consciousness provided the Association with more members than might otherwise have been the case, while many activists were certainly motivated by the organisation's political nature. Although patriotic and nationalist, the Association also declared its intention of acting independently of political parties, following its own principles and concentrating on its own success and prosperity.[19] The Association experienced years of slumps and difficulties before it became firmly established. By the early 1900s, it came under the guidance of a set of officials who brought a slow, intermittent, but undoubted revival. This revival also coincided with a general upsurge and participation in cultural activities.

As well as the G.A.A. the emergence of the Gaelic League was the most significant feature of the cultural revival then taking place. Founded in Dublin in 1893 the Gaelic League has since strived to preserve Irish as a spoken language, to inspire the study and publication of existing Irish literature and to promote a modern literature in Irish. In this context of diverse cultural developments, Gaelic sports gradually began to emerge as an important facet of Irish identity.

By 1909, with every county represented on Central Council, the G.A.A. finally became a genuine national body. In addition, the fortunes of the Association became increasingly tied with those of the growing Irish Ireland bodies of the Gaelic League and Sinn Féin. Indeed, notwithstanding the obvious positive effects that the contemporary development of organised sport had on demoralised Ireland and the

Association, much of the initial vibrancy of the G.A.A. derived from the political and cultural mood of the time.

In Ireland, the early years of the twentieth century witnessed a new optimism for matters Irish. The Association inherently demonstrated opposition to non-Irish sports at the expense of Irish ones, while the first years of the twentieth century were important for the development of the 'bans'. These referred to 'foreign' or non-Gaelic/non-native games that were seen as contributing to, and driving, the anglicisation of Irish society. They were viewed as continuing the process of the social and cultural colonisation of the country and they provided some of the mechanisms for the obliteration of Irishness. As British sports were seen as an extension of British authority, as well as cultural, social and political domination, to those who engineered the bans, they were viewed as instruments of cultural and national resistance, of encouraging native games and showing loyalty to national culture. Essentially, the first ban amounted to an organised boycott (participating or spectating) of recognised British games played in Ireland. A ban was also imposed on those who wished to participate in Gaelic games but who were considered to be part of the occupying military machine, the Crown Forces that helped enforce the colonisation of the country: that is, members of the British armed forces and the Royal Irish Constabulary (RIC). In relation to the sporting activities that forthwith slowly began to prosper in Ireland, De Burca states:

> These pastimes now passed for ever out of the hands of people like landlords, military and police, who belonged to a class that was opposed both to nationalist political aspirations and to nationalist cultural ideals.[20]

Mullan refers to:

> The pre-GAA Victorian sporting elite – the high professions, the higher echelons of urban commerce, the officer corps of the military and even the upper echelons of the state civil service, by virtue of a centuries-old system of entrenched Protestant control dating from the Penal Laws – were automatically assigned and isolated to the Anglo-Irish camp of modern sport.[21]

Not for the last time this century, and not in any way restricted to

Ireland or the Irish, sport became a repository of a national identity: in this instance, one that contested the dominance of another 'national' identity. The alliance of the G.A.A. in Ireland with nationalism was a regional variation on an almost universal theme. Two decades before the G.A.A. was born, the Czechoslovakian Sokal Gymnastic Association was formed. The threat of Germanization and the loss of Czech cultural identity motivated leading patriots to revive Czech cultural activities:

> to combine physical education and fitness with specific political objectives – primarily the Czech struggle for national independence. . . in the face of Austro-Hungarian political and cultural oppression.[22]

For Mandle:

> the use of sport to proclaim national distinctiveness was a British invention: imitations might be made in Melbourne or Tokyo, even in Thurles, Co Tipperary, but imitations they were, not originals.[23]

Combining with the contemporary cultural revival in Ireland, the Irish language movement of the late nineteenth and early twentieth centuries attracted women activists. In turn, this also encouraged them to perform an important role in the playing and promotion of Gaelic sports. In Ireland, as elsewhere, sport has frequently been a male preserve.[24] However, a women's version of hurling, camogie, developed within the G.A.A. thus establishing women's contribution to the revival of Gaelic sports. The first first recorded camogie game was played in Navan, County Meath in 1904, between Keatings and Cuchulains of Dublin. Cumann Camogaiochta na Gael was founded at a meeting in Dublin's Gresham Hotel in 1932. In Britain, within two years, twelve camogie clubs existed in London, Manchester and Liverpool, although the game experienced a marked decline by the time of war a few years later.

The years following the 1916 Easter Rising saw the G.A.A.'s support for the revolutionary nationalist movement further establish it as an important body in Irish society, although the years of the War of Independence (1919-1921) and the Civil War (1922-23) clearly also had a detrimental effect on the Association in many areas. Indeed, much of the 1930s had passed before Ulster began to function in a similar way to other provinces: the hostility experienced by the Association in

Unionist-dominated Northern Ireland proving a severe handicap to the expression of native Irish culture and identity. In fact, it might be argued that it was only after the foundation of the Irish Free State that the G.A.A. was firmly able to establish itself and henceforth flourish, liberated from any substantial political or military preoccupations or obstacles.

In 1906 there were seven hundred and fifty G.A.A. clubs throughout the country, one thousand three hundred and seventeen by the 1927 Congress and almost two thousand, including those in Britain and the USA, by the mid-1930s. By the second decade of the new century, the G.A.A. was resolutely established as one of the foremost cultural bodies in much of Ireland. For Purcell, the G.A.A. and the League combined to reawaken the ideal of nationhood, a concept beyond party and class.[25]

The 1920s witnessed a rising wave of popularity for the Gaelic sport of handball. During the same period minor (under-age) Gaelic sports competitions began. At the Easter Congress of 1925, National League Games in hurling and football were inaugurated. The same Congress also decided that 'no club be called after a living person or after any political or semi-political organisation'. New peaks in the standard of play, growing attendances and the building of Croke Park in Dublin, also marked important developments. With the welcome entry of Queen's University in Belfast to the G.A.A. in the 1930s and the expansion of third level education in Ireland, university Gaelic sports began to develop.

Since the 1950s, and the 1960s in particular, the parish G.A.A. club in Ireland has become an important focus for leisure and social activities in the locality. The revival of traditional music and other forms of native culture contributed to a growing strength and significance for the G.A.A. An effective administrative machine and adequate financial resources have also contributed to its importance in Irish life.

At the 1971 Easter Congress held in Belfast, the G.A.A. showed a measure of pragmatism when it viewed the Ban on G.A.A. members attending, promoting and participating in foreign games (rugby, soccer, hockey and cricket) as lacking in contemporary necessity and relevance, a feeling that had been emerging for a number of years. Such sports were on the whole now viewed as international rather than British and many people in Ireland wished to participate in world renowed games as well as native ones. Ban policy ceased being viewed as a requirement for the preservation and promotion of native games: Crossmaglen delegate, Con Short, moved that the appropriate rule be deleted from the official guide. The success of the removal of the Ban from the constitution and rules of the G.A.A. became obvious when, during the 1980s and 1990s, there was widespread acclaim shown towards the Irish soccer squad that achieved popularity in international soccer competitions. Ironically, notwithstanding sporting competition from soccer as the pre-eminent world game, the widely acclaimed Irish soccer successes of the 1980s and 1990s also coincided with an era of great progress, classic games and vibrant attendances in Gaelic sports. This has continued throughout the early years of the new millennium and has been particularly the case in the province of Ulster, where many sports-minded people also display a passion for soccer. Nonetheless, since the 1990s, a number of All-Ireland champion teams have emerged from Ulster and a growing interest in Gaelic games in the province revealed to G.A.A. activists fearful that native sports would lose their appeal in the face of British or global influences, that it was possible to exist and prosper side by side with other sports.

In the 1970s the basic aim of the Association was re-defined as:

> the strengthening of the national identity in a 32-county Ireland through the preservation and promotion of Gaelic games and pastimes.[26]

Gaelic games have either been played or continue to be played in countries that have traditionally hosted Irish ex-patriot communities; among them, the USA, Canada, England, New Zealand and Scotland. By the new millennium, there were over three hundred G.A.A. clubs outside of Ireland, including about fifty in New York and a similar number in Australia and New Zealand. Gaelic football is also played in Asia and the Middle-East, while a European County Board, mainly concerned with organising matches between ex-patriot communities in major European cities, was set up in 1999. Britain has the most extensive G.A.A. set-up outside of Ireland with approximately one hundred clubs, dozens of universities and colleges, and several hundred schools participating. The history of the G.A.A. has become one of the outstanding stories of modern sport.

1. Bairner, 2001, p.74-75.
2. From the Irish Parliament of William 111, National Library of Ireland.
3. Whelan, 1993.
4. de Burca, 1980, p. 5.
5. Sugden and Bairner in Allison (edt), 1986, pp. 90-117.
6. Purcell, 1982, p. 10.
7. G.A.A. Official Guide, 1994.
8. Purcell, p. 46.
9. Michael Davitt on the Celtic invasion of America in 'Sport', Dublin, 25/8/1888, from Healy, 1994.
10. Purcell, p. 48.
11. Mullan, 1995, p. 269.
12. Quoted from Mark Tierney, 'Croke of Cashel', in All-Ireland Final match programme, 17/09/95, p. 78.
13. Holt, 1989, p.240.
14. The Fenians was the name of the mid nineteenth century Irish organisation who engaged in military struggle against Britain for an independent Ireland.
15. Holmes, 1994, pp. 81-98.
16. de B˙rca, p. 26.
17. Whelan, pp. 27-31, also Mullan, pp. 268-289.
18. Rouse, 1993, pp. 333-363.
19. Purcell, p. 103.
20. de Burca, p. 100.
21. Mullan, p. 283.
22. Flanagan, 1991, p. 26 in G A Carr, the Spartakiad: Its approach and modification from the mass displays of the Sokol, in the Canadian Journal of history of Sport, vol XV111, May 1987, p. 87.
23. Mandle, 1987, p. 14.
24. Holt, 1996, pp. 231-252.
25. Purcell, p. 123.
26. G.A.A. Rule 1.

Chapter 3

The Irish in Scotland: Political and cultural identity

IMMIGRATION: CHANGING SCOTLAND

Scotland has been home to a migrant Irish population since the early nineteenth century, but particularly since the years of the exodus from Ireland during 'an Gorta Mor' (the Great Hunger) of 1845-51. It has been estimated that around 300,000 refugees migrated to Britain during the Great Irish Famine, with 100,000 arriving in Scotland.[1] Throughout the post-Famine years of the mid-nineteenth century, during the first quarter of the twentieth, and more erratically for the rest of that century, substantial numbers of immigrant Irish entered Scotland, most eventually settling in the west-central belt in and around Lanarkshire and greater Glasgow. During this period, numerous areas in west-central Scotland changed in their religious and social composition as Irish Catholics in particular streamed in. Towns and villages such as Coatbridge, Carfin, Plains, Clelland and Glenboig in Lanarkshire, areas of Glasgow like Calton and the Gorbals, and districts of Paisley, Port Glasgow, Greenock and Dumbarton, absorbed many of these Irish, assisting in their social and economic growth and development.

A number of people who came from Ulster were Protestants whose forebears' roots lay mainly in Scotland and who had been part of various plantations and colonisation periods of Irish/British history. However, there has been little research done with regard to this movement of people.[2] Nonetheless, as the primary identities of this group of migrants have long been a variety of Scottish, Ulster and British in nature, they have integrated and assimilated into the wider communities they settled amongst in Scotland.

By 1851 the census recorded 207,367 Irish-born in Scotland: around seven per cent of the population.[3] By this period McCaffrey estimates that there was around 150,000 Catholics in the country although the figure of 332,000 by 1878 may be a more accurate estimate and a better indicator of the number of Irish Catholics coming to Scotland during the period of Famine and for several decades afterwards.[4]

Proportionately, in relation to the size of the Scottish population, more Irish emigrated to Scotland than to any other country. This figure is striking when one considers that the vast majority of Irish and their offspring eventually settled in a thirty-mile radius around greater Glasgow and Lanarkshire. Collins estimates that around eight per cent of all Irish-born emigrants went to Scotland from 1841 to 1921 and most Irish immigration to Scotland took place during this time.[5] Although after 1921 emigrant Irish continued to arrive in Scotland, Scotland declined as a significant focus of settlement, although the post-World War II economic boom in Britain increased immigration from Ireland and resulted in thousands of people from Ulster, from Donegal in particular, arriving once more.

COMMUNITY POLITICS AND CULTURAL IDENTITY

Despite a paucity of research on Irish Catholics in Scotland, a number of academic publications indicate several aspects of their experience and is evident that the cause of Irish independence was important to many within the diasporic community in the nineteenth and twentieth centuries. Politics and identity linked to aspirations of Irish independence have always had a strong resonance for the Irish and their offspring in the diaspora, no less amongst those in Scotland. These aspirations and identities are significant in relation to understanding the Irish experience beyond the island of Ireland.

As early as 1823, the few thousand Irish who lived in the Glasgow area formed an offshoot of Daniel O'Connell's Catholic Association, which identified with the political nationalism then stirring at home. The O'Connell Association in the nineteenth century organised a number of street demonstrations whilst during the Daniel O'Connell centenary celebrations in the Partick area of Glasgow in August 1875, Home Rulers were attacked by hundreds of Orangemen and fighting lasted for days.[6]

By the 1870s strong Irish political feelings were evident amongst the by then much larger Irish community in the west-central belt. In November 1871, a Glasgow branch of the Irish national movement, then known as the Home Government Association, was formed and its leader, Isaac Butt MP, was on hand to deliver the local body's inaugural address. In 1893 Ulster Protestant immigrant and nationalist Home Ruler, John Ferguson, was elected to Glasgow Council.

In the late nineteenth century Glasgow, Lanarkshire and their environs, contained noteworthy associations of the Irish National League, then the primary body advocating Irish home rule. Indeed, one of the largest branches of the Home Rule movement in Britain in the 1890s was to be found in the Lanarkshire town of Coatbridge on the outskirts of Glasgow, which was also 'able in one year to donate more funds to the League's treasury than almost any of the great cities'.[7]

Marching and rallying by groups, associations and societies were a widely practised community and cultural activity in early twentieth century Scotland: these were expressions of political, religious, cultural and community solidarity. In 1912, at the annual demonstration of the Ancient Order of Hibernians (AOH) in Hamilton, over 30,000 Irish nationalists were reported to have taken part. Resolutions were passed congratulating Redmond and the Irish National Parliamentary Party, and the meeting resolved to assist them by every means within its power in its endeavours to place the government of Ireland in the hands of the Irish people. After the march:

> the procession of the different contingents, headed by their bands and banners, through the town formed an imposing spectacle, which was witnessed by thousands of spectators. Forty-five different bodies marched in the procession which was led by the famous O'Neill War Pipe Band, Armagh.[8]

A year later, 50,000 Hibernians took part in a procession in Kilmarnock, before being addressed by Belfast nationalist MP and national AOH President, Joseph Devlin.[9]

On 30th August 1919, in the Lanarkshire village of Glenboig, twenty nine male divisions and fourteen female divisions marched in the annual demonstration of the Lanark County.[10] Even in the east of the country, where far fewer Irish settled, a crowd of 500 marched during the summer of 1920: AOH divisions from Cowdenbeath, Lochgelly, Lochore, Dunfermline, Methil, Kelty, Inverkeithing and Cardenden were headed by the Lochgelly Flute Band, political speeches were heard and finance was raised for the Cowdenbeath Church Building Fund.[11]

In 1929, 35,000 people took part at an AOH parade in Dumbarton, 40,000 took part in Hamilton in 1930, 10,000 participated at a rally in Edinburgh in 1931 and 30,000 walked in a demonstration held in the Lanarkshire town of Blantyre in 1932.[12] At one of the last major rallies held in Scotland shortly before the outbreak of World War II, 40,000 people collected to march in the strongly Hibernian village of Carfin, Lanarkshire.[13]

The Irish National Foresters remained important amongst the plethora of Catholic and Irish bodies in Scotland until at least World War II. By 1936 the Foresters still retained over 5,000 in its juvenile section alone.[14] Nevertheless, the growth of the Ancient Order of Hibernians in Scotland rivalled the strength and marching prowess of the Foresters, although membership of both organisations frequently overlapped: the AOH was similar to the Foresters, at least in relation to its members' Catholicity, politics and Irishness, as well as its friendly status. Both organisations demonstrations served a number of functions and they allowed the Irish to congregate, to maintain a sense of community and celebrate Irishness and Catholicity.

Although significant numbers of the Irish diaspora in Scotland attended these later marches, the inter-war period was also a time when many Catholics' Irishness became increasingly privatised due partly to the political and cultural climate of the time. This period was also crucial to expressions of Irishness for many decades thereafter.

There are Scottish, Lithuanian, Italian, Polish and other influences within Catholicism in Scotland, but the vast majority of Catholics in the country originate from Ireland. Early in the new millennium there remained an Irish-born population in Scotland of around 50,000 people and more than 100,000 others who have an Irish-born parent and who constitute the second generation Irish. Nonetheless, most of the Irish community is now third and fourth generation whose grandparents and great-grandparents migrated from Ireland during the second half of the nineteenth and early part of the twentieth centuries. The Irish in Scotland are a multi-generational community.

The Irish community has contributed significantly to many aspects of modern Scottish society; to the rise and establishment of the Labour Party, the building of the country's industrial infrastructure in the shape of roads, railways and shipping, as well as iron, coal and steel production, it has been a significant contributor to the establishment and development of the National Health Service, particularly through nursing, and has influenced the artistic and sporting practices and expressions of Scotland in the shape of acting, popular song, comedy, art, football and boxing. The education sector has been developed in Scotland with a significant contribution from Catholics of Irish descent. These are features that form some of the principal contributions of the Irish to Scottish life.

Nonetheless, the Irishness of this community of Irish migrant origin varies enormously, and like other more indigenous and migrant groups in Scotland, the Irish are not a homogeneous entity or community. Gaelic sport in Scotland provides amongst other things, one avenue to reflect on this community in Scotland at the beginning of the twenty first century.

In this light, although the 1984 G.A.A. centenary celebrations in Ireland were also important for the Association's membership in Glasgow, the occasion was hardly a celebration of the G.A.A.'s place in Irish culture in west central Scotland or amongst the Irish diaspora there. Indeed, not only was the Gaelic Athletic Association of little relevance to most members of that community, so also were Gaelic sports. In Scotland in 1984 the G.A.A. was a small moribund organisation that had little bearing on the Irishness of the wider diaspora. In 1984 the G.A.A. in Scotland had a presence, but it was only as a diminutive organisation that few within the Irish community, even for those who esteemed their Irishness, were aware of.

1. J E Handley, 1964, p197
2. For existing research see McFarland, 1986 and Walker and Gallagher, 1990.
3. Therefore also a figure that underestimated the Irish presence because it did not consider the offspring of those born in Ireland.
4. McCaffrey, 1983, p276.
5. Collins in Devine, 1991.
6. Handley, 1964, p. 257.
7. From John Denvir, The Irish in Britain, from the earliest times to the fall of Parnell, 1892, p. 447, quoted in Gallagher, 1987.
8. Mitchell in Devine (edt), 1995, pp. 31-70.
9. Glasgow Observer, 6/9/1913.
10. Ibid, 26/7/1919.
11. The Star, 17/7/1920 and 21/8/1920.
12. Ibid, 7/9/1929, 6/9/1930, 5/3/1931, 3/9/1932.
13. Ibid, 18/8/1938.
14. The Star, 25/4/1936.

Chapter 4

Birth and evolution: The early G.A.A. in Scotland

GAELIC SPORT AND THE DIASPORA

There is a dearth of records, published research and studies relating to the historical, sociological, political and contemporary experience of the Irish in Scotland. In terms of the early G.A.A. in Ireland, the Association's own records lack depth and structure. In addition, due to the political situation in Ireland at the time and the resultant semi-secrecy within the G.A.A., many of the Association's early records, where these exist, are unreliable.

Nonetheless, it is clear that by the turn of the twentieth century, the G.A.A. was making progress amongst the Irish abroad as well as at home. For example, by the mid-1890s New York had some twenty G.A.A. clubs operating. Notable also is that in the early years of the G.A.A. much of the Gaelic sporting revival often centred on hurling.[1]

Although there are reports of hurling being played in London in 1775, these were rare occurrences.[2] By 1885 the first G.A.A. club in Britain was founded in Wallsend near Newcastle-on-Tyne, an area rich in Irish migrants. In a more formal sense, the Gaelic Athletic Association was founded in London in 1895 though it was around 1903 before Central Council in Dublin began reporting on Gaelic activities in Britain. An early event bridging the Irish Sea occurred in May 1887 when the Celtic Hurling Club of Dublin travelled to Scotland to play Glasgow Cowal Shinty Club at Celtic Park, home of Irish immigrants' sporting soccer champions, Celtic Football Club: Cowal winning 11–2. The return game was held two months later at which Michael Cusack refereed. Again the Scottish team won, this time 2–0.[3] It was not until 1932 that an Irish side gained revenge with a 6–1 defeat of the Scottish representatives at the 1932 Tailteann Games in Dublin.

Reflecting the sense of patriotism often experienced by Gaelic minded people, one of the first teams affiliated to the G.A.A. in London was Robert Emmets Club of Marlybone. The idea of calling a club after a perceived patriot has been a hallmark of G.A.A. clubs since the founding of the Association. When the Tuam Krugers Club was founded in County Galway around 1900, the club's name was a statement with regards British colonialism and the Boer War underway in South Africa and a clear identification with Britain's adversaries in that conflict.[4]

In Ireland in the late nineteenth and early twentieth centuries political awareness and consciousness were among the factors that attracted people towards the G.A.A. A review of Irish and Catholic newspapers in Britain reveals a similar mindset for the Irish in Britain and invariably political resonances had an influence upon G.A.A. activists there. Political activism was important to the development and shaping of the Association and the involvement of many Irish Republican Brotherhood (IRB) members with the G.A.A. reflects this. In London Michael Collins was secretary to Geraldines G.A.C. and treasurer of the London County Board. Collins of course was eventually to rise to national and international prominence as one of the main participants in the pivotal years of the struggle for Irish independence from 1916 to 1922. He fought in the Easter Uprising of 1916, became director of intelligence in during the War of Independence and chief Irish plenipotentiary during the Treaty debate in London.

Sam Maguire, whose name the All-Ireland football trophy bears, was born to a Church of Ireland family in Mallabraga, near Dunmanway Cork in 1879. Maguire was an outstanding footballer who played for Hibernians in London (winning four championships in a row, 1901-1904) and who captained the London County team to three All-Ireland finals between 1900 and 1903. He was elected Chairman of the London County Board in 1907. A member of the Gaelic League, as Major General and Chief Intelligence Officer of the Irish Republican Army in Britain, 'during the war of independence, all major republican operations there were largely under the control of Sam Maguire'.[5] Liam MacCarthy, who was to give his name to the All-Ireland Hurling Championship Trophy, also played Gaelic sports in Britain. He became treasurer of the London County in 1895 and President in 1898. MacCarthy was second generation Irish, born in London of Cork parents who had emigrated to England in 1851. It was MacCarthy who recruited Michael Collins to the republican movement in 1909.

IRISH CULTURAL IDENTITY IN SCOTLAND

In 1895, one of the main Irish Catholic newspapers of the time, The Glasgow Examiner, printed a letter complaining at the lack of Irish cultural activity connecting to the Gaelic revival in Ireland.[6] A positive response seemed forthcoming. The same year, the William O'Brien Gaelic Class was formed which became a branch of the Gaelic League before the year had ended.[7] This event thus marks the establishment of the Gaelic League in Glasgow, only two years after its founding in Dublin. Over the next few years the Gaelic League underwent a significant growth among the Irish communities of greater Glasgow and Lanarkshire.

The first record of a G.A.A. club in Scotland is to be found in 1897. The Glasgow Examiner carried news that:

> a large and enthusiastic meeting of young Irishmen of the city was held in the Young Ireland Hall, 8 Watson Street. . . for the purpose of forming a branch of the Gaelic Athletic Association in Glasgow. . . As this is believed to be the first branch of the G.A.A. ever established in Scotland, the committee hope that Irishmen of the city will rally round them, and, by joining the club, give them encouragement in their efforts. . .

It was agreed by those present that the Red Hugh O'Neill Gaelic Athletic Club be set up to include all branches of Irish national pastimes – hurling, football, running, jumping, boxing, dumb-bell and Indian club exercises, etc.[8] The club was to be non-sectarian and membership was restricted to respectable young men of Irish birth or parentage, and of good moral character.

It is likely that it was the politically active amongst the Irish community who gave birth to the Red Hugh Club. The location for engagements (Young Ireland Hall) was well established as a place for nationalist meetings and there seems to have been some overlap in membership of those of the Irish National League and the new club: John Brolly and Joseph McFaulds (or McFalls) being involved in both bodies. Tom Fergie of the Ormond Club was designated trainer and Mr P Honeyman became president. Other members included Peter McCann, J Healy, W Flanagan, J Keegan, J Moran, H O'Brien, G Glavin, A Gillies, J Neillis, E McGovern and J O'Brien. Nonetheless, although the club was reported as being in regular training and preparing for a match against a London side, reports of hurling activity in Glasgow quickly died.

One of the difficulties inhibiting a Gaelic sporting revival among the ex-patriot community was the growing significance and emphasis on soccer in working class areas of Britain. In the second half of the nineteenth century the growth of soccer was swift as it pervaded and was taken up by communities all over Britain, including by the Irish who were firmly situated within the country's working-class. As was the case generally in Britain and in much of its Empire, sport was to have a growing social and cultural importance during this period and it increasingly began to make news on prominent pages in the popular press. In many ways these developments were mirrored in Ireland with the growth of the Gaelic Athletic Association.

The 'Athletic Notes' column in The Examiner was written by Celtic Chairman John McLaughlin and his focus on Celtic alerted people to the presence of the club helping promote Celtic amongst the Irish communities of the west of Scotland. Other sports such as cycling and athletics attracted some attention in The Examiner, but with a spectrum of sporting events regularly organised at the home of Celtic, and with these sports dominating the relevant newspaper columns, Gaelic sports faced an uphill struggle. The Glasgow Examiner and Glasgow Observer, the main Irish and Catholic media organs of the period, gave their undaunted support to Celtic Football Club. Soccer was booming at the time and these newspapers reflected this.

The Examiner prioritised Irish affairs and events in a way that reflected the immigrant community's close ties and links with events in their homeland, particularly religious, social and political occurrences. Despite this, there were few sports reports emanating from Ireland. Such details were limited though one Examiner account in early 1897 did report on the erecting of a replica 'Cross of Cashel' to the memory of Dr Croke. Croke was seen as, 'one of the most valiant and strenuous defenders of the birthrights of the Irish people'.[9] Despite the sentiments, this report remains one of the few references to the early G.A.A. in Ireland on the part of the Irish Catholic press in Scotland.

Within the immigrant community, Irish political, social and cultural activities were plentiful. The Irish National League, Irish Independent League, Ancient Order of Hibernians and the Irish National Foresters, added to the plethora of Catholic bodies as well as Celtic Football Club, meant that by the end of the nineteenth century, Irishness in Scotland was expressed via an array of outlets.

As the founding of Red Hugh O'Neills G.A.A. club and the establishment of the Gaelic League in Glasgow demonstrated, events in Ireland were reflected in an 'Irish Ireland' response in Scotland. This cultural revival was also reflected in the regular Gaelic League columns that emerged in The Examiner newspaper from August 1896 onwards. By 1897, it was reported that there were seventeen branches of the League in Ireland, four in England as well as one in Glasgow, the latter based in St Francis Parish in the east of the city. In 1899 Padraic Pearse visited Glasgow's League to encourage its growth. On his next visit in 1902 he spoke admiringly of the League in the city.

> Then there was only one branch of the League in the city – the Glasgow branch – which was then in its infancy. Now there were a dozen branches and outside London with its vast Irish population, there was no centre where the language movement had made such progress as in Glasgow.[10]

Pearse was welcomed to Scotland by Glasgow-born Hugh McAleese, who along with his brothers, Cormac and Charles, was also present at the founding of the first branch of the League in Glasgow.[11] In relation to the growth of the Gaelic League in Scotland, Handley informs us:

> By the turn of the century, the Gaelic movement in the West of Scotland had seventeen branches in the Glasgow district. Later years saw the establishment of centres in Paisley, Blantyre, Motherwell, Hamilton, Wishaw, Coatbridge, Carfin, Renton, Kilsyth, Barrhead, Denny, Johnstone, Dumbarton, Ayr, Port Glasgow and Greenock. In the east of Scotland, classes were opened for a time at Dundee, Edinburgh and Leith. . . taught by Glasgow Gaels. . . All labour was voluntary and unpaid. . .[12]

Over the course of the first decades of the new century, the expansion of the Gaelic League in west central Scotland was to be particularly significant in relation to the evolution of Gaelic Athletic Clubs.

The dominance of Celtic Football Club as an Irish cultural and social activity was shown in 1900 when it was reported that there existed the possibility of a new Irish sporting club emerging in Glasgow which would appeal to the followers of Celtic and Hibernian, the latter Irish immigrants' soccer representatives in Edinburgh in the east of the country. However, any potential threat to Celtic was discounted on the basis that the only club that could possibly emerge in the financial climate of the times would be a hurling team and there was no genuine competition on the part of Gaelic sport in Glasgow. One of the important figures involved in the first few years of Celtic Football Club was Member of Parliament, William McKillop, who gifted a cup to the Armagh G.A.A. in 1907. The cup became the Armagh County's Championship trophy until it was replaced and later returned to Scotland in the 1990s to be played for as the O'Fiaich Cup. Regarding the issue of another Irish sporting club in Glasgow, Celtic's John McLaughlin showed a degree of appreciation, if not support, for the growing G.A.A. when he stated in The Examiner:

> Such a club would in no way be antagonistic to the Celts. Indeed, the Celts have already shown their interests in the Gaelic game by bringing over two or three hurling teams from Ireland. If the Gaelic enthusiasts in Glasgow succeeded in forming their teams we have no doubt that the Celts would not be averse to giving the use of the Paradise for the purpose of an exhibition game. Such hurling clubs already exist in London and Manchester and are affiliated to the Central Executive of the Gaelic Athletic Association in Dublin.[13]

In Ireland, Irish Irelanders hoped to reverse many of the features of British influenced colonial Ireland and to reinstate what they perceived as more native ways, including a revival of the Irish language and Gaelic sports. Abroad, in Scotland and elsewhere, Irish Irelanders wished to promote a similar set of values and cultural practices to be learned, preserved and celebrated by the people of the diaspora.

By early 1901 the Rapparees Hurling Club was formed in Glasgow, a club that became one of the most significant founded over the course of the twentieth century. One of the founders of the new club was Proinnsia O'Maonaigh who suggested that they should be called after his former team in Dublin, also the Rapparees. Initial training took place at Woodend Park, Jordanhill, ground of Jordanhill Football Club. Yet again a close association with the Gaelic League in the city is apparent in that subsequent sporting activities were reported alongside League activities. Hurling meetings in Glasgow were also held in the League Rooms in the National Halls, at 52 Castle Bank Street, Partick.

Links with the Gaelic League are further evidenced in an overlap in membership: John Keegan, T McGettrick, and D and P Cronin were some of the members of both the Partick Branch of the Glasgow League and the Rapparees Hurling Club. George Shorten from Ballingeary County Cork, an influential figure in initiating the Rapparees, was also a well-known Gaelic League activist. Shorten returned to Cork in early 1902. Although some Gaelic football was played by the Rapparees as well as efforts to begin a regular team, hurling continued to dominate. The first game participated in by the Rapparees was against the Caledonian Shinty Club at the latter's ground at Possilpark, Glasgow, in May 1901: the Irish side was beaten 5-2 by the Glasgow team.[14]

In March of 1901 the Whiteinch Hurling Club, The Faughs, was formed from the Whiteinch Branch of the Gaelic League. Govandale Park, the ground of the Benburb soccer club, became the new team's home ground. The following month The Examiner reported that a new club, Eire Og, had been formed in Port Glasgow. After the first match held at Battery Park Greenock, between winning side Rapparees and losers Eire Og, both teams finished the day's festivities by singing the rallying songs of the League. A few months later the Cuchulin Hurling

Club began in Polmadie area of the city. In mid 1901 at a meeting in the Grand National Halls, the Rapparees decided to formally affiliate to the Gaelic Athletic Association in Dublin.[15] By the middle of the following year such were the numbers attending Rapparees activities that it was decided to form another club from the excess of players. In May 1902, at a meeting in St Patrick's School, Coatbridge, the Patrick Sarsfield Branch of the Gaelic League initiated a hurling club, again reflecting the close ties in Scotland between the Gaelic League and Gaelic sporting activities as well as the growth of the Irish Ireland movement amongst the diaspora beyond the island of Ireland.

In August a match took place between the newly formed Sarsfields and Rapparees. After the visitors had been taken on tour of local Catholic schools and Churches, the match commenced in the West End Park at Langloan, a strong Irish quarter of Coatbridge. Around three thousand people attended the match won by the visiting club.

In March 1903, the Carfin Branch of the Gaelic League along with local priest Father John O'Dea, a former hurler from the Killaloe Diocese in Clare, organised a hurling match in the village between the Rapparees and Cuchulains. This match took place with the intention of promoting the sport and initiating a team in the area. By now the Rapparees were considered to be the champion hurlers of Scotland. A few months later a Carfin team was successfully started. Called Faug-an-ballaghs (later referred to as Fag-an-Bealach – meaning 'Clear the Way'), they played their first fixture against another Lanarkshire side, Wishaw Shamrocks. This game is noted for the first references in Scotland to goals and points being scored (some previous games involved goals only), a factor relevant to the developing ties with Dublin and the growing standardisation of the rules of the game. This particular game was followed by a Gaelic football match between local Irish miners and railwaymen, won by the former with a one goal advantage.[16] May 1903 witnessed a hurling match in Carfin between the local club and Patrick Sarsfields from Coatbridge. Both clubs' links with the Gaelic League was again apparent in this fixture with around one hundred Gaelic Leaguers accompanying the hurling team from Coatbridge to watch the game in Carfin.

By mid 1903 developments in Irish Gaelic sports in Scotland had begun to gain momentum. This year marks the first mention in records at Croke Park regarding Gaelic sport in Scotland: Central Council of the G.A.A. receiving 'an application from the Scotland County Board for permission to have two representatives from every club on the Central Committee'.[17] With five clubs now affiliated to Dublin, by June there was talk of forming a county board to 'have full jurisdiction over all matches played by affiliated clubs in Scotland'.[18] This was achieved before the month had ended.

The clubs represented at the first meeting of the Glasgow and West of Scotland County Board were; Rapparees (delegates – Murray and Corbett), Wishaw Shamrocks (Moran and McLaughlin), Fag-an-bealachs Carfin (O'Neill and O'Timmoney), Patrick Sarsfields Coatbridge (McCourt and Graham), Finn MacCumhails Anderston and Partick (O'Brien and Dougherty), Hibernians Pollockshaws (McDade and Gallagher) and Cuchulains Polmadie (O'Connor and Hayes). By the time of the first meeting of the new county the following week, the anticipated affiliation by clubs from Greenock and Shettleston took place:[19] nine clubs formed the first county in Scotland in 1903 and Lanarkshire-based Rev John O'Dea was unanimously chosen as president.[20] By July of the same year an organised hurling league was underway.

The first county in Glasgow had high expectations. By August 1903 it was noted by the exiles in Scotland that London had won the All-Ireland hurling title from Cork and suggested that such a feat was possible for the G.A.A. in Scotland a few years hence. With a good year behind them, the Board in Scotland saw themselves to be preparing for the 1904 All-Ireland Championship. Although there were players with no hurling background playing the game, at the time there were also a number of skilled hurlers in the west of Scotland. In late 1903, The Star observed that for a forthcoming game between Rapparees and Wishaw Shamrocks:

> As the majority of the members of both teams have fought and gained honours in many a Gaelic athletic gathering in the old country, a good hurling match should be the result.

The teams taking part were:

Rapparees: Hennessy, Murray, Moroney, Cody, J Ryan, P Ryan, Jas Ryan, Laffan, Linehan, O'Flynn, Devitt, O'Carroll, W Nagle, D Nagle, Shanahan, Herbert and Reid.

Shamrocks: O'Mahoney, Mullane, Regan, Nagle, O'Kelly, McGlynn, O'Brien, Dilworth, Crilly, O'Callaghan, Smith, Murray, Collins, O'Dougherty, Green, O'Kelly and O'Neill.[21]

The surnames of the participants as well as the comments noted from The Star suggests that a number of those playing the game originated from the hurling counties of Munster and generally the southern half of Ireland. One historian believes that many of the Rapparees had played with Tipperary and Cork teams before emigrating to Scotland.[22] Numerous references had been made over the previous few years to Tipperary players in particular making their mark on the game in Glasgow. In one match between Sarsfields of Coatbridge and the Rapparees, a former Tipperary hurler called Delaney who had latterly played with Southern Rovers in Dublin, took part for the Glasgow team.

Progress continued and by the end of the momentous year of 1903 it was reported that two junior hurling clubs had been formed in Lanarkshire, Desmonds in Wishaw and Dalcassians in Carfin. There was also talk of clubs starting in Hamilton and Motherwell and another county board being assembled in Lanarkshire. By early 1905, the G.A.A. in Scotland had acquired the status of a 'Province', which had the same rights and privileges as the other Provinces of Ulster, Connacht, Munster, Leinster and London.

The promotion of the game in Scotland continued apace. During March 1904 the Brian Boroimhe (Brian Boru) Gaelic club from Blantyre in Lanarkshire affiliated to the County. Later in the year, the Blantyre club played its first official football match at Dunbeth Park, the home of Sarsfields from Coatbridge.[23] By the middle of the following year a match was reported between Patrick Sarsfields of Coatbridge and St Margarets' of Airdrie.[24] Around the same time, there was word of Gaelic clubs functioning in Cleland (Lambh Dearg) and Shieldmuir, Motherwell (Lord Edwards).[25]

The Star reported:

> During the coming year there will be plenty opportunities for any Gael who holds the welfare of his national, manly pastime of any account in the reformation of the 'sea divided gael' into a compact and self-reliant nation to take a true man's part.[26]

The theme of true gaels exclusively playing the sports of their ancestors was of course a recurrent one for those involved in Gaelic pastimes. One Gaelic activist in Scotland went so far as to criticise the Irish and Catholic bodies (in this case the Robert Emmet Club and the William O'Brien Branch of the United Irish League) who played soccer amongst themselves or faced other clubs for that purpose. For this particular writer the only way to become a real athlete was to play Gaelic games.[27] Nonetheless, the fact that such obvious politically Irish Ireland bodies like the Emmet and O'Brien associations were playing soccer partly reflected the dominance of that sport, including amongst the Irish community, in Scotland. It also demonstrated that despite the growth in Gaelic sporting activities, at the time many within the Irish community were beginning to look to soccer as a cultural expression of their Irishness. The explosion of soccer clubs within the Irish Catholic communities at the time, particularly in the Glasgow and Lanarkshire areas, is further evidence of this.

Nevertheless, during this period Irish cultural and national identities also found expression in a growing demand for Gaelic sporting activities in Scotland. In June 1905, Scotland and England played a hurling fixture in the city of Liverpool.[28] Ryan, Lanigan and Fitzpatrick were three of the players from Scotland who participated in a game won by the gaels from England. As England's Gaelic representatives from London (whose chairman was Liam McCarthy) had won the All-Ireland only two years previously, the team from Scotland reckoned they had achieved much in a short space of time. As a reflection of this progress, in early 1906 a Gaelic football league got underway. Both hurling and football were played at a special meeting between Ulster and Scotland in Belfast in 1905. At Easter three years later, an England versus Scotland fixture was arranged for London.

The new 'Provincial Board of Scotland' comprised Cunningham and Fitzpatrick from Lanarkshire and Fitzgibbon and Flynn from Glasgow, with Coatbridge representative John McCourt elected President.

McCourt was an energetic cultural activist who was also involved in the Hibernians, the League of the Cross, and the Irish National Foresters among other bodies. McCourt's own club Patrick Sarsfields was affiliated to the Glasgow part of the province, though this is likely to have been as a result of the Lanarkshire Coatbridge club having been in existence prior to the formation of the Lanarkshire board.[29] By early 1906 the Lanarkshire County had nine affiliated clubs including Gaelic football clubs, Sons of Erin from Carfin and St Patricks of Wishaw. Indeed, the board hoped for further expansion of the Association in Scotland. Its members especially looked to the Irish Irelanders of Lanarkshire and from the Ancient Order of Hibernians, who at a convention in Dublin in 1905, pledged to support Gaelic games as well as the Irish language.

The continued expansion of Irish cultural activities in west central Scotland was reflected in the decision of the Provincial Board to compete in both the All-Ireland provincial football and hurling championships of 1906. Over the course of the next few years, football or hurling clubs sprang up in Springburn Glasgow (Clan na Ghaeldhilge), Coatbridge (Eire Og, hurling) and Kinning Park Glasgow (Lambh Dearg, football). Mr Denis Brogan, 'a self-made Donegal tailor',[30] and a well-known member of the Gaelic League, presided over the fund raising gathering that helped launch the latter club.

Brogan's support for the new G.A.A. club again reflected the close ties and frequent overlap in membership of both associations. One branch of the Gaelic League in Glasgow, 'Craobh na nIonmanaidhthe', was viewed as particularly energetic at this time. Its membership was bolstered by a large number of men who had migrated from south-west Ireland, a part of the country where many spoke Irish as their first language. At one point this particular branch provided six language sessions as well as classes in singing and dancing. During March 1906, the Branch also produced two plays, 'An Dochtuir', and 'The Lad from Largymore'.[31] In 1909, it was reported that the same branch entertained eight hundred guests at a Saint Brigid celebration.[32]

By April 1908, The Star reported that young Irishmen had met to form a Gaelic football and hurling club at the Hibernian Hall in Kerse Lane, Falkirk.[33] The founding committee, included Messrs:

W Burke, J Nagle, M Dongan, J O Neill, J Devine, W Byre, P McCann, W McMonagle, P McClosky, M Murphy, P McBride, S Kellagher, P Gormerly and F Gilhooly.

In the same year efforts were made to begin a hurling club in Dumbarton.[34] Other Glasgow Gaelic clubs like the Cavan Slashers (who later joined with Eire Ogs in Glasgow) and Fianna Éireann, were also mentioned in the Gaelic columns of the newspaper, showing the strength of Gaelic sport during this period.

The year 1906 was eventful for Irish gaels in Scotland. In Lanarkshire, the first ever hurling championship was won by the Brian Boru Club from Blantyre.

Table 4:1 **Lanarkshire Hurling Championship 1906**

	P	W	L	F	A	Pts
Brian Boru	7	7	0	26	9	14
Lord Edwards	6	4	2	22	14	8
Shamrocks	5	2	3	20	12	4
Fag-an-Bealagh	7	2	5	12	19	4
Lambh Dearg	7	1	6	9	20	2

The same year, Fag-an-Bealagh (possibly playing football under the name of 'Sons of Erin') from Carfin won the first football championship, though overall it was Glasgow that continued to dominate. Before a crowd of over fifteen hundred people in the provincial hurling championship held at Shawfield Park, the home of Clyde Football (soccer) Club, Lanarkshire's representatives Brian Boru's were beaten by the experienced Rapparees Club.

Glasgow's experience was again reflected in the provincial championship of that year. Earlier, in a challenge match in England, a strong representative team from Scotland beat Tyneside 5:12 to 2:5. For the Ulster (Antrim) versus Scotland (Glasgow) 1905 All-Ireland hurling quarter-final match (held in August 1906), eleven members of the Rapparees Club were chosen, four from Cuchulains and one each from Lord Edwards and Shamrocks of Wishaw. However, the Scottish-based side believed that tiredness, arising from having to travel to the match in Ireland, had a negative effect upon them and this resulted in a narrow 3:13 to 3:11 defeat. Around the same time Leinster (Kilkenny) defeated the English representatives (Lancashire) 3:21 to 0:5.

In early 1907, the Glasgow and Lanarkshire county boards amalgamated to form a new provincial committee. The following year, St Marks Parish of Carntyne (now Shettleston) in Glasgow formed the first handball team within Gaelic circles in Scotland. The first record of a handball game being played amongst the Gaelic fraternity is in mid 1908: St Marks beating the resolute and capable Rapparees in the contest.[35] During September 1908, Lambh Dearg's from Kinning Park paid a visit to Belfast to play Seaghan an Diomais. The match, played at Seaghan's Park on the Whiterock Road was won 1:12 to 1:8 by the home side. The closeness of the result reflected the high standard of play of the Scottish-based team: the home side apparently having the pick of the best players in Belfast for the match. The following year Rapparees hurlers visited Nenagh in Tipperary as well as Cork to play local sides in challenge matches. For the 1908 All-Ireland Championships, London was chosen to represent Britain in football while Scotland was chosen for the hurling competition. London lost to Dublin in the final while Scotland failed to travel for its semi-final against Tipperary.[36] In 1910 Glasgow defeated Antrim 1:13 to 0:7 in the quarter-final of the All-Ireland Hurling Championship. The county subsequently lost to Dublin 6:6 to 5:1 in the semi-final played at Jones's Road.37

In early 1909, the G.A.A. in Scotland reflected its concern with the advance of the Irish language when it joined the debate on the use of Irish in Irish universities. In January of that year the Province passed a resolution that was forwarded to the secretary, Coisde Gnotha, Gaelic League, Dublin.

> That we, the Scottish Provincial Council of the Gaelic Athletic Association, demand that the Irish language, both oral and written, be made an essential subject for matriculation and up to the point where specialisation begins in the new universities.[38]

Around this time Gaelic football began to come more to the fore among some small sections of the Irish community in the west of Scotland. The first ever football league competition was held during

1909 and was only decided on the final day of the season: Eire Og from Coatbridge beat Kinning Park's Lambh Dearg in front of a crowd of three hundred spectators. The Coatbridge team that won the first league title was:

> Plunkett, Carvil, Harknett, Wroe, Walsh, Carville, Maguire, Kelly, O'Neill, Kernan, Darcy, Byrne, O'Brien, Hughes, Devlin, Dunn and Carolan.

To the credit of the Coatbridge representatives, The Star reported:

> It would be but natural for the good Gaels of Coatbridge to feel proud of their achievement, but they carry their honours modestly, as befits men who are good footballers and good hurlers and who take an active practical interest in every phase of the Irish movement as regards the Irish language and industrial revival.[39]

The Irishness of Coatbridge's significant immigrant population also attracted positive comment from Belfast MP Joseph Devlin who visited Scotland during the St Patrick's celebrations the following year. When Devlin visited Coatbridge, Dr Charles O'Neill, the Coatbridge MP who represented South Armagh, was encouraged to welcome Mr Devlin to a United Irish League meeting in the town's Theatre Royal on Main Street. O'Neill commented that Devlin:

> would not need any pressure to force him to come there to witness such a demonstration of Irish power and loyalty.[40]

In November 1911, at a meeting in Upper O'Connell Street in Dublin, Central Council reported that Scotland was still making steady progress in the formation of Gaelic clubs and that additional clubs had affiliated to the relevant committee in Ireland during the year. However, the many positive signs of a Gaelic revival amongst the ex-patriot community in Scotland was continually qualified by setbacks and in many ways the first decade of the twentieth century represents the highpoint of Gaelic sports activity in Scotland.

1. Irish Post, 10/11/84, pp. 12-13.
2. This on a field where the British museum now stands. Irish Post, 3/11/84.
3. de Burca, p. 75.
4. Minutes of Central Council, 1900, pp. 31-32.
5. The Sam Maguire Cup, Cumann Luthchleas Gael, Dublin, 1986.

6. Glasgow Examiner, 20/4/1895.
7. Ibid: 24/8/1895.
8. Ibid: 11/9/1897.
9. Ibid: 30/1/1897.
10. Glasgow Observer, 14/6/1902.
11. Hugh McAleese died aged ninety in 1966.
12. Canning, 1979, originally from J E Handley, The Irish in Modern Scotland, Cork University Press, Cork, p. 233, 1947
13. Glasgow Examiner, 24/11/1900.
14. Feeney, 1995.
15. Glasgow Examiner, 15/6/1901.
16. Ibid: 23/5/1903.
17. Central Council Minutes, p. 149, 4/10/1903.
18. Glasgow Examiner, 13/6/1903.
19. Ibid: 4/7/1903.
20. O'Dea returned home in May 1904 and died in an accident in 1934
21. Glasgow Star, 5/9/1903.
22. Feeney S, Conradh na Gaelige (Gaelic League) in Scotland, 1895-1995: A centenary celebration (published by the author), 1995.
23. Ibid.
24. The Star, 6/5/1905.
25. Ibid: 15/7/1905.
26. Ibid: 5/3/1904.
27. Ibid: 4/2/1905.
28. Central Council minutes, May 1905.
29. McCourt probably originated from Dungannon, County Tyrone.
30. Gallagher, 1987, p.97.
31. Feeney, 1995.
32. Ibid.
33. The Star, 18/4/1908.
34. Ibid: 18/8/1908. Patrick Costello, James Fynan and M Joyce were important activists in Dumbarton's hurling circles at this time.
35. The Star, 29/8/1908.
36. Irish Post, 10/11/1984.
37. Gaelsport G.A.A. Youth Annual, 1984.
38. The Star, 22/1/1909.
39. Ibid: 7/5/1909.
40. Ibid: 18/3/10.

Chapter 5

The vicissitudes of Gaelic sport in Scotland

GAELIC SPORTING STRUGGLES

After the inspiring years of the first decade of the new century, the subsequent intermittent nature of Gaelic sports activity is reflected in the fewer reports on official hurling or football in the second decade of the new century. In 1911 an article in The Star stated:

> Bad as things are, there is no reason why the G.A.A. should not again be a vigorous body amongst the Irishmen in Scotland and particularly among those congregated in Glasgow and throughout the West of Scotland.[1]

It appears that the Rapparees were the only side being credibly sustained at the time, although The Star newspaper reported that despite the many hundreds of hurlers in the area, a lack of opposition was in danger of rendering the club 'blue mouldy'.[2] Gaelic sports in west central Scotland did not suffer from a lack of Irishness, for Irish activity remained plentiful; the Irish Foresters, the Irish National League, Celtic Football Club and the Ancient Order of Hibernians, with thirty-four divisions in the central belt of Scotland, were clear signs of Irish activity. However, during this period Irishness did not translate into a vibrant G.A.A. As was the case in parts of Ireland at the same time, the G.A.A. in Scotland struggled to acquire the status and vibrancy required for its good health and promotion.

Nonetheless, despite its struggles the G.A.A. also experienced encouraging episodes as well as those characterised by a lack of activity. By the middle of 1912, Eire Og Hurling Club in Coatbridge was reported to be again recruiting, practising and organising. Occasional challenge matches took place and there was newspaper speculation of clubs being rekindled in Wishaw, Whiteinch (Glasgow) and Greenock. The Owen Roe O'Neill Gaelic football club was founded in Coatbridge in late 1912. The Club held an inaugural function in a hall in the town's Coatdyke area: forty members signed up and the evening was rounded off with the singing of the emerging unofficial Irish national anthem, 'A Nation Once Again'. Around the same time Coatbridge's Eire Og met Sarsfields of Greenock in the first match in the Jersey Hurling Tournament. Although Wishaw Shamrocks failed to field in the tournament, matches did take place and the final was played in November of that year with Greenock's Sarsfields the victors over the Rapparees. The final teams were:

> **Sarsfields:** J O'Conner (captain), D West, J West, J O'Callaghan, S Tabb, C McCarthy, J Dillon, D O'Brien, W Perry, T Hirshaw, M O'Leary, D O'Leary, E Flynn.
>
> **Rapparees:** W Hennessy, L Hudson, D O'Donnoghue, H Ryan, F Mooney, M Minogue, D Minogue, J Minogue, P MacKay, J McCarthy, J Darragh, M Fitzgerald, R Morrisey.[3]

During November 1912, the Cork Free Press reported a match in 'Bonny Scotland' noting the predominance of hurlers from Passage West in Cork, who played in the Greenock Sarsfields team and were 'keeping the cult of the caman well to the fore' among the Irish in Scotland. The local Cork economy had been suffering and the Free Press reported that the young men were now employed as apprentices at the Greenock shipyards. The paper lamented that its young men had to leave home and also the demise of the club they once played for.

> All veteran South-East Cork Leaguers will be specifically interested, as it will show that though the famous old Passage club is non est at present, its members are keeping the memories of the dear old days green by indulging in the home pastime.

The newspaper hoped that better times 'when the trade of Passage will revive', would allow the young men to return to their native Cork.[4]

1913 was a landmark year for Irish hurling and football gaels in the west of Scotland. In April G.A.A. clubs again resumed as a constituted provincial board. The Scottish Province's representative, Eamonn O'Fhlionn, won assurance at a Central Council meeting in Dublin that the 1913 All-Ireland quarter-final provincial hurling match involving Scotland would, for the first time, be played in Glasgow. This was in response to previous complaints from members in Scotland that constant travel difficulties were hindering their chances of progress in the competition. It was also part of an initiative on the part of the G.A.A. authorities in Ireland 'to boost the game in Britain'.[5]

The following month the Province announced its biggest news to date. In June, Kilkenny, previous winners of a number of All-Ireland Hurling titles, was to visit Glasgow to play against a select of members in Scotland. This provided the Board in Scotland with a major incentive for promoting the game and for installing a degree of enthusiasm and anticipation into clubs which had until recently been struggling to field regular sides. Training and practice matches became more common as the Provincial selectors looked over players with a view to picking the best for the match with Kilkenny.

During May, the Rapparees beat the previous year's winners Sarsfields of Greenock to lift the Hurling Championship of Scotland.[6] When, on the twenty first of June 1913 the spectacle of Scotland versus Kilkenny took place at Celtic Park, the supremacy of the Rapparees side was reflected in their having seven players included in the representative Scotland team. Teams on this occasion were:

Kilkenny: J Power (Mooncoin), J Keoghan (Tullaroan), J Rochford (Three Castles), M Garrigle (Erin's Own, Kilkenny City), D Kennedy (Tullaroan), P Lanigan (Erin's Own), T MacCormick (Erin's Own), P Clohossay (Tullaroan), D Doherty (Mooncoin), S Walton (Tullaroan/ Captain), M Doyle (Mooncoin) and J Kelly (Mooncoin). Reserves, J J Brennan (Erin's Own) and D Welsh (Mooncoin).

Scotland: M Morrohan (Rapparees, Glasgow), L Hartnett (Eire Og, Coatbridge), D Donoghue (Rapparees), B O'Neill (Wishaw Shamrocks/ Captain), J McNulty (Rapparees), F Stephens (Shamrocks), J Tabb (Sarsfields, Greenock), E Flynn (Sarsfields), J Phelan (Eire Og), W Fitzgerald (Rapparees), W Dwyer (Rapparees), O'Connor (Sarsfields),

> J McCarthy (Rapparees) and P MacGearailt (Sarsfields). Reserves, P Dwyer, McDonnell and R Welsh.

The Kilkenny side were well represented by players from the Tullaroan and Mooncoin clubs, two of the strongest sides in the County who played in the first Kilkenny championship in 1887. Further, these years marked a particularly successful time for Kilkenny: winning seven All-Ireland titles in a ten-year period as well as the championship in the same year they played at Celtic Park.

Sports reporter for The Glasgow Star 'Man In The Know' Tom Maley (brother of the Celtic manager, Willie) enthused at the wonderful spectacle that took place at Celtic Park. Maley was particularly taken by the appearance of the Rory Oge O'More Pipe Band who the Celtic directors arranged to appear again at Celtic Park the following August. Although The Star was dominated by soccer reports, particularly those pertaining to Celtic, 'The Man In The Know' was enthused by the hurling exhibition match. Writing in the following week's Star, Maley reported:

> The game itself was a revelation to those of us who look upon football as the last word in competitive sport. . . The players covered more ground than any football fifteen could do in the allotted time and space; their ambidextrous strokes were a combination of golf, baseball, cricket, and tennis swings, and all the time eye and muscle had to synchronise, the ball timed with the utmost accuracy, and sent either to a waiting comrade or as near the opponents' goal as possible.

Although Maley was stirred by the game, and despite his remarks being indicative of the struggle that Gaelic sports experienced, his comments were also viewed as important for Gaelic sports enthusiasts in Scotland.

> It goes without saying that hurling, as we saw it, at Parkhead, is the king of the outdoor games, but I don't suppose it will ever make headway in a country given over to Association football.[7]

Initially, the G.A.A. in Scotland drew great store from the match. Although the Scottish representatives were beaten by a score of ten goals and five points to four goals and two points, the game was considered a 'decided success'. However, the Kilkenny men had shown the Scottish-based players a lesson. Kilkenny were more fit and in fact the local G.A.A. considered the visitors champion sprinters as well as hurlers. W Dwyer of the Rapparees seemed the only player on the home side who had the capacity to match the visitors although the defence also received plaudits.

The Kilkenny Journal reported that five thousand spectators had attended the match, a figure that may have been an optimistic estimate. In a stadium that could reputedly hold eighty-two thousand people, even five thousand would not look substantial. The Journal also spoke highly of the facilities at Celtic Park commenting that it was lamentable that they themselves did not have a similar structure at home.[8] At the post match celebrations, Luke O'Toole, General Secretary of the G.A.A., announced that forthwith Scotland would become part of the new Provincial Council of Britain. This would mean that Scotland would now have to compete with the other counties in Britain, London, South Wales and Lancashire, to qualify for the All-Ireland championship.[9]

Although the game at Celtic Park was viewed as having the potential to promote the sport amongst the Irish in Scotland on this occasion it met with competition. On the same day at Whifflet in Coatbridge, the annual demonstration of Irish National Foresters (Coillteoiri Naisiunta na hÉireann) took place, an organisation that had branches all over the west central belt and to which many Catholic families were attached. Many thousands of Catholics attended this demonstration that might otherwise have gone to Celtic Park.[10]

Indeed, the Irish National Foresters (INF) is an apposite example of how it was often bodies other than the G.A.A. that consumed much of the cultural and social time as well as commitment, energy and expressions of the Irishness of the community in Scotland. The Foresters functioned as an insurance, welfare, friendly and political association, and was one of the most obvious manifestations of the Irish presence in Scotland, continuing links with home and heritage in Ireland. A vast number, if not the majority, of Catholic families amongst the diaspora in Scotland, contained some members of the Foresters. Towards the end of the nineteenth and throughout the early decades of the twentieth centuries, the I.N.F. was a primary Irish organisation in Scotland. In 1903, a decade before the famous hurling encounter at Celtic Park, the

I.N.F. held a well-attended sports day at Celtic's stadium, such events also reflecting the intimacy Celtic Football Club had at the time with other Irish cultural, social and political organisations and activities.[11] With an estimated 100,000 members in Scotland on the eve of the First World War, men women and juniors, the I.N.F. held the allegiances of many members of the Catholic Irish in Scotland.

While the Foresters, Hibernians and the Irish National League took up the political, social or welfare time of many of the Irish and their offspring, and Celtic Football Club dominated their sporting interests, 'native' Irish games enthusiasts found it difficult to establish Gaelic sport activity as an important part of the repertoire of outlets for Irishness. Hurling and football continued in Scotland over the next few years but there seems to have been little resurgence as a direct result of the high profile 'international' at Celtic Park. With the advent of 'the Great War' the following year, and the gradual unfolding of a pivotal stage in Ireland's struggle against British rule, the cultural and political landscape which the Irish in Scotland experienced was on the verge of cataclysmic change.

1. The Star, 8/3/1912.
2. Ibid: 22/3/1912.
3.Ibid: 13/9/1912.
4. Cork Free Press, 30/11/1912.
5. Irish Post, 17/11/1984.
6. The Star, 23/5/1913.
7. Ibid: 27/6/1913.
8. The Kilkenny Journal, 28/6/1913.
9. Glasgow Star, 27/6/1913.
10. The INF (Irish National Foresters) began in 1877 as a breakaway from the Ancient Order of Foresters after political disagreements. The INF grew rapidly and soon became the largest friendly society in Ireland. It supported Irish nationalism and its constitution called for 'government for Ireland by the Irish people in accordance with Irish ideas and Irish aspirations'. It also spread throughout the Irish diaspora worldwide and by 1914 the order had a quarter of a million members in over 1,000 branches. With the establishment of the Irish Free State and the gradual expansion of the social welfare system, the INF went into decline in much of Ireland and Britain. However some branches, particularly in the north of Ireland, continue to exist.
11. The Glasgow Star and Examiner, 26/7/1913.

Chapter 6

Dislocations and the First World War

POLITICS AND CULTURE

From among the Irish diaspora in Britain, many thousands departed their adopted home to fight in World War I. With the War, conscription and Ireland's struggle dominating the period, throughout Britain, Irish social and cultural organisations were detrimentally affected. In London, a 'golden era' of G.A.A. activities came to a close and this period witnessed the disbanding 'of club after club'.[1] Likewise, many non-Irish social organisations were also damaged by the convulsions caused by War. For example, in Scotland shinty was ravaged by the effects of the First (and Second) World War and the subsequent economic and community dislocations 'could have brought the [Shinty] Association to its knees'. Like many Irish organisations, shinty survived rather than thrived.[2]

During the War years the popular press in Britain was often dominated by reports of those killed in action in France or elsewhere. In Scotland, the columns of Irish and Catholic newspapers were replete with names of young Catholic men, the vast majority either Irish-born or of Irish forebears, also slain in the War. Almost inevitably many of the previously strong Irish organisations in the west central belt of Scotland were decimated as they lost large sections of their membership, and indeed, much of the next generation of leaders and organisers. Even when the war ended, with morale low and the unenviable depression of losing family and friends, as well as widespread economic suffering, some local organisations never regained their vibrancy.

However, not all community activities, Irish or otherwise, ceased completely or diminished and this era also represents a highly politicised one for people in Britain. Although many Irish and their offspring had been drawn towards the expanding Labour Party for a number of years, this did not pre-empt them from also looking towards their origins, heritage, past family, community histories and experiences, for other aspects of their politics.

Since the beginning of the War Ireland had undergone a political and social convulsion. The political situation there also meant a new and more revolutionary impasse developed among Irish immigrant communities in Scotland and elsewhere. In areas of Lanarkshire and Glasgow, long at the forefront of Irish politics and cultural activities, the nineteenth century cry of 'God Save Ireland' and 'A Nation Once Again' were replaced by the 'Soldiers Song': a song which by 1926 had become the Irish National Anthem. Gaelic enthusiasts in Scotland noted that members and associates of the G.A.A. were significantly involved in the 1916 Rising; Padraic Pearse, Sean McDermott, Con Colbert, Michael O'Hanrahan and Eamonn Ceannt, all leaders during the Rising, were executed in its wake. Others like Austin Stack and Michael Collins received prison sentences for their part in the insurrection. In Kerry, due to the involvement in Sinn Féin activities of so many of its members, the County found it was unable to field a team for the belated 1917 All-Ireland Championship.[3]

As in Ireland, by 1919 in Scotland the more revolutionary Sinn Féin Party replaced the Irish National League and other older pro-Irish political bodies. Organisations such as the Hibernians also lost members though there was an overlap of membership with a number of these bodies. Although the cultural landscape appeared to be severely weakened at this time, events in Ireland meant that the Irish political scene acquired a new vibrancy and meaning and many peoples' energies were devoted to political activities rather than cultural ones. Local branches of Sinn Féin emerged from the immigrant areas where the G.A.A. was also active (Cumann); in Motherwell (John O'Leary Cumann), Port Glasgow and Greenock (Padraic Pearse Cumann), Glasgow (James Connolly Cumann), Clydebank (Joseph Plunkett Cumann), Hamilton (Patrick

Pearse Cumann, Burnbank), Govan (Michael Mallin Cumann), Mossend (Padraic O'Domnal Cumann – which had at least two hundred of a membership), Denny (Cormac Carrigan Cumann), Shotts (Sean MacDiarmada Cumann) and in Coatbridge there were at least three branches organised (Michael Mallin, Fr Griffen in the town's Whifflet area and Coatdyke's Thomas Ashe).

Even in popular Loyalist-Unionist-Orange strongholds such as Caldercruix and Larkhall in Lanarkshire, Sinn Féin Cumann also existed amongst the small Irish Catholic communities. It is estimated that the number of Sinn Féin branches in Scotland rose to around eighty during this period while the number of people who directly became involved in the developing Irish Republican Army was around three thousand in the Glasgow area alone.[4] Clearly the political situation in Ireland dominated within the Irish community in Scotland (indeed, it was a pre-eminent issue among the general population). So much so, that Eamon de Valera later revealed that the Irish in Scotland had contributed more money to the Republican struggle in Ireland than any other country, including Ireland itself.[5]

Large Irish and Catholic cultural and political demonstrations in Scotland continued throughout this time. In 1921, barred from entering Glasgow, the nationalist-minded Archbishop Daniel Mannix, an Irishman who resided in Melbourne Australia, spoke to the ex-patriate Irish community of west-central Scotland. His open-air rally held in Whifflet Coatbridge, attracted over 50,000 people, thus illustrating the Irish political conviction of the diaspora during these years.[6]

Nevertheless, this period of political activity also marked the zenith of popular pro-active Irish nationalist support in Scotland. The years 1922-1923 saw the eruption of the fratricidal conflict of the Irish Civil War. Gallagher believes that the Irish in Scotland became confused and 'war wearied' as the fight in Ireland became more complex than 'simply' driving the British out. Confusion over the situation in Ireland, along with anti-subversive actions on the part of the British authorities in Scotland, also contributed to many in the immigrant community becoming less inclined towards pro-active republican activities. Gallagher believes that crucially for the Irish in Britain:

> the spectacle of Irishman killing Irishman greatly weakened Irish political and cultural movements in many British cities where these activities had reached a high pitch only a short time before.[7]

As far as Gaelic sport was concerned, in Ireland the effects of the Civil War upon the youthful G.A.A. can be seen in County Clare where, until 1925, two rival County Boards were set up, one composed of pro-Treaty and the other of anti-Treaty gaels. As with even the most basic family unit the G.A.A. experienced the Civil War from each perspective having supporters on both sides of the divide.

Although in 1925 local Coatbridge Sinn Féin activists were instigating meetings in an attempt to revive the organisation there and beyond,[8] the British social and political climate had changed dramatically and other factors in Britain were usurping the capacity for Irish-focused political activities. In addition, the political parties that emerged in the new and independent 'Free State' of Ireland had lesser need to create a British dimension than had their forbears in the Parliamentary Party and Sinn Féin. Forthwith, politicians and revolutionaries in Ireland looked less to the diaspora for support. In Britain, the Labour Party and trade unions served as incorporatist agencies by diverting the attentions of the Irish towards matters seen as more immediately relevant.

Significantly, the commonalities arising from the experience of the War and the subsequent developing political, social and cultural hegemonic ideologies and symbolisms of the British state gradually impinged upon Irishness in Britain. At the same time, Irish parties began to weaken in Britain as Ireland (for the time being) played a less significant part in the British political agenda. A new era of politics in their adopted home began to impress upon many aspects of the immigrants and their offspring's lives. With the Irish Free State adjusting to its recently found independence, the new Northern Ireland state developed as a violent sectarian entity, largely hidden from the eyes of the public in Britain. As a result Ireland's historical struggle declined in the immigrant consciousness. Although many Irish in Britain became involved in bodies such as the Anti-Partition League, and a branch of Fianna Fail was founded in Glasgow, Irish politics ceased to stir the same level of activity as in pre-partition days. Allied to this, emigration from Ireland to Scotland declined dramatically after the First World War while many Irish in Scotland began to acquire new party political allegiances that were the product of their everyday social and economic circumstances.

Despite affinity with and loyalty to Ireland, many Irish recognised that they could be more influential in a local setting which, after all, was the situation they found themselves in and in which many of their aspirations were henceforth applicable. So began the Labour Party's deep reliance on the Irish in west-central Scotland: the main beneficiary of Irish immigrants changing political experiences and perspectives. The lessening role of Irish political activities, combined with the growth of the immigrant community's ties with local politics through links with the Labour Party, gradually supported a changing political attachment with their country of origin for many immigrants and their offspring.

Over the next few decades, the context of social, cultural and political lifestyles in Britain were transformed as the assimilation of the Irish intensified. The developing political system, the advent of progressive educational change and the slow growth of the mass media meant that 'common' cultural pastimes and traits developed as never before as these homogenising forces and agents began to take hold. These factors drew people towards actual and perceived shared public experiences that helped produce conventional and popular features of identity. In turn, these began to have a significant impact on the solidarity and communal nature, as well as the self-image, of the Irish in Scotland. Such alterations invariably introduced a challenge to existing identities, especially those that had a strong grounding in ethnic and religious beliefs and attitudes.

At a cultural and identity level, such experiences and perspectives also meant that the Irishness of the immigrant community was disadvantaged as Scottishness and Britishness became significantly privileged discourses involved in social, cultural and national identity formation. Although Irish immigrants and their offspring maintained strong links to Ireland and Irishness, the 1920s and 1930s also marks a watershed for the kind of unity that had previously existed within the Catholic Irish community.

Possibly much more significant than any of the factors relating to social, cultural and political change was the climate that existed during the decades after World War I whereby being perceived or 'labelled' as Irish and Catholic could be considerably problematic. This was a time when Catholics of Irish origin were mixing more with the wider society but also when there was significant anti-Catholic and anti-Irish activity, attitudes and identities that had consequences for everyday living in Scotland.[9]

INTER-WAR CULTURE, IDENTITY AND GAELIC SPORT

As 'agents of change', the Great War, War in Ireland, the increasing salience of Labour activity and rapidly changing social and economic conditions marked a watershed in Irish activities in Scotland. The vibrancy in Irish activities is reflected in the pre-War period when the Irish Catholic press contained numerous adverts and reports on the Irish National League, the Irish National Foresters, the Irish Independent League, the Ancient Order of Hibernians, Sinn Féin Cumann, the Gaelic League, the Irish Literary Association and an array of county and provincial associations, including Tyrone, Monaghan, Armagh, Cavan and Derry in particular, Connacht and Leinster, as well as a number of sporting bodies from athletics to swimming clubs. In addition, a variety of Catholic associations such as the League of the Cross, the Catholic Men's Society and the Catholic Truth Society were active organisations among the immigrant community. The most significant cultural and social facet of Irishness for the rest of the twentieth century also prevailed through Celtic Football Club. Nonetheless, for most of these bodies, decline in the face of a new cultural and political context ensued.

As far as G.A.A. history is concerned, little Gaelic sporting activity can be identified in the first few years after the War. Certainly some clubs played an occasional game such as a Pearse Harps versus Patrick Sarsfields football match during 1920[10] and another hurling club was founded in Coatbridge in the same year.[11] However, generally there were few official football or hurling games organised.

In 1921 an attempt was made to reinvigorate the Gaelic sporting scene. The Association in Scotland was re-organised and twelve clubs were represented at the first meeting held in Glasgow chaired by Maurice Frieze. Frieze, who lived in Rutherglen, gained more prominence two years later when he was arrested when British police swooped on thirty-eight suspected prominent republicans in Scotland and seventy-two in England. With the assistance of the new pro-treaty Free State government, the suspects were deported to Ireland where they were imprisoned in Mountjoy Gaol in Dublin. By the end of the Civil War they had been released[12] while the following year the deportees from Scotland received £17,000 in compensation for the unwieldy way they had they had been dealt with.[13]

Distinct from the politics of some of its membership, the noted Glasgow G.A.A. meeting was also important for the presence of two women, Misses Mullen and McKenna representing the Glasgow Camogie Club.[14] Subsequently, 1922 marked the first time Gaelic sports in Scotland became manifest among the women of the immigrant community. Under the auspices of the Camoguidneacht Association at least one camogie match took place the following year, between Granuailes of Glasgow and Taras of Gourock. The teams who participated in that match were:

Granuailes: J Donnellan, T MacBride, J McGranahan, L Gallagher, M McGowan, M O'Connor, L Canney, L McLeod, A O'Reilly, B Gormley, M B Marr and B Lynch.

Taras: G McDonald, M Flavin, R Kelly, Butson, Dorrien, Brennen, McElhinney, Healy, McKenna, Morrisay, Foley and Doyle.

By 1922, football and hurling began to be played more regularly and teams in both Glasgow and Lanarkshire areas temporarily found a new lease of life. Along with some of the established teams in Glasgow and Lanarkshire, others clubs began in Hamilton (Emmets), Springburn (McCurtains Gaels), Kinning Park (O'Tooles), whilst gaels in Dumbarton responded with two clubs, Dr Crokes and Cuchulains.

THE TAILTEANN GAMES

As a result of the Civil War, most G.A.A. activities in Munster and Connacht had come to a halt whilst the G.A.A. in Ulster continued to labour amidst its own particular circumstances. During this period, only in Leinster were fixtures fulfilled, notably for the first time since 1916.[15]

Nevertheless, despite the range of difficulties presented by the First World War and the struggle for Irish independence, the Association in Ireland avoided the political fission that might have destroyed it. After the Civil War, the new Irish Free State Government partly looked to sport to answer some of its problems.

A degree of 'Celtic spirit' was reflected among Irish and Scotland's Highland gaels when in 1922 a select hurling team from Glasgow played the Skye Shinty Club in a compromise game. Although the hurlers won the first half of the match under the rules of the G.A.A., the game was won by the Skye club with a final score of five goals and one point to three goals.[16]

The Skye representatives were additionally requested to attend the proposed 1922 Tailteann Games in Ireland, a national festival of athletics, art, music and poetry in the new Irish Free State. These games were intended to revive a tradition going back many centuries when they were originally instituted to celebrate the life of Queen Tailte. The first games had reputedly hosted competitors from all over Ireland and had survived uninterrupted until 1169. Although the proposed 1922 Games failed to materialise, revived Tailteann Games did take place in Dublin in 1924, 1928 and 1932. As an exercise in state building and projection the Games were primarily viewed as being sponsored by the post-Civil War Cumann na nGaelheal Government.

Until the founding of the Irish Free State, athletics in Ireland were under the control of the G.A.A. However, until 1924 Irish athletes had to compete for Britain or else emigrate and adopt the colours of another country. Protests to the International Amateur Athletic Federation by British representatives also persuaded the I.A.A.F. only to accept athletes from the Free State, viewing athletes from the North as being from a different country. This went against the hitherto united Irish effort involving athletes from the whole island and the subsequent confusion and division split athletics in the Free State for many decades. The 1924 Tailteann Games partly reflected these troubles. The games aimed to stress the independent sporting and cultural nature of the Irish people.

The G.A.A., provided many of the leading officials as well as the main stadium. Eventually joining the Irish on this occasion was a team of shinty players from Scotland.

An early shock to the festival hosts came when the Scottish shinty team beat an Irish hurling side 2-1. However, by the time the hurling tournament got underway, the Irish hurlers had regained their self-respect. The tournament produced the following scores:

Table 5:1

Tailteann Games 1924: Gaelic football and Hurling/Shinty scores

Ireland	4:3	America	1:3
America	4:2	England	3:2
Scotland	7:3	Wales	5:1
Ireland	5:4	Wales	2:6
Ireland	9:3	England	4:7
Wales	6:2	England	5:3
America	6:6	Scotland	2:3
Ireland	10:1	Scotland	4:5
Ireland	4:6	America	3:2 (final)

The team that originated from Scotland was led by James J Jackson, whose parents were from County Monaghan. In later years, Jackson, based in the Kings Park area of Glasgow, was also to become one of the founders of the Irish National Association in Scotland.

One game of Gaelic football was held at the games when the home side beat the G.A.A.'s English representatives 3:9 to 2:3. The team titles suggested an international dimension, though in reality it was more of a diasporic tournament as many countries were represented by participants originally from Ireland or of Irish descent. Purcell comments on how many Irish viewed the games:

> the contingents of exiles from the United States, Canada, Britain, New Zealand, Australia and South Africa gave our people a sense of pride in realising how our small island had contributed to the building of other and more powerful nations in every quarter of the globe.[17]

Despite thousands of people attending, the games were not regarded as an unqualified success. The Glasgow Star and Examiner condemned the expense being laid out whilst Sinn Féin and other groups boycotted the games in protest at the Free State Government's imprisoning of republicans.[18] Nine days before the games commenced the Government released the last of these prisoners, including Eamon de Valera, Austin Stack and Sean McCarthy, although the Republican boycott remained.

The Tailteann games, initially seen as being revived after a lapse of seven and a half centuries, were again held in 1928 and in 1932, though not on the same scale as the 1924 event. On these occasions there were no football or hurling representatives from Britain and the games failed in their aim of reflecting pride in the antiquity, survival and identity of the Irish people. After taking office in the 1930s De Valera's new Fianna Fail Government ended the Tailtean experiment.

IMMIGRATION

Aside from a few positive signs of Gaelic sporting activity, and although Central Council in Dublin sent a Mr McGrath to Britain to re-organise the sport, little more was heard of hurling, Gaelic football or camogie in Scotland for a number of years. Notably missing since 1914, it was 1927 before Britain returned to compete in the All-Ireland championships, by that time having the status of junior footballers and hurlers.

The slowing down of Irish immigration to Scotland after the First World War is vital to understanding the lack of vibrancy, energy and organisation involved in Irish activities in Scotland during this time. Census figures showed that the Irish-born population of Scotland had declined from its peak of 218,745 in 1881, to just over 200,000 at the turn of the century, to 159,020 by 1921. Moreover, by this time, 88,397 had been born in the area of Northern Ireland and 70,623 born in the new Irish Free State. With the G.A.A. taking until the 1930s before making a significant impact upon much of Ulster many Irish immigrants to Scotland had themselves experienced very little by way of a grounding in Gaelic sport. In addition, many immigrants were women who had employment and familial priorities as opposed to the sporting and cultural ones more frequently displayed by male members of the diaspora. Further, Irish cultural activities were always constrained by the fact that most Irish immigrants to Scotland were preoccupied with surviving, rather than having the time and energy to organise and participate in deeds considered cultural.

1. Irish Post, 17/11/1984.
2. Shinty: Sport of the Gael, BBC Scotland (television), 1993.
3. de Burca, 1980, p. 139.
4. Gallagher, 1987, p. 90.
5. O'Connor, 1970, pp. 141-142.
6. See Gallagher, p. 93-94.
7. Gallagher, 1987, pp. 94-97.
8. The Star, 9/1/1925.
9. See chapter 6.
10. The Star, 28/2/1920.
11. Ibid: 17/7/1920.
12. Ibid: 17/3/1923.
13. Gallagher, 1987, p. 97.
14. The Star, 17/12/1921.
15. de Burca, 1980, p. 161.
16. The Star, 15/7/1922.
17. Purcell, 1982, p. 192.
18. The Star, 30/8/1924.

Chapter 7
Anti-Irish racism and anti-Catholic prejudice

THE FUTURE IN THE PAST

The vibrancy of the cultural life and identities of any migrant community in their new country of residence is determined by numerous factors. These include the condition of their culture and identity in the country departed, the well being of their culture and identity on entering their new environment, and the ability or fervour the migrant goup has to maintain, promote and celebrate these. Critically, the potential vitality of the existing culture and identity will be considerably fashioned by the social, economic, political and cultural environment encountered by the migrants in terms of the area of settlement and their reception, acceptance or otherwise, on the part of the host community. This vitality will be affected also by any social, economic or political progress achieved by the migrant community in the years after arrival in the host country. The aforesaid combine to determine the richness or poverty of the culture and identities that are brought with the migrants as well as the capacity of the new community to remember, articulate and celebrate these in their new setting. Other factors will also partly determine developments, one of the most significant being the pre-migration established historical, cultural, social, economic and political relations that exist between the host and donor countries.

Reflection on several historical aspects or periods in the story of the Irish in Scotland, including Scottish national and cultural identities, nineteenth century press reports and the important inter-war period of the 1920s and 1930s, assists not only an understanding of Irishness in modern Scotland, but also ethno-religious relations and cleavage. In a similar vein this is important to a greater appreciation of the place of the G.A.A. in relation to the Irish diaspora in Scotland.

In Scotland, 'Presbyterianism was not just a state religion but, for more than three centuries, defined the Scots to one another and to the rest of the world'.[1] Additionally, Muirhead opines that: 'in Scotland anti-Romanism had become a religion and a way of life'.[2] Although Protestantism in Scotland has long been multi-dimensional, involving social, political, moral, philosophical and spiritual aspects, it is the relationship between Scottish Protestantism and the anti-Catholic dimensions of Presbyterianism, as well as the ethnic distinctiveness of Catholics from Ireland, that have had a significant impact on relations between Protestants and Catholics in Scotland.

Since the sixteenth century Reformation, a significant anti-Catholic culture has existed in Scotland, one that has varyingly infused many aspects of social and political life. Partly reflecting the significance of anti-Catholicism in Scotland prior to Irish-Catholic migration, two statistics singularly demonstrate this in the city of Glasgow in the 1790s. One commentator relays that at this time there were only thirty-nine Catholics in the city but forty-three anti-Catholic societies. Devine notes sixty anti-Catholic societies in 1791.[3]

Nonetheless, anti-Catholicism has been a complex culture and identity and has involved many different strands and elements over both time and place. The arrival of Irish Catholic immigrants to Scotland during the nineteenth and twentieth centuries added ethnic and racial aspects to traditional anti-Catholic antagonism.[4] Anti-Catholicism, with a new potent ethnic element, subsequently became a framework for influencing many features of everyday life from employment and education, to sport and politics.

For much of the nineteenth century, the Irish huddled together in the worst parts of towns and cities and coming from an unsophisticated peasant society, they often found it difficult to adapt. For some immigrants, particularly those from the west of Ireland, linguistic differences further inhibited acclimatisation to their new circumstances. In addition, Irish Catholic refugees and migrants to Scotland were confronted with an environment and climate they found hostile, alienating and prejudiced against their faith and ethnic background.

A range of stereotyped attitudes towards the Irish flourished in the nineteenth century and these negative attitudes manifested themselves within various facets of Scottish life. Victorian times were characterised for example by 'No Irish Need Apply' notices, a common warning in the employment columns of the contemporary press and the walls and entrances of employment concerns. Pamphlets, lectures and tracts against Ireland, the Irish and Catholics, as well as their 'rudimentary' schools, were common during these decades, a time when Scots were developing a great sense of national pride in their education system.[5] A cultural and ideological polemic was waged by many sections of society against Irish Catholic immigrants, thus demonstrating that the Irish were generally viewed with suspicion and hostility in Scottish society.[6]

Writing of the small Irish immigrant community in nineteenth century Scotland, Handley reports that the Irish were subjected to all sorts of 'verbal abuse and mockery': the newspapers of the districts where there was an Irish presence were among the chief purveyors of this denigration. Handley quotes a number of newspaper articles having such titles as 'gims of the Emerald Isle' and 'bhoys from the land of the bog and the shamrock'. In addition, 'Ape-faced' and 'small headed Irishmen', 'a cruel Tipperary visage', 'a malicious-looking Irishman' and 'a blackguard-looking creature with a plastered face' are all specimens from the North British Daily Mail during the nineteenth century.[7] When the comic reporting became exhausted it usually ridiculed the incomers as the 'low Irish'.[8]

For Handley, the hostility with which the Irish in Scotland were met stemmed from economic, political and religious reasons, which in turn shaped the discourses in relation to Irish Catholic immigrants.[9] Commentators such as Finn and Curtis concur and consider this antagonism racist.[10] Handley also argues that the chief reason for native animosity was the fact that the immigrants were Catholics, the fewer Ulster Scots Protestants of the north of Ireland who also arrived in

Scotland in their thousands apparently assimilating easily with their former kith and kin.

Close inspection of the columns of the North British Daily Mail, Glasgow Courier, The Witness, Bulletin, Glasgow Chronicle, Glasgow Constitutional, Glasgow Herald, and Scottish Guardian among others, reveals an abundance of animosity towards the Irish in Scotland. Some newspapers like The Scotsman based in Edinburgh were occasionally more favourable towards the immigrants, but this was the exception rather than the rule. A discourse of superiority, domination and rejection was also evidenced by the census report for Scotland in 1871.

> As yet the great body of these Irish do not seem to have improved by their residence among us; and it is quite certain that the native Scot who has associated with them has most certainly deteriorated. It is painful to contemplate what may be the ultimate effect of this Irish immigration on the morals and habits of the people, and on the future prospects of the country.[11]

One significant factor used to negatively distinguish the Irish from the native Scots and British population generally was their 'Celticism', defined as:

> Their religion and their perceived Irish nationalism. As 'white negroes', the Irish were regarded as 'dirty' and 'diseased', a contagion within Victorian England [Britain] and a threat to it.[12]

Such historical reporting on the Irish is fundamental to appreciating how the wider society viewed the offspring of Irish Catholic immigrants, as well as to how they perceived themselves. This context is important in relation to contemporary Irish identity: that is, the Irishness of the progeny of Irish immigrants in Scotland. This is also crucial to understanding 'sectarianism' in modern Scottish society.

These representations indicate that the Irish were largely seen and prescribed as a racialised minority. As this minority began to become a more permanent feature of industrial Scotland, its offspring began to be 'sectarianised' in a related racialised fashion. Amongst other things, this has meant they have been subsequently identified not by their differing accent and place of birth, but by their town or village of residence, some of their cultural tastes and practices, but primarily, identified via their Irish names and Catholic religion: traditionally uncovered through unearthing whether a Catholic school was attended or not. A number of authors allude to the resultant discrimination faced by this community.[13]

Although it would be erroneous to characterise or stereotype all Scots with this prejudice, the history of ethno-religious cleavage in Scotland has meant that opposition, discrimination and intolerance towards the Irish immigrant community and its offspring has been extensive and has clearly had wide resonance. The inter-war years in the twentieth century were a particularly significant period when such manifestations became mainstream within Scottish society. Indeed, this period is important to understanding contemporary and modern expressions, as well as manifestations and representations of Irishness in Scotland.

Cooney asserts that as late as 1938, the Church and Nation Committee of the Church of Scotland emphasised: 'the elementary right of a nation to control and select its immigrants'.[14] This contention on the part of the Church was formed solely with Irish Catholics in mind. Brown states that from around the time of the Education Act (Scotland) 1918, until the outbreak of the Second World War, there was an 'official' Presbyterian campaign against the Irish Catholic community in Scotland.[15] This campaign was both institutional and popular, and is viewed by Brown as an attempt at 'marginalising, and even eliminating an ethnic minority whose presence was regarded as an evil, polluting the purity of Scottish race and culture'.[16]

This was a fertile period for such activities as well as a time when they were acceptable to and supported by many people in the wider society. Such sentiments found expression in popular literature, for example in the works of Andrew Dewar Gibb (later to become Regius Professor of Scots Law at Glasgow University) and of journalist George Malcolm Thomson.[17] Political activists, like Alexander Ratcliffe and John McCormick, gained success at the ballot by declaring similar anti-Irish and anti-Catholic opinions. Other significant political figures at the time reflected these widespread sentiments regarding the Irish in Scotland. Conservative Member of Parliament, Lord Scone, believed that:

> culturally the Irish population. . . has not been assimilated into the Scottish population. It is not my purpose to discuss now whether the Irish culture is good or bad, but merely to state the definite fact that there is in the west of Scotland a completely separate race of alien origin practically homogeneous whose presence there is bitterly resented by tens of thousands of the Scottish working-class.[18]

SOCIALISATION

The remarks of people like Scone were primarily aimed at the offspring of immigrants from Ireland, as by this time they outnumbered migrants born in Ireland who lived in Scotland. The remarks partly reflect the historical, religious, cultural and national position of Irish Catholics within Scottish and British societies. These attitudes towards Irish-born or descended Irish Catholics were conceived within a context of Britain's historic relationship with the island of Ireland and the embedded anti-Catholicism that dominated or filtered through much of Scottish life. Notably, persons born in England who lived in Scotland also outnumbered those who were Irish-born in Scotland at this time, though they were not a focus for grievance.

After the mass influx of Irish to Scotland during and after the Famine, for a number of decades this community led a relatively sheltered existence, surviving as marginalised, even 'ghettoised' Irish Catholics in society. Although in the decades after the First World War society opened up to a new era of economic, social and political developments and thinking, this period also represented a time of more structured, systematic and mainstream opposition towards Irish Catholics in Scotland. The marginalisation they had become largely accustomed to acquired new features and expressions that were public and particularly active and virulent.

For the Irish diaspora in Scotland, the postwar era thus represents a time of significant divergent experiences from those of the pre-war age. In terms of the solidity of this community, the damaging effects upon the diaspora of a more complex phase of national conflict in Ireland, the incorporatist influences of Catholic education largely controlled by the British state,[19] the incorporatist consequences arising from the positive opening up of British society in a social and political sense and, related to this, the development of the common cultural features and experiences of the twentieth century, all contested and diminished the Irishness of the immigrant community.

In the 1920s and 1930s, a heightened anti-Catholic and anti-Irish atmophere intensified an environment that Irish Catholics believed was already customarily hostile and discriminatory towards them. This accelerated the inclination and willingness of the Irish community in Scotland not to declare or publicy disclose its Irishness, and unnecessarily expose itself to the prejudice, bigotry and racism that existed. Although an ongoing process for the Irish, this period was crucial to the development of Irishness in Scotland and made a critical impression upon the communty's self-perceptions as well as their confidence and capacity to articulate being Irish (and Catholic). The complex and multi-varied racial hostility and religious prejudice encountered by the Irish has long marked that community's experience and has had a monumental influence in the inclination and ability of those of Irish descent to esteem their Irishness in Scotland.[20]

Irishness has remained important to many within this community, as is reflected in the vigour of Irish identity in early twenty first century Scotland. However, Irishness might simultaneously also be considered fragile, elusive and inarticulate. Distinct from the anti-Irish and anti-Catholic environment that has long prevailed in Scotland, the particularly forceful and aggressive era of racism and prejudice incited during the 1920s and 1930s, can also be seen as a time that in turn provoked an intensification of a willingness of the Irish to privatise their national, cultural and ethnic identities as a response to the prevailing environment.

This period represents a time whereby the Irish in Scotland, in an effort to contend with adversity, were to become – consciously or unconsciously – less obviously Irish. Indeed, this might be represented as a time when an increasing number of Irish became more Scottish, or at least began a process of constructing a more Scottish identity than ever before: this in an effort to be accepted, to divert unwanted negative attention, and to acquire and gain the social and economic passport and credentials for advancement and acceptance within Scotland.

In the context of negative portrayals and representations as well as active hostility, many Irish were hesitant and fearful about being publicly and negatively associated with Ireland or the Irish Catholic immigrant community. A changed or more diversely constructed social and cultural identity may or may not have dampened some of the antagonism of those who were anti-Irish, but a less distinctive Irish identity and community within Scottish society might relieve its worst features. Such change also had the potential to reassure those hostile and antagonistic to Irishness that there was less economic, social or political 'threat' on the part of the Irish Catholics in their midst. If the Irish were to be a permanent fixture in Scottish society and could not be physically ejected, then rather than negatively effect a perceived purity in the Scottishness of the host community the Irish required to be assimilated. Irishness remained unacceptable, but the Irish might be more acceptable and tolerated if they disavowed their Irishness and became more Scottish. In this sense, the Irish were being 'put in their place', they were being assigned a status in Scottish society that they were required to accept. One of the contemporary contradictions to emerge from this is the paradox expressed in the attitudes of anti-Irish and anti-Catholic Scots, or at least those Scots who do not accept the Irishness of the Irish descended in Scotland who esteem and celebrate their Irish heritage, culture and identity, that, 'you should go back to Ireland' or, 'you're not Irish anyway, you're Scottish'.

One example of this change taking place in the inter-war period is an increasingly discrete and less visible Irishness reflected in a mounting Catholic emphasis within the previously sure Irish political, cultural and religious organ, The Glasgow Star and Examiner. To a lesser degree Irish politics and cultural activities continued to be reported in Catholic newspapers but as they receded in prominence, they did so at the expense of solely Catholic or religious matters. Sport in general and news relating to Celtic Football Club in particular also suffered in this newspaper. Newspapers like as The Glasgow Star became less partisan and engaged in a struggle to be viewed popularly as disinterested in things Irish and political: more often than not, ignoring Irish and political affairs altogether. A product of this process was the gradual diminishing of news in relation to Ireland and the Irish as 'the Irish in Scotland'. The

Star was one newspaper that began a trend amongst Catholic newspapers in Scotland (The Glasgow Observer was to emerge as the Scottish Catholic Observer) reflecting a gradual shift towards focusing on articles Scottish, rather than matters Irish, as was previously the case. A product of this process was the diminishing power of what had been up until then the distinctive Catholic-Irish press to act as a formative influence and purveyor of Irishness as well as agent of Irish cultural maintenance, source of knowledge, community solidarity and celebration.

Up to that time, the focus and discourses of these newspapers reflected the Irish background and origins of the mass of their Catholic readership. However, this reporting and news began to be replaced by an emphasis on the portrayal of matters and stories that were essentially pre-Reformation, and therefore pre-Irish migration, 'Scottish' Catholic. Articles such as 'Catholic Scotland', 'How the Highlands held the faith' and 'Scotland's martyrs' began to predominate. These stories were important to a Catholic history of Scotland, but not only were they of limited relevance to the history of the Irish Catholic community in Scotland, they represented a transformation in the traditional and established narratives of Irish Catholic life as had previously been represented, portrayed and celebrated.[21] They partly symbolised the official omission of these narratives from the only public news organs that positively addressed Irishness in Scotland. This was also designed for the purpose of a reconstructed cultural alignment – away from Irishness and towards Scottishness. If it was better to be seen as less Irish and more Scottish then these newspapers became vehicles for the transmission of that message within and beyond their Catholic readership. Finally, with the death in 1934 of Derryman Charles Diamond, owner of much of the Catholic and Irish press in Britain, a new era for Irish ethnic newspapers dawned. By 1935, The Glasgow Star announced its forthwith 'strictly non-political' position whilst its 'aims and ideals [were subsequently] devoted entirely to the Catholic cause', defined only as 'Scottish' as opposed to 'Irish' Catholicism. [22]

SOCIALISATION THROUGH EDUCATION

Paralleling these changes, for the second and third generation Irish taught in state Catholic schools in Scotland (and Britain generally) there was a virtual absence of references to Ireland or the Irishness of the pupils, their families or communities. Therefore, a significant reference point and aspect of the lives of these pupils was omitted from the school curriculum, as well as from most other sources in relation to public memory or celebration in terms of the wider society. Officially, in the teaching of social subjects in particular, little or no reference was made to the ethnic or national origins, narratives and historical or contemporary experiences of this community. In this context, Doyle states:

> the history curriculum has always held a primary position in the transmission of national identity and national values and the history textbook has been an important tool in this process.[24]

In this process, other histories, specifically those relating to Scotland, Britain and the British Empire and British cultural norms, were (and have continued to be) 'imposed' upon children who were, and are, from fundamentally different backgrounds than the majority in society. In the state Catholic schools' curriculum a cultural conformity towards Scottishness and Britishness was engendered which was supported by a growing mass media that similarly ignored the Irish Catholic presence in Scotland and Britain. Although Catholicism was partly 'protected' and promoted through the state Catholic system, Irishness and numerous links with Ireland became for some of the diaspora, hidden, inarticulate, omitted, secondary, subordinate and less familiar. The Irishness of this community was generally ignored, unacknowledged, and in many ways, Ireland and being Irish became a less accessible identity.

This process is contrary to the modern educational rationale that seeks to educate children utilising their own environment, circumstances and cultural experiences to facilitate learning and crucially, integration. Indeed, according to Hickman, the most significant process served through state funded Catholic education – distinct from questions of faith – has been that of the assimilation of the Irish as opposed to their integration. In line with the thinking of Lord Scone and others like him, assimilation – meaning the obliteration of Irishness – rather than integration – meaning Irishness living side by side with Britishness and Scottishness – was desirable. This has also meant that for those conscious of the diminishing of their and their community's Irishness, a greater and more conscious effort was required to be affirmed for the maintenance, promotion and celebration of Irish socialisation and identity formation amongst Irish offspring in Scotland.

For some of the Irish community, to be viewed as Scottish increasingly became a mark of acceptability, respectability and success. For some immigrants and their offspring, Ireland represented the poverty and oppression of a past they were socialised into forgetting: indeed, they had learned to become embarrassed about. A perception existed that to be seen as Irish was to be viewed as parochial, ignorant and ghettoised.[25] A less visible Irishness, internally and externally, amongst Irish immigrant offspring in Scotland, and a steady adoption of a new framework of identity for some, has always characterised aspects of the Irish experience in Scotland. However, the inter-war period represents an intensification of this process. Antagonism and hostility on the part of a variety of institutions, organisations and individuals throughout Scottish society helped create and sustain an atmosphere where to be seen as Irish meant that life chances were limited. Part of the Irish Catholic response to this hostility was a privatisation, dilution and even eradication of Irishness.

The emerging Catholic, increasingly Scottish Catholic, identity, which began to dominate the traditional Catholic Irish one in west central Scotland, consisted of strong assimilationist obligations. For Hickman, the promotion of assimilation was part of a conscious strategy to diminish the Irishness of this community, frequently allowing in the process the formation of a less threatening Catholic identity and practice. The Irish in Britain were being incorporated into the British State and in the process Irishness was replaced with British and Scottish identities.[26]

The traditional view of the Irish being different in religion, culture and politics, of being a community that in times of trouble in Ireland provided authorities in Britain with a perceptible element of concern, even threat, was partly – though never completely – changed by this strategy of assimilation. A speech by Archbishop Hindley in England summed up the growing dominance of Scottish (and English) and British cultural attributes over those that were arguably of greater significance to the immigrants:

> Such loyalty to God and our Sovereign, George VI, who has succeeded to the dignity and to the heavy responsibility which were laid down by his brother. In unswerving sincerity the 17,000,000 of Catholics throughout the Empire do homage to our new King, and declare their devotion to his person and their attachment to the royal family. . . [27]

Hindley's comments link with the argument of Scone and others like him, who desired the obliteration of Irishness and only tolerated assimilation. The comments also link with Hickman's research that stresses how British government policy, allied with the intentions of the English Catholic hierarchy, strove to lessen the Irishness and de-politicise, as well as 'civilise', the massive numbers of the offspring of the Irish in Britain.

Hindley's remarks can also be associated with those of Scottish Bishops Murdoch and Scott during the 'The Free Press' controversy in the nineteenth century when they made known their negative feelings regarding the vast majority of the Catholic community in Scotland being Irish rather than Scottish as a result of Irish migration and few Scots being Catholics.[28] Further, Hindley's comments parallel those of Scottish Bishop Hay in the late eighteenth century.

In the era prior to Irish Catholic immigration the few remaining Catholic Scots in the country persisted as an object for hostility. The dominant Protestant as well as widespread anti-Catholic identities of the Scottish people encouraged the remaining Catholic population in the country to maintain a low profile. This low profile and the subservient nature of contemporary Catholicism, was evident during the period of the passing of Catholic relief bills in 1788. Throughout this time of crisis, Bishop George Hay protested that Scots Catholics were innocent and loyal, thus emphasising the abstruse and servile nature of the native Scottish Catholic church.[29] Such comments pre-dated, but also anticipated an era in the twentieth century when the Catholic Irish became a focus for intense hostility. A frequent response from that community towards this enmity resembled that of Scottish Catholics in the late eighteenth century. The Irish also maintained a low profile amid a social and political hostility that targeted them and helped create a climate where expressions of Irishness, as well as Catholicism, were likely to attract unwanted antagonism.

1. Gallagher in Devine, 1991, pp.19-43.
2. Muirhead, 1973.
3. Murray 1984, P. 93 and Devine 1988 p.154.
4. See McFarland 1990, Gallagher 1987 and Devine 1991
5. Gallagher, 1987, p.32
6. Some newspapers like The Scotsman in Edinburgh were occasionally more sympathetic towards the immigrants, but this was the exception rather than the rule.
7. Handley, p.249.
8. Ibid. P.133.
9. Ibid. P.131.
10. Also see Finn 1991 and Curtis 1984 and 1988.
11. Handley, p.321.
12. MacLaughlin 1999.
13. See Handley P. 357, Devine (ed) 1995 and Gallagher 1997.
14. Cooney, 1982, p.19.
15. Brown, 1991, pp.19-45.
16. Ibid: p.21.
17. Gallagher, 1987, pp.168-172.
18. Hansard, 261, 22/11/1932.
19. Hickman, 1995.
20. See Bradley, 1995.
21. For examples see The Star, 11/1/1936, 12/12/1936 and 1/2/1936.
22. The Star, 7/9/1935.
23. M Hickman, 1990 & 1995. Much history teaching in Scotland has been traditionally been centred on British and English characters and events.
24. A Doyle, 2002.
25. Gallagher's otherwise excellent work 'Glasgow: The Uneasy Peace', also repeats and reflects the language and concept of the non-specific sub-theme of an Irish ghetto in the West of Scotland.
26. Hickman, 1995.
27. The Star, 26/12/1936.
28. See Bernard Aspinwall, in Devine (edt), 1991, p.91. He says that the Catholic Church has acted as a far more integrating force than critics allow. Hickman is also of the belief that the Catholic Church in England/Britain was actually a vital instrument in this strategy.
29. Cooney, 1982, p.14.

Chapter 8

A struggle for survival

IN THE CULTURAL AND SPORTING SHADE

By the 1930s the Gaelic Athletic Association in Scotland was facing its lowest ebb. It had long since struggled for recognition even amongst its own constituency in Scotland but with the changing social, cultural and political environment within which it existed, like many other expressions of Irishness in Scotland its opportunity for survival and progress was severely limited.

In July 1932 a letter from 'Old Faugh' in The Glasgow Star and Examiner confirmed a lack of Gaelic sporting activity in the west of Scotland:

> Is there such a thing in Glasgow or district as a hurling club or Irish Athletic Club. . . I used to play myself on ground in Possilpark, now used for a housing scheme. And I am sure there are a lot of people in Glasgow who if they had the chance would be only too pleased to join up in such a club. . . [1]

The question was to be partly answered by people like Thomas Flynn, Sports Convenor of the Irish National Association (64 Charlotte Street, later based at Risk Street off London Road, Glasgow), James Jackson and the Irish National Association (founded by Con Horgan a Glasgow-based schoolmaster from Cork), Willie Farrell (one time President) and Richard Ford. Ford was an Irish Catholic activist who had been president of the first branch of the Gaelic League founded in Scotland and who was later prominent in the Catholic Knights of St

Columba. It was as president of the Irish National Association that Ford, a former player with the Rapparees and over the previous twenty or so years renowned amongst the Gaelic fraternity for his lectures on 'Poetical Wild Flowers',[2] stated:

> The Irish National Association since its inception has used every means in its power to foster a love for the Irish arts and games among the young Irishmen and women in Glasgow. During the past session we have been amply repaid in the dancing and musical sections as the results of the recent Sinn Féin Feis in Glasgow show. We have recently acquired a commodious sports ground of six and a quarter acres at Marylea [adjacent to the Franciscan Convent]. . . We have a hurling field in the grounds and have started a hurling club. In passing I may mention that we have also a County Board of the G.A.A. . . [3]

Although a hurling club was founded in the early months of the following year, the truth was that the Gaelic Athletic Association was not flowering in Scotland.[4]

In early 1933, after initial contacts between representatives of the Irish National Association and the Southern Shinty League, an advertisement in the Glasgow Observer appealed for support for a new initiative:

> that the Irish people in Glasgow will give them the support it would receive in Ireland by turning out in large numbers to give the Irish team a hearty welcome and show that the exiles still hold dear the National games of Ireland.[5]

The result of the meeting was the arrangement of a compromise rules fixture between an Irish university hurling team and a selection of players from the Scottish Shinty League at Glasgow's Shieldhall Park, Hardgate Road in south Govan. The hurling team was composed of players from the University colleges of Dublin, Cork and Galway. The Glasgow Southern Shinty League selection shared a background of Highland birth and descent. The hurlers won the match by the only goal of the game.[6] Nonetheless, according to one report:

> the result was of secondary importance to the fact that this essentially Gaelic game was shown to have a large following in the West of Scotland and the possibilities for its development are attractive.[7]

In terms of the match itself, it was reported:

> Our Irish visitors put more play on the ball, changed and interchanged positions with fine understanding, made ground more quickly and the harassed Scots had to reveal to the full their renowned characteristics – doggedness and tenacity – to withstand periods of uninterrupted attacks. J Canning, one of Erin's priest forwards, scored the goal after 18 minutes play, netting from short range. . . The second half was more evenly contested: indeed at times the speed of the play exhilarated.[8]

The G.A.A. in Scotland looked anxiously for revival. In October of the same year, Rev Daniel O'Keeffe of St Charles' Kelvinside Glasgow, Rev Daniel Horgan of the Irish National Association, acting as an intermediary for the G.A.A. in Dublin, along with Padraig O'Keefe (often known as Padraig O'Caoimh), Secretary of the G.A.A. in Ireland and Patrick McNamee, secretary of the Ulster Council, met with officials of the Camanachd Association in Scotland, 'with a view to unifying the rules of hurling and shinty'.[9] Among the Camanachd representatives were ex-provost Skinner from Oban and Messrs Fletcher (Glasgow) and Patterson (Beauly). The result of the meeting was that future games between hurling and shinty representatives would be directed by the attending members at this meeting: they would 'settle points of divergence in the unified game'.[10] Nonetheless, the Camanachd Association officials finally decided not to compromise on their rules for games in Scotland although some accommodation might be made for future international games.

Hutchinson states that government officials in Edinburgh and Whitehall learned of the contact between both Associations and made representations to the Camanachd body stressing what it termed as the 'anti-British political flavour' of the G.A.A. Reid also suggests that a cultural and religious 'unwillingness' to associate with Catholics on the part of the Camanachd members, who were also members of the Free Church of Scotland, may also have been a factor in their not wishing to pursue friendly relations with the G.A.A.[11] For Hutchinson, it was the shinty players of Scotland who lost out. The refusal to understand, or as a result of a 'distorted' understanding of, the G.A.A.'s origins and evolution as part of the struggle for Irish independence and the willingness to accept government views meant:

> self-imposed solitude in the country to which the Irish had introduced it [shinty] 1500 years before.[12]

Irish feelings were more positive on Irish-Scottish matters. At the annual meeting of the Gaelic Athletic Association's Ard Comairle held in Thurles, County Tipperary in the following year, the Council claimed:

> The position in Scotland, so long uncertain, has been transformed during the past year by special re-organisation and an understanding with the Camanacht Association in the Western area.[13]

Despite plans and expectations, nothing appears to have been done during the rest of the year. At a variety of junctures during the twentieth century some efforts were made to substantiate competition between hurlers in Ireland and shinty players in Scotland: this was especially true between some Irish and Scottish university sides. However, the Scottish shinty authorities did not welcome the Irish competition and in 1964 the Camanachd Association went so far as to pronounce itself to be 'firmly against any links' with Gaelic sports in Ireland, requesting its members not to patronise any compromise game that might be organised. In 1971, Blessed Oliver Plunkett School from Dublin travelled to play Oban High School. Hutchinson believes that this event meant that, 'the ice was broken'. Since then, clubs in both countries have played each other and a number of 'international' compromise rules matches have also been held.[14]

In 1934 the Gaelic Athletic Association celebrated its Jubilee: fifty years as a major institution in Ireland. The newspaper of the Catholic Irish in Scotland, The Glasgow Star, was moved to comment:

> . . . the G.A.A. is the healthiest lay movement we have in Ireland and is the one continuous platform for unity of action that nationalists have developed. The controlling body of the Association have brought it safely through the dark and dreary days of external and internal trouble, and their outspoken loyalty to the Faith of their Fathers is all the guarantee we need that in piloting it successfully through the political shoals of today.[15]

Another attempt was made to revive the games the same year and a hurling match at the Clontarf Park grounds in Marylea (Merrylea) was arranged as an opener to the revival. During August, Rovers from Cambuslang met the Fitzgeralds of Glasgow with the former winning by three goals and two points to one goal and three points: the match was refereed by Rev Daniel O'Keeffe. Pater, Dwyer, McCallion and Haugh scored for the Rovers whilst M J McCann and Sugrve replied for the Fitzgeralds.

> A most encouraging feature of the game was the good play shown by the neophytes under the skilled guidance of veterans of national reputation in Ireland. Among them were former heroes of hurling of Glens of Antrim, Tipperary, Clare, Limerick, Sligo and Cork. The Scottish Provincial Council has started well. . . [16]

Despite some optimism, it was August 1934 before the revival was further reflected in press reports. A meeting on the part of the Clontarf Park Committee believed that:

> for the development of Gaelic games and outdoor amusements. . . an optimistic feeling prevailed. Sincere thanks (were) accorded to many patrons for their generous donations and through the gift of 7 sets of hurleys from the National Council, G.A.A., Dublin a promising future is believed to be secure. . . Having turned with jealous eyes to the flourishing condition of Gaelic games in London and America, the apathy still prevailing in Scotland was deprecated. The important bearing of our games on national character of which we are so justly proud, cannot be exaggerated. The idea of a national recreation ground where the people throughout the city (Glasgow) are drawn together. . . cannot be sufficiently stressed. . .

Gaelic pastimes as an aspect of guarding against the excesses of industrialisation and urbanisation, and the cultural and national security afforded by the Association in an often hostile land, at least for this particular writer, recreated some of the ideals of the original founders of the G.A.A. He continued:

> How the glad thoughts of happy associations in Clontarf Park where all hearts beat in unison in the friendly Celtic way, where friends meet friends once more – all for each and each for all – can enliven many a weary hour in the office, the salesroom or the factory or lost amidst the mass of swarming humanity. Remember that procrastination is the thief of time, an earnest appeal is made to the youthful exiles – boys and girls – scattered throughout the city to take immediate advantage of the long-looked-for opportunity and to assist the good work already begun under their patronage and memberships.[17]

Yet despite the existence of committed Gaelic enthusiasts and continued attempts on the part of the Irish National Association, who were at the forefront of Irish activities to revive Gaelic games and other Irish pursuits and pastimes, few successes resulted. Probably the last reference made to Gaelic games played in Scotland for a number of years can be found in the Glasgow Observer of October 1934.[18] A hurling match was arranged between sides from Glasgow and Lanarkshire. Played at Lanarkshire Park in Motherwell, the Glasgow team won the game with six goals and two points against five goals and two points. The teams that took the field were:

Glasgow: Dwyer, Lillies, Howe, McCallum, Ahern, Gallagher, Burns, Martin, Butler, Gillian, H Dolan, Walsh, Hughes and McCarran.

Lanarkshire: T Kiernan, Myles, H McCann, M McCann, McAlinden, D Dickson, Lambert, O'Connor, H Kiernan, Boylan, Devlin and Sugrve.19

This game in Lanarkshire was probably the last competitive hurling match to be organised in Scotland for a number of years. Canning believes that like the First War, World War II decimated the G.A.A. as it did many other organisations.

Hurling, whatever about Gaelic football, virtually disappeared from the Scottish scene. The influx of Irish to Scotland had dried up to a mere trickle and consequently the youth and material of the G.A.A. games simply did not exist.[20]

Although being Irish and Catholic often represented diminished life chances and negative labelling, and despite Irish bodies suffering severe decline in the decades after the First World War, Irishness remained important to many within the Catholic community in Scotland as is partly reflected in the thousands who followed Celtic Football Club and the 40,000 who turned out for a demonstration by the Ancient Order of Hibernians at Carfin in Lanarkshire in August 1937. Nevertheless, as had long been the case, Gaelic sports struggled to rise above the status of a 'minority sport', even within a minority community.[21] Few families who were Irish or who had Irish antecedents had any affinity for these uniquely Irish sports.

By the 1940s popular and public Irish cultural activities, and Gaelic sports in particular, were at a low ebb in the west of Scotland. It was some years before Gaelic enthusiasts recognised that for Irish sporting activities to survive and become popular, a concerted effort was required to recruit young people of Irish antecedents. Indeed, Gaelic sports activity, as a facet of being Irish in Scotland, would require to be introduced as a new sport to many of those with Irish forebears. Nonetheless, in the immediate years after World War II, a revival in Scotland did take place, 'chiefly attributable to the post World War II situation when Irish immigrants found great demand for their labour in the vast building and construction developments' then underway.[22]

1. The Star, 20/8/1932.
2. Ibid: 20/9/1912.
3. Ibid: 27/8/1932.
4. Ibid: 14/4/1934.
5. Glasgow G.A.A. Centenary Brochure, 1984.
6. The Star, 13/5/1933.
7. Glasgow G.A.A. Centenary Brochure, 1984.
8. Ibid.
9. The Star, 9/9/1933.
10. Ibid: 21/10/1933.
11. Information from Dr I A Reid via interview with Donald Skinner, grandson of Provost Skinner.
11. Hutchinson 1989, pp. 186-187.
12. Minutes of Central Council, 1934.
13. Hutchinson, 1989, pp. 186-187.
14. The Star, 22/9/1934.
15. Glasgow G.A.A. Centenary Brochure, 1984.
16. Ibid
17. This match was played on 29th of September.
18. Boylan was probably Michael Boylan who originated from Ballina, County Mayo. A number of this family are believed to have subsequently emigrated from Motherwell to the Pittsburgh Steelworks in the U.S.A. Information from a member of Boylan family in Motherwell.
19. Glasgow G.A.A. Centenary Brochure, 1984.
20. The Star, 28/8/1937.
21. Michael Fallon in Glasgow G.A.A. Centenary Brochure, 1984.

Chapter 9

Gaelic sporting regeneration

SURVIVAL: RETURN TO GAELIC SPORT

For most of the 1930s Gaelic sporting activities in Scotland existed in a state of flux, much of the period characterised by little if any specifically Irish sports. It seems that an occasional informal game of Gaelic football played on Glasgow Green, one game noted was that between a Gweedore select and a Glasgow-based side, was the only Gaelic sporting episode evident at the time.[1]

In fact, it was the late 1940s and a new era of Irish migration to Scotland before G.A.A. activities began to re-emerge in west central Scotland. After a few long term visits prior to World War II, aged twenty-five, John Keaveny finally emigrated to Glasgow in 1943. A native of County Sligo, Keaveny began to socialise with others in Glasgow who originated from Ireland. This occurred mainly at the numerous ceilis held around the Glasgow area in venues like the A.O.H. Hall in Greenvale Street Bridgeton, as well as in the Fianna Fail Club in Clyde Ferry Street Glasgow.

Along with several other Gaelic-minded individuals, Keaveny took over the running of G.A.A. affairs in Glasgow from earlier Association figures such as Tom Flynn and Tom Gillespie. The Gillespie family were well known Donegal republicans from Buncrana, whose members had participated in the struggle for Irish independence in the first quarter of the twentieth century. Gillespie, and subsequently his son Diarmuid (also Dermot), encouraged others such as Rory Campbell to become involved in G.A.A. affairs.[2] Campbell's people had come to Scotland from County Tyrone; his father also previously involved in republican activities prior to the onset of World War II.[3]

Formerly a Gaelic footballer in his native Geevagh, County Sligo (and also a former County Junior Championship winner), Keaveny settled in East Kilbride during the mass re-locations of much of Glasgow's population to Scotland's 'New Towns' during the 1950s and 1960s. Along with Eoin Kelly a native of Fermanagh, Rory Campbell and Charlie Quinn, the latter having emigrated from Dromore in County Tyrone in the 1940s, he was instrumental in re-forming the Glasgow G.A.A.: the formal inauguration taking place at the Catholic Diocesan Centre near Charing Cross in Glasgow.[4]

Part of Keaveny's importance to the Association was that he was one of the first to encourage the game amongst those of Irish descent in the west of Scotland. This reflected in Motherwell's Thomas Davis Club that chiefly comprised players born in Scotland of an Irish background. These included Frank McIlheney and Gerry Gallen, the latter also a member of the Gaelic League. Gallen's father emigrated from Donegal, his mother from Tyrone, while his wife originated from Leitrim.[5]

In Lanarkshire matches were played at Carfin's Glenburn stadium, at the time owned by the Heffernan family, and still utilised as a dog-racing track until the late 1990s when the land was turned into a housing development. Son of the original owner, Pat Heffernan had played with the Thomas Davis Club when matches were played at this venue during the late 1940s and early 1950s. Heffernan's mother came to Scotland from Cavan whilst his father's side were earlier immigrants from west Munster. South east of Glasgow, Orion Park in Carmyle became the ground of another new club, Tara Harps (under Jimmy McMenemy, Con Maguire and Paddy Ward) based originally at the Irish Club in Greenvale Street in Bridgeton Glasgow. Formally the A.O.H. Hall this subsequently became the Tara Social Club.

This Gaelic sporting resurgence was initially sparked with the first Gaelic football club to emerge after the war when a few members of the Gaelic League, overlapping their membership with that of the Four

Provinces Social Club in Paisley, began a fundraising venture. This was organised mainly in the form of weekly ceilis in the School Wynd Hall to finance the founding of a club. On raising the sum of £100 the membership decided to purchase a football strip for the proposed Paisley Gaels Club, later to be known as Clan na Gael. The Club was born due in the main to the efforts of Father James Nevin from the local St Mirrin's Parish, Plunkett Cairns, Packy McCusker, Eoin Kelly, Seamus McManus and Frank McCarron.

Over the latter few years of the 1940s Paisley Gaels, in addition to several other teams, began to play Gaelic football on an ash/blaze pitch near St Agnes' Church in Lambhill, Glasgow: courtesy of local priest, James Fennessy. The experience of playing on ash meant that improved playing conditions became a priority for G.A.A. members. Although hurling had dominated amongst the Gaelic fraternity during the first fifty years of Irish Gaelic sports in Scotland, it was Gaelic football which would provide the revived Association with its future.

From the Gorbals area of Glasgow arose the Eire Og Club. This club was organised by Jimmy O'Donnell, Josie Rogers and John McLafferty, and consisted mainly of recent immigrants from the Rosses and Gweedore areas of Donegal, with Gerry Galvin a notable outsider from Roscommon.[6] During this period the St Eunans club was founded in Clydebank. At around the same time arose the Padraic Pearses club that had its base in the Fianna Fail Cumann's Club in Glasgow's Rutherglen Road, the only branch of Fianna Fail to be founded outside of Ireland. Most of the players playing with the club were originally from the Donegal gaeltacht, although some team members were second generation Irish.[7] A team also emerged from within the Irish community in Edinburgh, organised by John Doran and situated within St Mary's Cathedral Parish in the city.

The first re-born Glasgow Championship was won by Eire Og against Pearses. The Eire Og team consisted of;

> A Gallagher, Joe O'Donnell, N Boyle, Jimmy O'Donnell, Dan Gallagher, Jimmy Gallagher, Owen McElwee, Michael O'Donnell, Josie Sweeney, Charlie McFadden, Jerry Galvin, Packie O'Donnell, Sean Boyle, Willie Boyle and Tommy Boyle.

Soon after this Championship winning season Eire Og disappeared from the scene. In 1952 Pearses, led by organisers John Quaile, Paddy McCafferty, Jerry Shields, Louis Wilson, Liam Murphy, P McFadden, Fred Sweeney and John Lally, won the Glasgow Football Championship, celebrating with a visit and game against Baillieborough, Cavan county champions. The match ended three points apiece. During this time, although small in size in comparison to many other sports, Gaelic games in Scotland were regarded as being of a high standard. The Pearse team that played in Ireland was:

> P Comiskey, P O'Donnell (capt), T Conway, G Friel, P Reilly, H Friel, B McDonald, P Friel, S Barrett, J Donnelly, Bro Cornelius Lean, P Boyle, F Irwin, M Friel, E Friel.[8]

Some of those involved in Gaelic football also managed to form a hurling team, Eugene O'Growney's, whose secretary was M Gibbons.[9] Although the club had little or no hurling opposition, it did play a game in Mussleburgh and encountered a number of University and College shinty sides (Edinburgh, Glasgow, Dundee College and a Perth-based club) in compromise matches. Partly reflecting an era of increased migration from Ireland, a number of other Gaelic football clubs clubs were initiated during the 1950s. Roger Casements in Clydebank (secretary, Willie McDermott), St Francis' in Falkirk (sec Peadar Flaherty), St Patricks' Greenock (sec S Loughery) and St Colmcilles in Edinburgh (sec Owen Coll). Round Towers (under Jack Hunt and Frank O'Neill) based in the Kildara Club, Earl Street in Scotstoun, and also Fintan Lalors Gaelic football club from Govan was also founded, the latter taking part in the 1954-55 championship.[10]

The postwar building revival in Britain and the continued poverty in much of Ireland meant a resurgence of Irish migration to Scotland. Although smaller than previous waves it entailed many thousands of Irish arriving in the Glasgow area in particular and this was significant enough to give rise to a new Glasgow County Board to conduct G.A.A. affairs in Scotland. Forming the new Board were chairmen at the time P McCafferty and Fr Joseph McElholm along with Rory Campbell, S McManus and Mick McNulty. On Easter Monday 1950, the Board organised an Aeridheacht at St Mungo's Sports Grounds in Glasgow.

Irish dancers and combined bands from the Irish National Association and Sean Ward's Ceili Band provided entertainment while Gaelic football teams represented a Glasgow/Tyrone select against a Glasgow/Donegal select: a game won 3:3 to 2:5 on the part of the Donegal team.

Tyrone: T Gallagher, McLafferty, Boyle, O'Donnell, Brady, H Friel, T Friel, McKenna, McAleer, J Sweeney, P McGuire, Dyer, Keaveny, Mulvey, P O'Donnell: subs F Lynch, O'Hare, Liam Docherty.

Donegal: McColl, Coll, McBrearty, Diver, McIlroy, J Gallagher, P Ward, McFadden, Barr, Galvin, Dougan, J O'Donnell, O'Hare, Thomson, H Gallagher: subs R Friel, T Sexton, Long.

PLAYERS, CHAMPIONSHIPS AND PEARSE PARK

In June 1950, Central Council in Dublin sponsored an exhibition Gaelic football game between two senior county teams from Ulster, Derry and Antrim, at Moore Park Govan, the home of St Anthonys junior soccer club. The match ended Antrim 3:11, Derry 2:8. Teams and officials stayed at the Beresford Hotel, later to become part of Strathclyde University's Halls of Residence. The Ulster guests were welcomed by the Glasgow County Board at a ceili reception held at St Simon's Hall Benalder Street Partick in Glasgow. In addition, players and officials from both counties were taken as guests to visit Canon Taylor and the Lourdes Grotto at Carfin in Lanarkshire:[11] this visit echoing that of half a century before when the Rapparees of Glasgow visited Sarsfields of Coatbridge, the visiting team being taken on tour of local Catholic schools and chapels. On the same day as the visit to Carfin, a Glasgow team played a Derry-Antrim select at Glenburn Stadium in Carfin.

Arising out of a visit to Scotland by Patrick McNamee, Ulster representative on the Central Council, Glasgow was reinstated to the British junior football Championship to play London at New Eltham Park, on August 23rd 1952. London narrowly won the match 1:10 to 1:8. Reflecting the high standard of play evident at least eight of the Scottish-based players had previously played county football in Ireland, including Hudai Beag Gallagher who had won Railway Cup medals in 1942 and 1943.[12] The Glasgow-based side that represented Scotland was made up from players:

Jerry Galvin (Roscommon), Tony Coll (Derry), K McSherry (Leitrim), Eoin Kelly (Fermanagh), Tom Conway (Mayo), Sean Barrett (Monaghan), Pat O Meara (Tipperary), Con McKenna (Monaghan), Tony McGee (Fermanagh), John Doherty, Tommy Boyle, Hudai Beag Gallagher, Michael Friel, Paddy Boyle, Eddie McBrearty, Joe Rushe, Willie McGee, Paddy Diver and Tommy McGinley (all Donegal).

During this period of a resurgence of Gaelic football activities further games took place in Ulster involving clubs from Scotland. In 1954 Glasgow played Antrim at Casement Park and later travelled to Clones to meet Monaghan. Nonetheless, despite the prestige attached to these games, success eluded the Glasgow-based players.

Table 6:1 **Glasgow Football Championship winners 1950-1958**[13]

1949-50	Eire Og	1951-52	Pearses
1952-53	Clan na Gael	1953-54	Clan na Gael
1954-55	Pearses	1955-56	St Patricks
1956-57	Fintan Lalors	1957-58	Roger Casements

One of the most significant events for gaels in Scotland and indeed, for the future revival of the Association three decades later, was the purchase of an area of land in Glasgow in 1953. The main driving force behind the procurement of the potential G.A.A. park was Charlie Quinn, although its buying was initially opposed by officials like Gerry Gallen who thought the area too isolated and believed there were already reasonable crowds attending matches at Carfin. Quinn had long anticipated a piece of land the Glasgow G.A.A. could call its own and in his capacity as a travelling foreman he frequently searched for an appropriate space. An area at Eastfield in Cambuslang attracted him and it was purchased from people living in the USA, relations of two elderly women from Glasgow who had previously owned it.

Although Quinn had viewed a pitch so heavy with water 'there were ducks swimming in it', he managed to arrange for a number of workers to partly revive the area, an effort mainly carried out in the evenings after the work force had completed their normal course of daily work. Soon after the purchase of the land a park was drained and turfed. Quinn's sister, Molly, paid for huts from a source in Motherwell and these were to become the dressing rooms for almost half a century.[14]

A steering committee of Eoin Kelly, John Keaveny, Rory Campbell, Charlie Quinn and Reverend P J McGovern of St Roch's Parish in Glasgow, had helped raise money for the purchase of the six and a half acres of ground. Campbell, McGovern and Padraig MacNamee, the first Ulsterman to head the G.A.A. at Croke Park, became the ground's patrons.

Due to Glasgow's prevarications, those representing the County had finally to pay more for the ground than the price initially quoted. Central Council of the G.A.A. in Dublin loaned the Glasgow G.A.A. £300. Eoin Kelly added a loan of £50 to finally seal the deal whilst the committee raised the following donations:

Table 6:2 **Pearse Park Financial Contributions 1953**[15]

Fr P Burke	£2.00
Fr P J Brady	£2.00
Fr M Coakley	£1.00
Fr Gillespie	£1.00
Fr Hanrahan	£1.00
Fr M Lyne	£1.00
Fr Lowery	£5.00
Mr J McVey	£2.2shillings
Mr E McGowan	£1.1
Fr McHugo	£1.10
Mr J O'Byrne	£0.10
Fr Whyte	£1.10
Mr T Cassidy	£0.10
Mr F Carr	£0.10
Mr J Tonner	£0.10
Scottish Council, Anti-Partition League	£2.2
Fr O'Keefe	£2.2
Mr J McMenamin	£0.10
Fr Keegan	£1.00
Mr F Jordan	£1.1
J Colton	£3.15
J Kavanagh	£3.3
Fr D B White	£1.00
Fr Conway	£10.00

Chas Quinn £10.00
Gaelic League £20.00

The ground was formally opened with a match between Glasgow and opponents from Lancashire on September 13th, 1953.

1960s – 1970s

Despite a list of positive gains made by the G.A.A. in Glasgow, by the early 1960s once again the only Gaelic sport manifest amidst the large Irish community in the west of Scotland took place at Eastfield Park, Cambuslang. Indeed, possibly only for the foresight of the Gaelic stalwarts who had purchased Eastfield in 1953 and which had at least ensured a central and accessible G.A.A.-owned facility was available, there might have been no Gaelic sport at all in Scotland. Keeping Gaelic football alive at Cambuslang, individuals, mostly Irish-born and with a strong Donegal influence, congregated at the pitch, picked sides and played matches. The main organisers were people like John Quaile, Gerry Gallagher, Eddie McBrearty, Charlie Quinn and Eoin Kelly. However, the availability of players largely depended on how the building trade was functioning, many potential players involved in that industry. For one player during this era, the economic situation and the type of work in which many of the gaels were involved, meant that:

> there tended to be constant movement of Gaelic footballers. Players could be available one week and not free for several weeks. If the family was based in Glasgow you could have one player one week and then the next he would appear with his brother. This made team selection difficult, but when it operated to your benefit with lots of players available the strongest side could be fielded.[16]

During 1962 one of the highlights for the G.A.A. in Glasgow took place when around ten teams took part in a seven-a-side tournament. In 1963, in a challenge match in Liverpool, Glasgow played and defeated Lancashire Champions, John Mitchell's. Some of the players who participated in that victory were:

> Sean Sexton (Cavan), Paddy O'Donnell (Donegal), Paddy Boyle (Donegal), Gerry Galvin (Roscommon), Frank Corr (Donegal), Seamus and Pat Maguire (Donegal), Pat Kearney (Donegal), Eamonn Cullen (Donegal), John Brown (Donegal), John Langan (Derry).

The following year a Scottish-based side was well beaten by London in the British Provincial Championship. In 1964 the Glasgow team gained revenge for its 1963 defeat by beating John Mitchell's from Birmingham.[17] In 1965 a number of G.A.A stalwarts began training regularly at Eastfield Park. Eamonn Cullen (secretary), Clydebank priest Father E Burns (Chairman), Sean Moore an Aer Lingus employee (assistant secretary) and Charlie Quinn (treasurer) made up the County Board for that season. St Eunans, Padraic Pearses (which emerged from the Padraic Pearse Fianna Fail Cumann in Glasgow) and Clan na hÉireann evolved to become G.A.A. clubs of the period. The first championship of this era was won by St Eunans who subsequently drew with John Mitchell's of Liverpool in the Provincial Championship. The St Eunans team was made up from:

> Eugene Harkin (Clydebank), John Brown (Letterkenny), Pat Kearney (Inch), 'Farmer' Duffy (Letterkenny), Phil Welsh (Dungloe), Pat O'Callaghan (Armagh), Jim O'Callaghan (Armagh), John Brown (Glenties), Eamonn Cullen (Milford), Bobby Hamilton (Armagh), John McCaughey (Tyrone), Jim McKenna (Monaghan), Charley McGinley (Gweedore), Eddie McGinley (Milford), Barney McDaid (Letterkenny).

In 1966 County Antrim Champions St John's from Belfast visited Glasgow whilst St Eunans visited Manchester and defeated the local St Brendans club. The same year also witnessed the start of a new club, Clydebank-based St Brendans, which replaced the struggling Clan na hÉireann. This club was given birth by Father Burns, Eamonn Cullen and Eoin Kelly. In 1966, St Eunans again won the championship.

Although only three clubs participated in the 1967 championship, gaels traditionally regard this season as a high point of the 1960s: games being played on a regular basis at Eastfield Park. St Brendans shocked holders St Eunans to win the 1967 championship, and apart from only a few players, the winner's panel consisted almost entirely of Donegal-born players.

> Seamus Sweeney (Fanad), F Michael Sweeney (Fanad), Kieran McGhee (Fanad), E McGinley (Milford), Sean Sweeney (Gweedore), Donal McBride (Letterkenny), Seamus McGuire (Dungloe), Tom McHugh (Tyrone), George McHugh (Tyrone), Benny Gormley (Tyrone), Joe Sweeney (Gweedore), Anthony Kelly (Kerrykeel), Barney McDaid (Letterkenny).

The Scottish-based champions were subsequently beaten by one point in a British Junior Championship semi-final against John F Kennedy's from Leeds. Such a strong Donegal representation was also reflected in the instigation of an annual match at Eastfield Park between players from Donegal and those from the rest of Ireland.

Visits to and from clubs in Ireland also characterised this era and St Eunans Inch, St Joseph's Bundoran/Ballyshannon, Gweedore and Downing's, all from Donegal, Castleblaney Faughs Monaghan, South Kerry, St John's Belfast, Crossmaglen County Armagh, Clan na Gael Dublin, Bellaghy County Derry, John F Kennedy's Leeds and London Gaels, all participated. In 1968 there again remained only three teams in Glasgow though Padraic Pearses quickly demised. They were soon replaced by another Glasgow club, Clan na Gael. That year St Brendans retained the championship.

By 1969 St Eunans had demised, only to be replaced by another club, South O'Hanlons. One player in particular, Father Sean McGrath, a Fermanagh-born priest and former county footballer based at the priest training college (Kiltegans) at Buchlyvie in Stirlingshire, providing the club with a much needed boost of talent and coaching. Nevertheless, it was Clan na Gael who won the championship in 1969. This season also witnessed Glasgow defeated at Casement Park in Belfast by Down in the Ulster Junior Championship. According to one participant of this period, the quality of the County team was never truly reflected in positive results due to the fact that a number of the accomplished players did not travel when county matches were played away from Glasgow.[18] A similar situation was also to handicap future County squads in the 1980s and 1990s as players were reluctant to travel and contribute to County fortunes.

In relation to the quality of the game played in Scotland there were a number of players who had played both senior and minor football for their counties in Ireland; Neil Gallagher (Donegal), Anthony Gallagher (Donegal), Joseph Winston (Donegal), Tadg McGinley (Donegal), Sean McGrath (Fermanagh), Chris Kane (Dublin) and Michael Power (Waterford) the most prominent participants of this era. The most notable Scottish-born players of the period were Joe Pugh and Eugene

Herren (St Brendans), Pat McInerrin and Michael Mulkerrin (St Eunans) and Malky Mackay, John McGowan and Gerry Morrow of Clan na Gael. Mackay and McGowan were also soccer players with Queens Park whilst the son of the Mackay, also Malky, played with Celtic Football Club in the 1990s before playing in the English Premiership.

Table 6:3 **Glasgow Football Championship winners 1965-1969**

1965	St Eunans
1966	St Eunans
1967	St Brendans
1968	St Brendans
1969	Clan na Gael

In 1971 the Glasgow County concurred when the G.A.A. removed 'the ban' on playing 'foreign' sports, despite the efforts of Eoin Kelly to have the organisation in Glasgow vote against the move.[19]

In 1970 and 1971 the Glasgow Champions were accepted to play in the Ulster club championship. Around this time Glasgow played Clan na Gael of Armagh in the tournament. Although beaten 2:12 to 3:7 at Eastfield Park, Glasgow took great store from the fact that the winning club subsequently went on to become beaten finalists in the All-Ireland Club Championship.

To the detriment of the Association in Scotland, this period was characterised at County Board level with a number of long acrimonious meetings. More significantly on the playing side, by this time clubs in Glasgow were again experiencing a decline and subsequent reorganising. Much of this was to be the result of players and activists moving on to new employment in Britain or Ireland. The St Brendans Club was one example of this reorganisation, soon becoming Mulroy Gaels, called after the bay of the same name in County Donegal. Other St Brendans players formed Rosses Rovers (again called after a Donegal location) whilst they also drew players from Clan na Gael. During this time Crossmaglen Rangers visited Glasgow to play in the Ulster Junior Championship. In the east of the country, Father Eugene O'Sullivan from Kilkenny tried to give birth to a hurling side though he had to settle for a shinty team. Some of the footballers from the Glasgow area went east and played in a number of challenge matches against O'Sullivan's charges.

Despite a small organisation, the three existing clubs in Glasgow engaged in much rivalry, this due in the main to the regional basis of the clubs. However, one former player of this era described the rivalry as 'sometimes distasteful'.[20] Mulroy Gaels drew their players mainly from central and east Donegal. Significant figures for Mulroy were Seamus Sweeney, Eamonn Cullen, Donal McBride and John Connor. South O'Hanlons took most of their players from the six counties of Northern Ireland, while Rosses Rovers brought footballers from 'The Rosses' and west Donegal, although the club also contained players from other counties. Many of the Rosses team were Irish speakers and much intra-team communication was carried out in the native tongue.

One Rosses' player became a significant figure in the future revival of the sport in the west of the country. Father Eamonn Sweeney, a native of Ballycroy County Mayo, arrived at St Bridget's Baillieston in the east of Glasgow as a young curate in 1969. Drawn into the local G.A.A. by another Irish-born priest, former seminarian colleague at St Peter's college in Wexford, Neil Carlin from Derry, Sweeney began to play in the small and poorly organised local competitions. During this time clubs struggled to field regular sides and many games were played with teams lacking a full compliment. In 1970 the Irish Weekly newspaper included an article that attempted to revive the ailing Association in Scotland.

> As far as the clubs were concerned during 1970 the efforts of St Eunans and St Patricks as effective units were almost nil. Some individuals make token efforts, but no more. St Brendans found themselves with no opposition. . . The G.A.A. in Glasgow hope to have a social centre at Eastfield Park before the end of 1971. The presence of such a centre would ensure regular football as well as providing the very necessary social amenities. . . [21]

Despite Sweeney's attempts and partial success in attracting local-born players, a concerted effort to achieve this on the part of the Glasgow G.A.A. was absent. An exhibition game between a Donegal club side and a local select held at the Coatbridge home of Albion Rovers senior soccer team, which attracted a crowd numbering several hundred, failed to provide the impetus required. The ideas of Sweeney and his more forward-looking fellow gaels, with respect to a more significant G.A.A. within the community of Irish descent in Scotland, remained a dream for the time being.

1. Glasgow G.A.A. Centenary Brochure, 1984.
2. Dermot Gillespie subsequently immigrated to Canada from Scotland.
3. Interview, Rory Campbell.
4. The Fermanagh Herald, 23/1/1993.
5. This club demised in 1951.
6. Gallen was also manager of the Irish Club, formally the Top Hat Club, St Georges Road, situated in Glasgow's Charing Cross area. In the late 1950s this was a popular venue for early Irish folk groups as well as many of the show bands of the era.
7. Irish activist Rory Campbell remembers that although not overtly political, a number of the teams during this period were known as either republican or Fianna Fail clubs. He believes this was probably a reflection of the dominant views of their prominent members at the time. For some activists such as John Keaveny, he did his utmost to keep politics out of G.A.A. affairs during this period.
8. Glasgow G.A.A. Centenary Brochure, 1984.
9. O'Growney being one of the founders of the Gaelic League.
10. The Kildara Club was formally a hall of the A.O.H. and latterly owned by the O'Neill family that ran a famous school of Irish dancing in the city. The family moved eventually to the U.S.A.
11. Glasgow G.A.A. Centenary Brochure, 1984. Interviews John Keaveny and Gerry Gallen.
12. Glasgow G.A.A. Centenary Brochure, 1984.
13. Ibid.
14. Interview Molly Quinn. Quinn was also to make football shorts from flour bags purchased at Glasgow's Barrowland Market for Clan na Gael Football Club.
15. Ibid.
16. Ibid.
17. Ibid.
18. Ibid.
19. In Ireland twenty-eight of the thirty county boards voted in favour of 'the bans' removal.
20. Interview Father Eamonn Sweeney.
21. Irish Weekly.

Chapter 10

Ethnic and cultural revival

1984: YEAR OF RESURGENCE

There was little G.A.A. activity in Glasgow during most of the 1970s and early 1980s. During these barren years for Gaelic sports, Irish-born priests such as Eamonn Sweeney (Ballycroy) and Dominic Towey from (Kilmovee) Mayo and James Shiels of Derry (Bogside), tried to keep matters Gaelic alive in Glasgow. In particular, Eamonn Sweeney was to become a crucial figure in the latest regeneration of the Association in Scotland while other activists, some based in the Glasgow Irish Centre in Glasgow's Govanhill area, also helped commence a revival.

An occasional exhibition match against an English-based club summarised the Gaelic football witnessed in Glasgow during this time. Reflecting the poor state of play in Scotland, for Gaelic enthusiasts like Glasgow-based Mayoman Michael Moran, his desire to play organised football was only satisfied in his travelling regularly to Huddersfield in Yorkshire to play with Brothers Pearse. Since 1975 the annual Pearse Park family sports day and reunion involving a Gaelic exhibition match, a few organised games for children and the celebration of Mass, seemed all that Irish gaels in Glasgow could initiate. At this event a few hundred people attended, with a strong Donegal representation present. This event characterised the G.A.A. in Scotland, in reality, an organisation of little relevance to the majority of the immigrant diaspora in the west of Scotland.

Few second and third generation Irish who esteemed their Irish identity were aware of the G.A.A. in Glasgow or even that there existed such a way to express Irishness, distinct from, or complimentary to, supporting Celtic Football Club. Although a small group of gaels had maintained a semblance of the game throughout the 1960s and into the 1970s,the G.A.A. in Glasgow was poorly organised and was devoid of ideas and plans to develop the Association. The G.A.A. in Glasgow was small, attracted little publicity, and consisted of an unrepresentative group in that most of them were ageing activists of latter Donegal origin. Although Donegal sent thousands of immigrants to the Glasgow area, particularly in the post war years, migrants from many other counties also existed in Scotland. However, for those few who were aware or interested in the G.A.A, some felt excluded from G.A.A. activities due to a perceived parochialism that emerged from the overly Donegal based scene, with officials and players perceived to be content to play football virtually among themselves. Nevertheless, the biggest handicap facing the G.A.A. in Scotland was its apparent inability to reach out to the second and third generation Irish who knew little of Eastfield Park or Gaelic games in Scotland.

During the mid to late 1970s a further effort was made to give life to Irish culture in Glasgow. Following the example of many Irish communities in England, and wishing to reinvigorate much of the social spirit of the past, a number of Irish cultural activists in Glasgow, including members of the G.A.A., attempted to create conditions required for an Irish social club in the city. Although there existed numerous Irish public houses and clubs frequented mainly by Celtic football supporters or Catholics of Irish antecedents, no such formalised or organised structure had existed for a number of years in the city or its environs. As part of a plan to change this situation and re-organise and facilitate expressions of Irish identity in the Glasgow area, Irish cultural activists such as Margaret O'Dell helped raise money to purchase a new centre at Coplaw Street in the Govanhill area of Glasgow, an area with a significant Donegal influence.[1] Although for a time providing a social and cultural focus for Irish functions, by around 1982 the resultant club was in serious financial difficulties as a result of poor management and it was eventually forced to close. Similarly, in 1984 a branch of the successful Irish in Britain

Representation Group (I.B.R.G.) was also formed in Glasgow but it too demised after only a few years.

To celebrate the centenary of the birth of one of Ireland's foremost patriots and leaders of the 1916 Easter Uprising, Eastfield Park was renamed Pearse Park in 1979.[2] Padraic Pearse had a strong affection for all things Gaelic and had been a visitor to the city's Gaelic League in 1899 and 1902.[3] Linking with the park's renaming, to mark the centenary a joint G.A.A. and Pearse Centenary Committee organised a fund raising activity to erect a Celtic Cross at the ground. A match was also played between a Glasgow side and Huddersfield, the winning Glasgow team receiving the Pearse Cup as their prize.

In 1984 the small Glasgow G.A.A celebrated the centenary of the founding of the Association in Ireland. This included among other activities a match held at Pearse Park against St Richard's Gaels of Manchester. The Glasgow squad that participated in this match was;

> Fr Eamonn Sweeney, Eamonn Cullen, John Connor, Michael Moran, Pat O'Callaghan, Eddie McHugh, Harry Cook, Willy Murray, Sean McNamara, Sean McGleanon, Frank Conway, Dan McAlindon, Sean McReady, James Friel, Sean McCarry, Sean McMonagle, Pat Montgomary, Eddie Doherty, Owen Hegney, Seamus Sweeney, Sean McCaughney.[4]

The County also organised a team to play in an 'Exiles Tournament' in Ballina, County Mayo, an event held under the auspices of the Croke Park authorities to help celebrate the founding of the Association. Set in August, and also involving representative sides from New York, the 'rest'of the U.S.A., Australia, London and the 'rest' of England as well as other teams from Ireland, the Glasgow team failed to field a Scottish-based side: their Donegal-based playing contingent not arriving for the opening match. Frank Conway, Eamonn Sweeney, Mick Moran (all Mayo) and Harry Cook from Father Sweeney's parish in Baillieston, made up the Scottish contribution, additionally supplanted with players rounded up in the short time before the game.[5] For Sweeney, this negative experience further emphasised that a more youthful Irish-descended base had to be built if Gaelic football was to flourish in Scotland. Another function to celebrate the centenary of the Association, a successful dinner dance, was held at the Knights of St Columba Club in Moodiesburn.

During the period of celebrating the centenary, several G.A.A. activists began to advertise and attract a number of young men to take up Gaelic football with a view to reinvigorating the Association. Along with Eamonn Sweeney, successful Glasgow-based Donegal building and demolition contractor Seamus Sweeney and Eamonn Cullen, these G.A.A. enthusiasts slowly began to give birth to teams in their respective areas of Hamilton, Glasgow and Dumbarton.

Assisting their efforts, during 1984 the Evening Times in Glasgow carried an article on a young girl from Ireland who had come to the city of Glasgow for bone marrow treatment. Playing a role in the story, Sweeney was interviewed by the freelance journalist and he used the opportunity to draw the attention of the reporter to Gaelic football activities in the area. What resulted was a degree of publicity and essentially an advert for people to learn to play Gaelic football. A handful of young people responded and training and coaching under the auspices of Sweeney and Michael Moran began to accelerate with the help of the new additions. Those who subsequently arrived at Pearse Park trained over the course of the year until they comprised a team. Taking the name Pearse Harps, the club began to play challenge matches against the other developing teams, Mulroy Gaels of Glasgow, St Patricks, Dumbarton and Sweeney's new parish club, Clann na Gael, based at St Ninian's Hamilton. By the following year the first competitions began and Gaelic football was re-born in the west of Scotland. In early 1985 these four clubs took part in the first competitive championship and league set up for almost a generation.

By 2007, Gaelic clubs had formed (although most had also demised) in Glasgow, Coatbridge, Edinburgh, Saltcoats, Wishaw, Shotts, Paisley, Clydebank and Dundee. A number of minor (junior) clubs were also instigated in these areas. Minor initiatives such as these were recognised by the Croke Park authorities that subsequently chose Scotland as the county to experiment with a two-year pilot development scheme in 1995. Financed by the Dublin authorities the scheme was launched jointly by Scotland and Croke Park (including G.A.A. president Jack Boothman) at a reception held in Glasgow's Civic Chambers.

At the 1992 Glasgow County convention, a motion was proposed by Dundee Dalriada that reflected the growth in Gaelic sports in Scotland as well as their greater geographical spread since the late 1980s. The motion to name the County the Scottish County was defeated but an amendment by Sands MacSwineys delegates proposed that the principle of adopting a more encompassing name which resonated with the game's development and greater geographical spread was adopted: thus the name of the county was changed from Glasgow to Scotland.[6]

During the late 1980s and early 1990s the work of G.A.A. members John McCreadie, Jimmy Kelly, John Nally and Charlie McCluskey meant the County acquired a new proficiency. The participation of Tommy Main in the G.A.A. was also significant during this period. Since his involvement in G.A.A. affairs, Main initiated and contributed to a higher public profile for the Association and also organised or assisted in the organisation of a wide range of Irish cultural activities in the west of Scotland, particularly in Glasgow. Although some ventures were short-lived this was mainly a reflection of too few individuals dealing with an expanding Irish cultural scene. Amongst Main's achievements was his involvement with a number of successful Strathclyde Irish Festivals since 1989, which included a range of Irish cultural activities, ceilis, G.A.A. events, academic lectures, theatre, Irish dancing, concerts and bookfairs. In 1988 he was instrumental in constituting an Irish Marian Day at Carfin Grotto in Lanarkshire and in 1991 he also organised a Scor competition involving most G.A.A. clubs. In 1994 Tommy Main became one of the main founders of what was to become the largest G.A.A. club in Scotland, Tir Conail Harps. In the new millennium, Main also attracted a number of grants to fund activities pursued by the Tir Conail club. These included his appointment as development officer for Tir Conail supported by Dion the British-based Irish emigrant grant funding body.

In 1989 a Glasgow County representative squad travelled to New York to participate in an international seven-a-side tournament. Headed by Father Eamonn Sweeney, the Glasgow team lost three matches during the course of a poorly organised competition. Scotland also participated in the 1994, 1996 and 2002 international Gaelic football competitions held in Dublin under the auspices of the G.A.A. authorities. This competition was seen as important to those of the diaspora, as an instrument supporting Irish culture as well as demonstrating recognition of the efforts the G.A.A. membership beyond the the island of Ireland. In 1994, an under strength Scotland team was defeated by London 0:24 to 1:4 and North America 4:15 to 0:8. Scotland defeated Canada 0:11 to 1:7 in the play-off to avoid last place. Included amongst the various dignitaries who attended some of the related functions for the 1996 tournament were the G.A.A. Uachtaran, the Chairman of Bord Failte, the Lord Mayor of Dublin and the Minister for Tourism and Trade. This level of invitation also reflected the efforts of the G.A.A.'s international dimensions committee to pay due respect to its international membership.

Taking part in the 1996 tournament for the Dr Dermot Clifford Cup, held at the grounds of Dublin-based St Enda's of Ballyboden, were football sides from Australasia, Canada, London, New York, North America (eventual winners) and the Rest of Britain, as well as from Scotland. Scotland lost both matches against North America (3:12 to 0:5) and London (0:5 to 0:15), but participation in both the inaugural tournament in 1994 and the subsequent competitions of 1996 and 2002 reflected the progress of Gaelic football in Scotland since 1984.[7] In the 2002 tournament held at Naomh Mearnog's grounds in Portmarnock County Dublin, a Michael Hollinger-managed Scotland side defeated Europe, was narrowly beaten by the Rest of Britain and lost to North America.

The promotion of such a tournament also showed recognition of the place that the diaspora has in Gaelic sports culture. This paralleled increasing recognition of the Irish beyond the shores of Ireland by Irish President Mary Robinson that characterised her term of office during the 1990s: a recognition that was continued thereafter with the Presidency of Mary McAleese. Reflecting this new confident look towards its diaspora on the part of politicians and others in Ireland, Jack Boothman, President of the G.A.A. during 1996, recognised what the Irish have given to other lands as well as what Ireland has contributed to a sense of self and community for those who have had to leave the country.

> . . . when one considers the tragedy of emigration and the great haemorrhage of our people to foreign lands. They brought with them to those lands their music, their culture and above all the legacy that is the G.A.A. and Gaelic games. In turn, the G.A.A. provided them with a focus, a link with their homeland and a medium that stimulated togetherness and a sense of identity.[8]

Since the early 1990s several third tier educational establishments have been involved in inter-university competitions. They have also competed at British universities level and ultimately since 1997, in the Irish Universities competition, the Trench Cup. This universities Gaelic football initiative was largely driven by Peter Mossey from Gortin in Tyrone, a former student of and by the new millennium a lecturer at the University of Dundee. Teams from Stirling, Glasgow, Ayrshire, Strathclyde, Dundee, Abertay and Aberdeen universities have competed at this level since the 1990s. By 2007 dozens of universities across Britain had become involved in football, hurling and camogie competitions, and in Scotland since 2002, an annual hurling-shinty compromise rules challenge match. Many of the students taking part in university competitions have also become members of local G.A.A. clubs, although many others retain strong links with their home clubs preferring only to play in Ireland. In Scotland, the most obvious examples of this has been close relationships between Dundee and Abertay Universities and Dundee Dalriada, Paisley Gaels/Glaschu Gaels and the University of Glasgow, Tir Conail and Strathclyde and Caledonian Universities and Dunedin Connollys with Heriot Watt and Edinburgh Universities. Sands MacSwineys have had numerous members who also played at the Universities of Glasgow, Strathclyde, Glasgow Caledonian and Stirling. In 1994, a successful Dundee side won the British Universities Gaelic Football competition and the University of Abertay also from Dundee won this competition in 2001.

However, teams from St Mary's College Strawberry Hill in London set the standards in Britain in both men's and women's football; the men winning seven of twelve British championships up until 2006 and the women beaten only once between 1997 and 2006. Since the Championships moved to Pairc Na hÉireann in Birmingham in 1994, St Mary's men's dominance in terms of British football championship titles has only been broken on five occasions, by Dundee University in 1994, Liverpool John Moores in 1996, 1999 and 2006, and Abertay University in 2001. St Mary's roll of honour is impressive, but the history of the G.A.A. will set them apart for their exploits in February 2004 when they won the Trench Cup in Belfast. This was the first time that a British-based Gaelic football team at this level had won a major Irish national University G.A.A. trophy on Irish soil.

Although there has been a series of falls and decline in Scotland, steady and sometimes dramatic progress has also been made since 1984. Gaelic sports have been re-established and many have experienced Gaelic football in particular. Hundreds of Irish-born young people and several thousand more second, third and fourth generation Irish offspring, as well as hundreds from outwith the community, have participated in Gaelic games in the west of Scotland as well as other locations in the east of the country. A significant number of Glasgow and Lanarkshire schools have adopted the game. Several women's teams have existed in this period and small local camogie and hurling teams have also evolved periodically.

In 1992 a Pearse Park Redevelopment Committee was set up as a sub-committee of the County Board to raise funds to develop the county ground. Since then G.A.A. members as well as others previously involved in Gaelic sport in Scotland, like Billy Nugent and John Toal, have contributed to the task of organising, raising money and planning for the redevelopment of Pearse Park.

Related to this redevelopment, the Kilkenny visit to Celtic Park in Glasgow in 1913 was matched by the visits of Donegal, Derry, Mayo and Dublin senior footballers during the 1990s: three of the four having been recent winners of All-Ireland titles. In 1993, in front of approximately 2,000 spectators at St Aloysius Rugby Ground in the Millerston area of Glasgow, Donegal beat Mayo. In 1994 the north-west county defeated Derry and in 1995 it was Dublin's turn to be vanquished by the Ulster side. In 1996, the challenge took place between Tyrone and Dublin, the latter winning the Willie Dowd Trophy in front of around 1,000 people. An inter-county Celtic Challenge Cup has also been played for by a number of minor teams prior to each of these games. At a variety of Glasgow hotels, successful banquets were also held on the evening of the respective matches.

These visits were concerned with raising money to finance the cost of the restoration of Pearse Park in Glasgow, a ground not only handicapped by a poor surface and lack of volunteers to provide maintenance, but which was also dilapidated by virtue of having no suitable changing facilities. Within G.A.A. circles, it was generally felt that something should be done for the ground or the apparent potential for the game's development would be lost.

> If developments at Pearse Park do not proceed soon, Irish identity may not be enough to hold on to their [i.e., youngsters involved in G.A.A. activities] loyalty. At present we just cannot compete with soccer, rugby or any other leisure pursuits in terms of playing and after-match facilities.[9]

These fundraising efforts helped raise the finance to support a 'sportscotland' (formally Scottish Sports Council) grant, awarded in 2002 on a matched funding basis. However, this proved to be insufficient to build appropriate facilities and subsequently the money had to be relinquished. By 2007 the committee was in the process of exploring the commercial potential of Pearse Park and using this to provide the facilities required to sustain the presence of a 'home' ground for the G.A.A. in Scotland.

As a contribution to the celebration of its centenary year, in April 1997 the Scotland County welcomed the Sligo senior squad to Glasgow. Subsequently a Gaelic football match between the Scotland County and Sligo took place at St Aloysius Rugby Ground in Glasgow. The match finished with a convincing victory by the visitors of 7:21 to 1:4: Sligo winning the Willie Dowds Cup which until then had been played for between counties from Ireland visiting Glasgow. For the fourth year in succession, Scotland minors defeated their opponents in the Celtic Cup: this time they beat Lancashire 5:11 to 0:4. The Sligo squad were hosted by Sands MacSwineys over the course of their weekend in Scotland and completed their visit with attendance at the Scottish premier league soccer game played between Celtic and Aberdeen.

A NEW ERA

By 1997, a century after the first G.A.A. club was founded in Glasgow, a new confidence and articulation had emerged in relation to Irishness amongst the Irish diaspora. Many second, third and fourth generation Irish in Scotland were central to this process of revival. The re-emergence of the G.A.A. in Scotland also partly links with a re-surfacing and articulation of Irish identity in many parts of Britain.[10] This development adds substance to the argument of Isajiw:

> Much evidence indicates in North America ethnic identities persist beyond cultural assimilation and that the persistence of ethnic identity is not necessarily related to the perpetuation of traditional ethnic culture. Rather, it may depend more on the emergence of ethnic 're-discoverers', i.e., persons from any consecutive ethnic generation who have been socialised into the culture of the general society but who develop a symbolic relation to the culture of their ancestors. Even relatively few items from the cultural past, such as folk art, music, can become symbols of ethnic identity.[11]

It has been recognised amongst some observers that a change has taken place amongst many second, third and fourth generation Irish in Britain in that many have began to reassert their Irishness and, to display it in a number of styles and forms which, as well as being traditional, have also been unconventional. These displays have happened in a new social and cultural environment for Irishness in Britain, one less constrained by the long-established social and political pressures which Irishness in Britain has traditionally attracted.

Questions relating to Irish identity are important sub-themes of any analysis of the history, development and role of the G.A.A. in Scotland. Likewise, the history of the G.A.A. among the Irish diaspora, also gives credence to the arguments of a number of authors who believe that ideas of globalisation should be considered within a context of historical, cultural and spatial specificity.[12] The Association and its members retain a unique identity amidst a growing emphasis on 'global sports'. Gaelic sports remain a forum through which cultural, national and political identities are celebrated. Since the re-emergence of the G.A.A. in Scotland in 1984, thousands of young people have, at very least, experienced this aspect of Irish culture in Scotland.

1. O'Dell was for thirty years the longest serving president of the Gaelic League in Glasgow, the prime mover in the revival of the annual St Brigid's Cross making celebration in the city, assisted with the building of the Pearse memorial cross at Pearse Park, was much involved in Catholic Church activities and was formally a member of the Anti-Partition League in the West of Scotland. She was also associated with the visit to Glasgow of Eamon de Valera in the 1940s.

2. The Pearse Park Commemoration Committee consisted of Rev James Shiels, Sean Feeney, Rory Campbell, Rev Bernard Canning, Joseph Coyle, Rose Coyle, Margaret O'Dell, Eoin Kelly, Peter McAleer, Patrick O'Donnell, Padraig Roarty and Lena Tierney.

3. B Canning in Glasgow G.A.A. Centenary Brochure, 1979.

4. Glasgow G.A.A. Centenary Brochure, 1979.

5. Cook's parents came from Donegal and Kerry.

6 Irish Post, 12/12/92, p34.

7. Scotland County representatives at the international tournament in 1996 were; J Morkin, V Glennon, S Quinn, E Brennan, M Brennan (Paisley Gaels), D Kellett, G Quinn, B Grimes, J Bradley, S McGinley, P Markey, R Gallacher (Sands MacSwineys), R McHugh, B Grant, N Dillon, S Gavaghan, N Walsh, J McKeown, P Davies, M Joyce (Dunedin Connolly's), H Currie, D Nicol, J Hamill (St Patricks) and D O'Brien (Dundee Dalriada). M Hollinger (Paisley Gaels, Manager), S McGleenan (Sands McSwiney's Assistant Manager), K Friel (Paisley Gaels, Assistant Secretary) and I McGuigan (Paisley Gaels).

8. Jack Boothman, G.A.A. President, from programme for 'Irish Holidays International Football Tournament', 9th-13th Sep 1996.

9. T Main, Youth Development Officer Scotland, from match programme, Donegal versus Mayo, 7/2/93.

10. See The Guardian, 16/7/96, p3 for reference to increase in Irish cultural activities in Scotland.

11. Isajiw 1974, pp.111-124

12. See Rowe and Wood, 1996, p.524.

Michael Davitt
centenary conference

ST PATRICK'S COLLEGE
DRUMCONDRA · DUBLIN 9

COLÁISTE PHÁDRAIG · DROIM CONRACH · BAILE ÁTHA CLIATH 9

26 – 28 MAY 2006

John McCourt – Irish political and cultural activist from Lanarkshire during the early twentieth century. Member of Patrick Sarsfields Hurling Club, Coatbridge; First President of the Provincial Council of Scotland (G.A.A.)

Michael Collins

Terence MacSwiney

Archbishop Croke

T P Murphy (International Workgroup) and G.A.A. President Jack Bootham at St Jude's Primary School, Barlanark Glasgow for the launch of the Coaching Pilot Scheme 1994

President of Ireland, Mary Robinson is welcomed by local politicians on her vist to representatives of Glasgow's Irish organisations in 1992

Gaelic football summer school at Coatbridge 2006

Tir Conail Harps 2006

Fr Eamonn Sweeney and Mayo manager,
Mickey Moran, May 2006

May 2006 – Sands MacSwineys celebrate 20 years playing football

Damien and Ciaran McHugh welcome the Sam Maguire
to Coatbridge in 1994

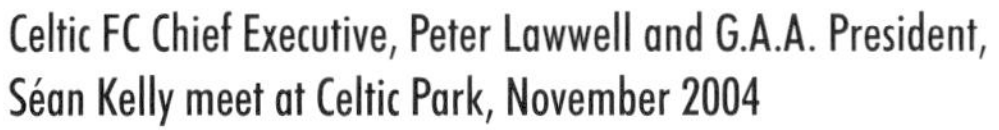

Celtic FC Chief Executive, Peter Lawwell and G.A.A. President,
Séan Kelly meet at Celtic Park, November 2004

St Patrick's and St Timothy's Primary Schools Coatbridge play Gaelic football , June 2006

Dunedin Connollys, Scotland Championship Winners 2005

Glaschu Gaels Women's Gaelic Football team, Scotland Championship Winners 2006

Dundee Dalriada, 2005

Shotts Gaels Camogie, 1997

PEARSE PARK
REDEVELOPMENT
FUND

Willie Dowds
Challenge Cup

DONEGAL
v
DUBLIN

2.30pm
St Aloysius Rugby Park
Millerston
Glasgow

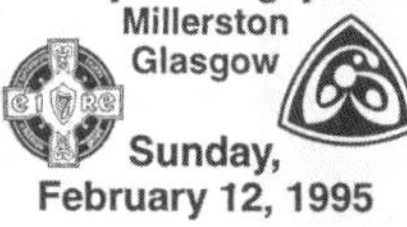

Sunday,
February 12, 1995

Under 13 Celtic
Challenge Cup
SCOTLAND
v
WARWICKSHIRE
1.15pm
£1

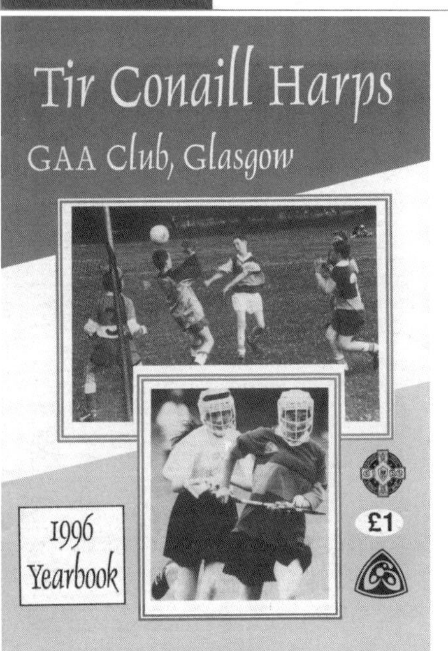

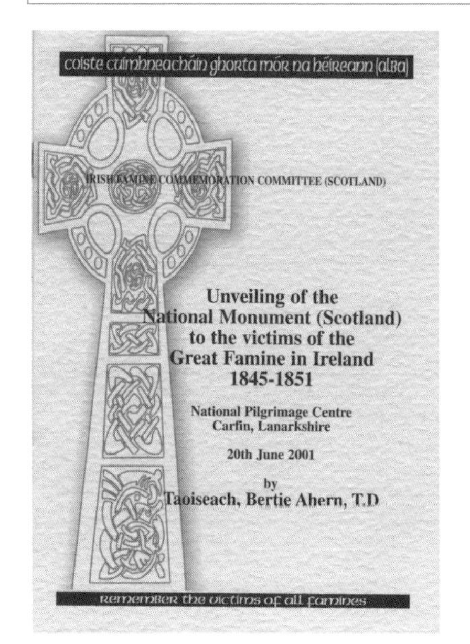

Glencovitt Rovers, Clydebank, 1992

Paisley Gaels, 1996

Jimmy McHugh, Anne Doherty, Anne McHugh and Owen Kelly, founding members in the 1950s of the Irish Minstrels Branch of Comhaltas Ceoltoiri Eireann, the first branch to be founded outside of Ireland

Scotland under-16 team vs. Warwickshire, 1996

St Patrick's, Dumbarton, 1996

Mulroy Gaels Captain Paddy Gavigan receives the 1997 Scotland Championship Trophy from Molly Quinn and Eoin Kelly

The Ancient Order of Hibernians parade in the Lanarkshire town of Coatbridge, c1971

Mulroy Gaels, c1991

Championship Winners in 1987, Beltane Shamrocks

St Patricks Coatbridge branch of Comhaltas Ceoltóiri Éireann with British Minister of State John Reid, local MP Tom Clarke, North Lanarkshire Provost Pat Connolly, MSPs Elaine Smith and Michael McMahon, Irish Consul Cliona Managhan and Irish Government Minister Conor Lenihan

Members of the Anthony Savage School of Irish Dancing on stage during St Patrick's Day celebrations in Coatbridge, 2007

Wall mural in Belfast in 2006 – 'Our revenge will be the laughter of our children'

Jewel in the crown of the Irish diaspora, Celtic Football Club and their fans at the UEFA Cup final in Seville, 2003

The Scotland County squad in Dublin at the 2002 international football tournament

Scotland Championship semi-final 2006, Dunedin Connollys vs Sands MacSwineys

The Paul Lennon Memorial Cup

Sands MacSwineys, 2006

Part 2
A sociology of Gaelic sport: Irishness, identity, politics & culture

Chapter 11

Narratives of belonging

INTERNAL REFLECTIONS

Despite intermittent successes before the resurgence of Gaelic sports activities in the 1980s, during the forty years after World War II, Gaelic clubs in Scotland also encountered many of the problems that had previously plagued Gaelic sports activity. For example, many Donegal immigrants in the Glasgow area were labourers and a significant number worked as tunnellers. This was a hard and dangerous employment often entailing weekend work at a time when others were attempting to revive Gaelic sports. This reflected in regular poor attendances for matches, occasional inferior standards of play and a general atmosphere of social and cultural isolation

Progress was further impaired due to the obscure nature of Irish activities in Scotland. For Liam Murphy, who played with the Pearses club in Glasgow in the 1950s, if the Irish were given media coverage it was frequently in a disparaging manner. More often, the Irish were ignored and their ethnicity and distinctiveness un-recognised. At times when Irish facets of life in Scotland were given attention, it was increasingly likely to be through a discourse and medium of ridicule and sectarianism. In Scotland, it has frequently been evident that to be seen as Irish, and often Catholic, has meant that relevant attributes are assessed in negative terms. This has also partly resulted in denigration of Irishness and a discourse of contestation within the community of Irish descent in Scotland.

In the 1950s many members of the G.A.A. in Glasgow were also fervent Irish Irelanders. All things Irish were viewed not only in a positive light, but a strong element of executing Irish cultural practice in as pure a form as perceived was demanded by such activists and these had to be adhered to in a way that was often regarded by others as exclusive and absolute. An aspect of this in terms of the G.A.A. was the strict enforcing of 'the ban'. As applied in Ireland by the G.A.A., soccer and other 'anglicised' games and pastimes were forbidden, in terms of participation and spectating. This meant that for Gaelic activists such as Rory Campbell and Eoin Kelly, they were also staunchly against 'foreign dances and entertainments'. This has also had the effect that despite Celtic Football Club long being adhered to by Catholic Irish immigrants and their offspring, as a soccer club, for some gaels Celtic was also looked upon as being a detrimental influence on the perceived purity of Irish identity. A consequence of such idealism meant that many potential players were excluded from the G.A.A. in the cause of creating a fastidious image of being 'truly Irish'.

The pre-occupations of some G.A.A. activists in west-central Scotland with their ideas of an Irish identity defined solely and exclusively in terms of Gaelic sports, ceili music and commitment to the Irish language meant that people like John Keaveny eventually lost interest in the local Gaelic scene. Although 'the ban' had relevance to the situation in Ireland and was supported by the G.A.A. in Glasgow, in Scotland Keaveny and many other Irish and their offspring were supporters of Celtic Football Club – a soccer club founded by and for the Irish in Scotland. Keaveny and others like him did not live in Ireland and lived in circumstances and a cultural environment that was different. Scotland was a place, indeed a diasporic space, where not only traditional expressions of Irishness could be manifest amongst the Irish diaspora, but where new expressions might be formed due to the differing social and cultural circumstances that prevailed. However, the enforcement of the ban in Scotland meant that as Chairman of the Association he could not attend soccer matches. As his young children began to mature, like many others of Irish origins they wished their father to take them to view Celtic matches. Partly in response to changing circumstances, but also as a perceived retort to a distinct lack of organisation and leadership on the

County Board, the practice of County Board members ignoring the conventions of time in an industrialised society and, with a frequent lack of discipline on the field of play, by the mid 1950s Keaveny left the Association. During the same period Gerry Gallen was also frustrated at the length of County Board meetings which 'seemed to talk of nothing and which resulted in a number of fruitless arguments'.[1] Gallen too eventually faded from G.A.A. activities in Glasgow.

Keaveny observed that the extreme actions he perceived on the part of some Irish Irelanders meant that many Irish were excluded from activities that were in fact, also keenly Irish for many people. Keaveny cited one example of perceived Irish exclusivism, when in the 1950s at an Irish ceili in Glasgow, a crowd from Greenock arrived to enjoy the function: all were of Irish origin. However, few had experience of ceili dancing and some requested the Pride of Erin Waltz. An argument ensued because some organisers felt their Irishness was being compromised. This antagonism resulted in the Greenock participants refusing to return to further ceilis.[2] Such occurrences has parallels with the Irish experience of half a century before when, in 1914, a G.A.A. official complained of the vast majority of G.A.A. members whose, 'nationalist sentiment begins and ends with the mere practice of kicking or striking a hurling ball'.[3]

In the 1990s such experiences were occasionally still evident. In March 1994, at a G.A.A. function held in Coatbridge, a Gaelic League activist provoked a minor argument. This function included a present-ation of the Sam Maguire trophy brought to Scotland by Mickey Moran, coach of 1993 All-Ireland Football Champions Derry. The Gaelic League member confronted a local G.A.A. activist regarding two guests not standing at the end of the evening for the playing of the Irish National Anthem – a custom not only at many Irish cultural events but also in terms of those traditionally held by the club concerned. The individuals who had not stood for the National Anthem had Irish-born parents, but they had little appreciation of the cultural practices of the G.A.A. and had a modest understanding of the environment they were socialising in. Although the official had recognised that these people had not respected club and G.A.A. conventions, he did not consider it important enough or was it his place or role to be seen to 'reprimand' these individuals. Nevertheless the League activist stated he would not return to a function held by this particular G.A.A. club. As far as this person was concerned, the club had not pursued this cultural practice with enough vigour.[4]

One writer on Gaelic sports in Ireland has intimated that such cultural exclusivism in adhering to a strict and formal interpretation of rules, and meanings of Gaelic sport in particular, has been a mistake, because it closed doors and created an ideal of purity which became exclusivist and narrow minded.

> It's an old Irish failing to become precious about these things. You can only speak Irish if you're born to it. Irish dancing isn't Irish dancing unless the participants are standing ramrod straight and stiff as corpses. Sean nos isn't sean nos unless its boring.[5]

Although Irish cultural activities faced a variety of limitations, barriers and constraints created by the wider society, other factors have also contributed to diminishing expressions of Irishness in Scotland and, as a consequence, the promotion of Gaelic sports activities. Former G.A.A. activist Liam Murphy describes how his parents felt no real purpose in passing on their Irish heritage to their children. He believes that one of the reasons for this lay in their lack of formal education resulting in an inability to pass on and articulate a positive sense of Irishness and affinity for Ireland. They also lacked a corresponding motivation, promoting and viewing their children as Scottish in that they saw this identity – as opposed to Irishness – as the best way and most appropriate credential to social acceptance, achievement and progress.

John Keaveny's experiences were similar to Murphy's parents in that his children were 'left to their own devices'. He recognised problems that Irish people had in Scotland and encountered some of them himself. Although also recognising that Scotland was a foreign land and a certain accommodation in attitudes had to take place amongst the Irish corresponding to their changed situation, he maintained caution in things Irish by 'being very careful here'.[6]

A further insight into this kind of approach to a new life in Scotland was implicit in a Donegal immigrants experience in Glasgow, when she spoke of losing her Irish language and learning English. She described this as learning to speak 'better'.[7] Murphy's father believed his son would find life difficult in Scotland if his background were known. He was surprised to find him earning an apprenticeship with a printing firm, a trade then popularly known to be anti-Catholic and native Protestant Scots. Experiences such as Murphy's and those of the Donegal migrant, who viewed loss of her native language as 'progress', are occurrences that invariably affected the self-perceptions, self-esteem and social construction of the identities of many Irish in Scotland, particularly during periods of overt hostility.

Some of the experiences of Afro-Americans in the U.S.A. reflect similar sentiments. U.S. television personality Marsha Hunt reported having only 'discovered' she was a black negro while watching a TV show as a child. She commented to her mother, that 'negroes are the funniest people'. Hunt's mother subsequently informed her that she too was a negro. Hunt's response was to deny this.

> What I actually meant that I had heard so many disparaging things about negroes that I did not associate that or my family with colour. I associated it with some sort of state of being that I had nothing to do with.[8]

The experience of those such as the Donegal migrant and Liam Murphy's reflects that an attitude has existed within the Irish community in Scotland that the best or the only way to make social progress, and to negotiate a decent existence, was in disguising their Irishness and privatising aspects of the past as well as their experiences and identities. Indeed, for many Irish who have encountered a hostility that has been perceived as reducing their own and their family's life chances, Irishness was largely discarded or became a factor of a past that represented poverty and oppression. Some immigrants felt the need to hide their place of origin in Ireland: this in case they were sent back home 'or there was a clampdown by the authorities on the number of people entering the country'.[9] A significant number of Catholics of Irish origins in today's west-central Scotland have little knowledge regarding the place of birth of their grandparents and great grandparents. In some extreme cases this also applies to Irish-born parents.[10]

Early in the twentieth century, P T McGinley of the Gaelic League castigated those Irish who came to the west of Scotland. He said many of them. . .

> abandoned their native language and customs, in the belief that the civilisation they found around them was superior to their own. In adopting the speech and habits of their neighbours, they forgot their origins and became anglicised. . . [11]

As a cultural activist McGinley undoubtedly saw himself as having a point to make, especially during a time of struggle to maintain and esteem the notion of being distinctly Irish, even in Ireland. The Irish have perceived themselves as being oppressed and downtrodden for centuries. Although many people throughout the nineteenth and twentieth centuries would be of a similar mind to McGinley and participated in Irish activities and often retained a strong sense of Irishness, it was the 1980s and 1990s before Irishness assumed a confidence that confounded many centuries of denigration, low esteem and denial.

Despite understanding his own social and cultural existence as ghetto like, and his social contacts as limited, Liam Murphy only became aware of being Irish when, after leaving school at fourteen, he was sent to carry out some work in the Fianna Fail club in Glasgow. There he met other young men of his own age group. They all had similar backgrounds that became a matter of conversation and exposure to an education not acquired from anywhere else. Questions began to be asked at home and Murphy developed a stronger sense of Irishness. Born in Glasgow and married to a Kilkenny woman, Liam Murphy had discovered that his parents were in fact resolutely Irish-minded, originating from Belmullet in County Mayo, an area retaining a positive Irish traditional identity. They were also Republicans, his father being a former member of the Irish Republican Army during the War of Independence and his mother a part of Cumman na Bann (the women's side of the movement). Both were to take the anti-treaty side during the Irish Civil War. However, Murphy heard little of politics at home. Only in visiting Ireland, reading books and becoming more independent as he got older, did his Irishness as well as his Irish political views begin to form.[12]

G.A.A. STALWARTS OF THEIR TIME

For others like Rory Campbell in Glasgow, as a second-generation youth in the 1930s and 1940s, the only way to confidently display his Irishness was, as for many others, in support for Celtic Football Club. During this period he found:

> no other way to be Irish. . . there was nothing around with a semblance of Irishness involved. . . but gradually, the scales fell off my eyes.[13]

Campbell discovered other more fulfilling avenues for Irishness in Scotland. Over the course of the next fifty years, he became an active member of the G.A.A., the Gaelic League (Conradh na Gaeilge, Glaschu), Comhaltas Ceoltóirí Éireann (Music and Musicians of Ireland) as well as Sinn Féin and Republican prisoners welfare groups.

Rory Campbell made a significant contribution to Irish cultural affairs in Glasgow especially through his involvement with the Gaelic League. Campbell viewed this aspect of Irish culture as being of primary importance and indeed recognised that learning the language of antecedent generations meant that one could learn the 'spiritual values of the past. . . it binds us to past generations'. Although rarely a Gaelic player, in the half century after World War II, Campbell held a number of offices within the Glasgow and subsequently Scotland G.A.A. By 1997, in the capacity of Irish language representative, Campbell remained a member of the G.A.A. in Scotland. By this time Campbell also remained one of the only operative links with previous generations of G.A.A. activists in Scotland. Rory Campbell died in August 2000.

Packy O'Donnell was a contemporary of Campbell's most active G.A.A. days. As a fourteen year old, O'Donnell arrived in Scotland from Dungloe, County Donegal to join his father labouring in Glasgow. O'Donnell also married into the Irish community of the west of Scotland, uniting with Kathleen Gillespie, niece of Tom Gillespie an important figure for Irish cultural activities in Glasgow during the period shortly before World War II. From the mid 1960s through the 1990s, Kathleen's O'Donnell's School of Irish Dancing organised classes in the Glasgow area and competed at a number of Irish dancing world championships.

O'Donnell was one of the top players in Glasgow during a period noted for its high quality of experienced Gaelic sportsmen. However, as for other stalwarts of the 1940s and 1950s, married life and children impacted on the time and commitment young players could devote to Gaelic football activities. Although being an ever present on the football scene for ten years until around 1958, like many other immigrants to the west of Scotland, O'Donnell also found that through his children he became involved in another Irish pastime of supporting Celtic Football Club: his sons interests being similar to many other young Scots-born Irish. Although O'Donnell recognised his family as retaining strong links with their origins, especially through holidays in Ireland and in his wife's Irish Dance School, and despite some involvement with the annual sports day held at Pearse Park in the 1970s, none of his family maintained a link with Gaelic sport. During O'Donnell's active days, few within the Glasgow G.A.A. had the foresight to expand the game to the second and third generation Irish.

Standing out among the other main links with previous periods is Eoin Kelly. Born in Ederney, County Fermanagh in 1946 aged eighteen Kelly migrated to Glasgow. His father was also an earlier migrant, working in Coatbridge's Phoenix Foundry in the first decades of the twentieth century. Kelly senior participated in hurling competitions involving Coatbridge clubs during this time before returning to Ireland to live. Notably, in relation to an understanding of G.A.A. history in Scotland, while working in Coatbridge he recognised that a significant number of migrants involved in Gaelic sport came from Munster.

Like many other immigrants, Eoin Kelly married a woman of Irish antecedents: her parents originating from Tyrone and Donegal. For almost fifty years Kelly was a Gaelic enthusiast, involving himself first with Paisley Gaels in the late 1940s, being instrumental in the purchase of Pearse Park, and along with Jimmy McHugh of Tyrone and several others, was a founder member of the Irish Minstrels, the first branch of Comhaltas Ceoltóirí Éireann outside of Ireland. Since the purchase of Pearse Park, but particularly since the 1970s, despite the dilapidated facilities, Kelly was also instrumental in maintaining – indeed, saving – the pitch at Pearse Park as a Gaelic football venue in the west of

Scotland.[14] In the early years of the new millennium Kelly returned to Dromore where he assumed the position of Chair of the local branch of Comhaltas. Eoin Kelly died in September 2005.

1. Interviews John Keaveny and Gerry Gallen.
2. Interview John Keaveny.
3. Rouse, 1996.
4. Interview with member of Sands MacSwineys G.F.C.
5. Humphries, 1996, p. 39.
6. Interviews, John Keaveny and Gerry Gallen.
7. Jimmie MacGregor, 'Across the Water' BBC Radio Scotland, four part series, 1st – 22nd November, 1995.
8. Marsha Hunt, 'God Bless America', ITV 24/3/1997.
9. Cassidy, 1996, pp.34-38.
10. Ongoing research into Irish identity in Scotland has reflected a number of interviewees only have a scant knowledge or do not recollect where in Ireland their relations originated. In one example this extended to an elderly lady's father who she knew as having migrated from Ireland but she was unaware from where.
11. Feeney 1995.
12. Interview Liam Murphy.
13. Interview Rory Campbell.
14. Interview Eoin Kelly.

Chapter 12

Cultural Contestations

PRIVILEGED DISCOURSES

Although never a completely homogeneous body, the nationalist, cultural and symbolic significance of the G.A.A. is well established in the history of the Association. As a traditional focus for the maintenance and celebration of Irishness this significance has also been reflected amongst some of the diaspora in Scotland.

Narratives of contested Irishness in Scotland can enlighten and sensitise us to a range of sources that can influence identity. Social identity is neither a neutral nor an innate phenomenon and social, national and cultural identities are learned, lived and expressed. Identities are imagined though they are no less real as the power of the human imagination is necessary for any conception of social identity.

One of the most significant aspects for the formation, maintenance, promotion and celebration of Irishness in Scotland has in fact been the way these have been traditionally omitted in many accepted public expressions in Scottish life. Despite the numerical, religious, cultural, political, economic and national significance of Irish Catholic migration to Scotland since the Great Irish Famine of 1845-51, such expressions have conspired to construct Irishness in Scotland at the periphery of mainstream social, cultural and political life. In turn, this has contributed to the production of Irish invisibility in Scotland. In this context it must also be noted that a paradox exists, whereby in the face of this invisibility, the Irishness of the supporters of Celtic Football Club has been conspicuously discernable and has allowed for the maintenance and celebration of Irishness, although in turn, this expression also simultaneously has the capacity to reveal marginalisation.

At a conference held at the University of Stirling in January 1997, consideration was given to a number of pertinent social and political questions that focused on the historical and contemporary position of Catholics in Scotland.[1] Apart from a small number of indigenous Scots, and those with origins in countries such as Poland, Lithuania and Italy, Catholics in Scotland largely originate from Ireland and although it can be crude to see Irish as equalling Catholic and vice versa, there is a certain accuracy in this portrayal and relevant issues concerning the Irishness of Catholics in Scotland were expected to be a part of conference proceedings. Nevertheless, during the discussion, two academic speakers expressed the view that the Irish in Scotland could be referred to historically but not contemporaneously. Only after a number of exchanges did one concede that discussants could talk about 'the ex-Irish' in Scotland. The Chair of the conference and his supporting professorial colleague offered a view that talk of the Irish in contemporary Scotland was illusory and that the greatest single immigrant grouping in society had 'ceased being Irish'.

In this light, comparatively few academic or popular books and articles address historical, cultural, economic and religious issues in relation to the Irish in Scotland, and a significant amount of published sources do so only within the boundaries of a 'sectarian discourse'.[2] Devine states with some surprise that, 'Irish immigrants in Scotland have not until recent years been effectively integrated into the wider study of Scottish historical development'.[3] In a related sense, a member of the Irish diaspora, Scottish-born writer and novelist Andrew O'Hagan, has lamented the dearth of reflective works on Catholic or Irish Catholic life in Scotland in the 1970s. For him, this means that there are few realistic or supportive references that can assist the formulation and transmission of his ideas and experiences.[4] Likewise, a Dublin-based interviewee stated that at school he learned of the Irish in the USA, Australia and England. Until he became interested in Celtic in Glasgow, he was unaware that a significant part of the Irish diaspora existed in Scotland.[5] Such perspectives constitute a view that Irishness in Scotland has been pushed to the periphery of the social, cultural and political narratives pertaining to every day life.

Textual, oral, historical, social and other such omissions are crucial to explaining events and outcomes. Devine makes the point regarding the building and exploitation of the British Empire that:

> The Scottish connection with the Caribbean colonies has, until very recently, rarely attracted much attention from Scottish historians.

As an example, he cites the Oxford Companion to Scottish History of 2001:

> The index contains only one reference to the West Indies, and that merely relates to the sale of Scottish coarse linen in the Caribbean. Slavery and the slave trade come off even worse. There is no index entry to 'slavery' and the single 'slave trade' reference is exclusively concerned with the campaigns of the Scottish missionary societies of the nineteenth century against the immoral commerce in human beings. The omission is surprising because the role of the Scots in the British Caribbean was deeply significant.[6]

Conspicuously, and with few exceptions, the Irish or Catholic experience in Scotland is largely absent from research, novels, histories and stories from Scottish literature and beyond. MacMillan points out that the Collins Encyclopedia of Scotland:

> has no entry for the Irish in Scotland or the Catholic Church. Foreign visitors to Edinburgh attended an exhibition a couple of years ago at the Scottish Record Office, recounting the history of immigration to Scotland. Large displays set out the history of the immigration of Flemish weavers, Jewish traders, Italian peasants, Asian shopkeepers, Chinese restaurant owners, black bus conductors, and rightly praised the contribution they had all made to Scottish society. The massive Irish immigration in the nineteenth and early twentieth centuries was dealt with in something like three sentences as follows:
>
> > 'in the mid-nineteenth century an increasing number of seasonal Irish farm labourers who worked in the summers in lowland Scotland stayed over due to poor economic conditions in Ireland. Many of them became a burden on the local Parish Poor Laws'[7]

Scotland's role in the colonisation of Ireland (which led ultimately to the creation of the Northern Ireland conflict), the Great Irish Famine, the massive economic contribution of the Irish to emerging industrial and then post-industrial Scotland, the Irish contribution to the advancement of the Scottish health services, to Christianity, to education provision, to political life (particularly through the Labour party), and of course, to Scottish sport (particularly soccer), has simply been omitted in this important text. In addition, the sectarianism and racism faced by many Irish in Scotland has also been silenced in this account. These omissions are repeated throughout much of the contemporary Scottish media.

MacMillan's account suggests that the frequent omission of the Irish in Scotland's recent history is evident throughout literature, oral records, contemporary media and other forms of communication and records. One example seems to bear out this observation. With over one hundred thousand of a population, the area formally known as Monklands in the west central belt of Scotland, has served as an important industrial, social and economic centre for one hundred and fifty years. Until the re-structuring of local administrative areas in the mid 1990s, it included the north Lanarkshire towns and villages of Airdrie, Coatbridge, Chapelhall, Glenboig, Calderbank, Plains and Salsburgh, among others. It is also an area that has attracted tens of thousands of Irish since the mid nineteenth century and is an area that provides a valuable source of information on the history of Gaelic sport in Scotland. Per head of population, no area in Scotland or Britain contains as many people of Irish descent as the former Monklands district. In 2006 it was reported in British and Scottish news reports that on the basis of people's surnames, Coatbridge was the most Irish town in Scotland.[8] Nevertheless, in the Monklands Official Guide of 1989 containing several thousand words and pictures illustrating social history, environment, leisure, sport, housing, industry past and present, educational facilities and local businesses, there is neither historical or contemporary references to the Irish in the area. Indicatively in 2006, the local newspaper in the Monkland's area, The Airdrie and Coatbridge Advertiser, failed to report – as the BBC and national press did – this noteworthy news item regarding Irishness in the town of Coatbridge.

In such accounts the Irish presence in the area is rendered invisible via omission and exclusion: this is a common technique in popular discourse that serves to ignore and distort basic essential facts while also demonstrating the subtleness of certain acts of prejudice.[9] Such omissions and distortions are repeated in much of the contemporary Scottish media.

The Scottish education system also reflects numerous gaps in historical, political and sociological texts where references to the Irish in Scotland might be expected, indeed, where they might enhance understanding of the relevant subject. For example, there is little reference in Scottish social, journalistic or academic circles concerning famine in Ireland, its roots in Britain's exploitation of Ireland as a colony, its effects on the diasporic Irish and its impact on subsequent Scottish history, society and politics. This is despite an interpretation that might argue that Irish migration to Scotland since this period is in fact fundamental to understanding a variety of social, religious, economic, health and political issues, particularly in the west-central belt of contemporary Scotland. If the host community refuses to recognise the reasons and context for inward Irish Catholic migration as well as 'positively' acknowledging the significant presence of this diaspora group, from its (the host's) perspective it has no need or it can avoid engaging in a recognition of the historical and contemporaneous experience of that group and the host community's negative role in a circuitous and sustained pattern of denial and deflection.

Maley makes a general point regarding education stating that through the curriculum children should be encouraged to be aware 'of the cultural diversity of the society they will inherit'. In the Scottish context he believes that Catholics of Irish extraction should be allowed 'access to their own cultures and histories'.[10] The implication Maley makes is that if they are not able to access this, then ignorance of their past and present constitution will dominate amongst Scotland's Catholic Irish (as well as the more indigenous population) while conceivably serving an assimilationist, acculturising or secularist agenda on the part of Scottish society and the British state.

Diasporic peoples are frequently cut off from the representation of important strands of their histories by a series of absences from spaces of cultural reproduction, in education, memorials and popular culture more widely. The population who experience this disjuncture most sharply are often those born and raised in one society, but whose parents, grandparents and great-grandparents, originate from a different one. This generally equates with a largely differing socialisation process to that learned by prior immediate family and community members in the ethnic and historical 'home'. At least some aspects of 'original' culture are passed on in privatised spaces and this may have a greater chance of occurrence in areas where large numbers of immigrants settled together and re-created numerous structures and cultural agents that promote re-production of ethnic and religious identities.

Often however, diasporic offspring exist in public spheres where their culture is underrepresented, only partly visible or, missing altogether. Immigrant practices, beliefs, attitudes and lifestyles, including those of subsequent generations, can also be viewed with varying degrees of hostility. This will invariably contribute to the context of second, third and subsequent generation identity formation: whether re-production and sustenance of ethnic and religious identities takes place and in what form.

> For colonised populations who emigrate to the former colonising state this may entail a more active suppression of dissident identities in order to avoid contestation and speed up the process of incorporation and acceptability into the national mainstream.[11]

Mary J Hickman shows that Irish history has been conspicuously excluded from curricula throughout Britain since the nineteenth century, not only from non-denominational state schools, but also from the distinctive Catholic school framework that operates within the state system and where the majority of children of Irish descent are educated.[12] Hickman argues that this has been a key element in the denationalisation of the Irish in Britain and their construction as good Catholic British citizens. The implication for Hickman is that the end product of such a revision can result in the Irish, in their diasporic setting, learning to become British, English or Scottish. That this occurs is not a natural or inevitable development but one that can be considered as part of constructed socialised process. The contested nature of this historical development is also implied with the re-discovery by third and fourth generation people of their ethnicity or, in their finding a new sense of respect for this ethnicity, one that their parents or grandparents had 'lost' or changed in response to their own experience within this socialisation process.

In simple terms, children whose origins lie elsewhere are taught histories often alien to their backgrounds. Indeed, sometimes they are oppositional to the histories of the nations and communities from where they originate. It is important to note that teaching history at school is only one – albeit a vital one in relation to age and the lifelong learning experience – of numerous important agents and sources of identity construction and socialisation.

> There are many political, social and cultural forces which exert and have exerted an influence on the formation of national and cultural identities, such as religion, family, community, mass media, art and literature. . .[13]

Despite the omission and denial of Irishness within the education system and in other spheres, research demonstrates that knowledge of their cultural background in Ireland cannot be erased from accurate reflections on the identities of the Irish diaspora. Such reflection remains relevant to any assessment of national and cultural identities in contemporary Scotland, including those related to Gaelic sport. Recent research in the 'Irish 2 Project' demonstrates that there continues to be second and third generation Irish in Scotland who esteem their Irishness: indeed, people who consider themselves 'Irish', not Scottish or British and who consider their Irishness as their primary cultural identity.[14]

Therefore Irishness can remain relevant in the personal, social and community composition of people born in Scotland whose parents, grandparents or great grandparents migrated from Ireland. Importantly, interviewees on the Irish 2 Project also reported a lack of recognition within Scottish society with regards to Irishness. Hickman and Walter note that the:

> well-documented evidence of the racialisation of the Irish in contemporary Britain and of discriminatory practices is consequently ignored.[15]

Cultural activities around sport, particularly soccer and Celtic F.C., Irish music and dance, political activities relating to Northern Ireland and the growth in the use of Irish forenames for children, are only a few examples that show Irishness remains a significant factor in west-central Scottish life. Further, and more significantly, the comparative strength of the Catholic Church and Catholic education in Scottish life are considerable manifestations of the impact made by Irish immigrants in society.

REPRESENTATIONS OF IRELAND AND IRISHNESS IN SCOTLAND

The Irish 2 Project and other studies reveal that Irishness (and Catholicism) is a significantly contested identity in Scotland. That this is an ongoing process and experience is evident via critical inspection of official and popular discourses in much of the contemporary Scottish media.

For example, for several weeks in early 2003 a debate ensued regarding the organisation of a St Patrick's Day Festival in the Lanarkshire town of Coatbridge. This debate dominated letters to the local newspaper and although some letter writers defended the celebration, reflecting one aspect of the contested nature of Irish identity in Scotland, much of the hostile comment asserted a belief that despite a majority of people in Coatbridge being of Irish descent, such a celebration should not take place. Interestingly, many correspondents to the newspaper emphasised the primacy of Scottishness over Irishness while paradoxically also recognising the presence or predominance of the Irish diaspora in the area. Frequently positioned within a 'sectarian' discourse were references to the Irish nature of the celebration.

> I read with some disappointment the article in last week's Advertiser regarding the proposed St Patrick's Day celebrations in Coatbridge. While I realise the vast population of the area we live in comes from Irish descent, I would think by now we would class ourselves as Scottish.[16]

> I personally feel that this planned festival is more linked to the Catholicism of the area and not of any great heartfelt link to the Irish. This is one of the many factors which results in the cancer of sectarianism, which still blights our society.[17]

> I am writing to express my utter disbelief at the shocking event held in Coatbridge. . . Why wasn't there anything similar to celebrate the Queen's Golden Jubilee?[18]

> I was dismayed to see the announcement of plans to hold a St Patrick's Day Festival in Coatbridge. . . How can this be organised when no corresponding celebration is ever planned for St Andrew's Day – you know the patron saint of the country we actually live in. . . Also, the majority of families with Irish heritage can only trace their links back to great-grandparents/grandparents etc. [19]

Such correspondence, along with newspaper editorials and journalistic commentary, frequently appears in the popular Scottish media and various ethnic and religious institutions and events can prompt similar responses on a routine basis. Matters Irish and Catholic in Scotland are often a focus for critical comment and contestation.

Relevant to the ommision and marginalisation of Irishness is the history of negative representations of Ireland and Irishness that are deeply embedded within Scottish and British societies. Such representations can be seen as important for the formation and sustenance of the Irishness of the Irish diaspora in Scotland.

One example of the detrimental reporting of Gaelic football, and Irish activities generally in Scotland during the 1950s, took place in the wake of a seven-a-side Gaelic football tournament at Roseberry Park, Shawfield, Glasgow.

> Gaelic football played by sturdy sons of the Ould Country wasn't quite what we expected. . . There are a multitude of rules, multiplied from football, I suspect, so that more rules can be ignored. . . they can kick it, punch it, EVEN HIDE it!. . . [20]

Forty years later such negative and distorted reporting on matters Irish prevailed. In 1991 The Sunday Scot, a short-lived newspaper owned by Glasgow Rangers chief shareholder and chairman David Murray, ran a story headlined, 'Gael, Gael, the Celts are here! This article alluded to the 'well known and widely understood' stupidity of the Irish, utilising embedded notions of the Irish as developed over many centuries of British colonialism in Ireland.

> The Sunday Scot looks at some of our zanier sports. The big centre

> controls the ball with his hand, swivels in the box and balloons the ball wildly over the bar – and the football crowd go wild with delight. Sounds a bit Irish. . . [21]

A Glasgow journalist also adopted stereotypical notions of the 'thick Paddy' language of degradation when reporting on a Tyrone versus Dublin Gaelic football exhibition match held in Glasgow in 1996. He wrote:

> . . . Tyrone rallied to end the game at a rather respectable scoreline of two goals and eight points for Tyrone to the Dubs' three goals and fifteen points. I know: it sounds daft and bear in mind that this is an Irish sport. . . [22]

Similarly, a Glasgow newspaper on reporting an upsurge in Gaelic football activities in the West of Scotland, and relating the story to former international football goalkeeper Pat Jennings from County Down, declared:

> Where else but in Ireland would you hear a group of supporters shout 'Up Down'.[23]

This is of course a humorous story arising from a play on the juxtaposing of words opposite in meaning to each other. However, again the phrase, 'where else but in Ireland' explicitly invokes the British cultural stereotype of the 'stupid' or 'thick' Irish. Writing about a Gaelic football match in Glasgow between two of Ireland's best footballing counties, an Evening Times journalist spoke of two teams set to 'knock the daylights out of each other'.[24] Such frequent and widely accepted representations on reporting Gaelic sports and matters Irish has been unlikely to reflect the merits of Gaelic sports or serve the promotion of Irishness amongst the offspring of the Irish in Scotland and beyond. Such narratives concerning Irishness in Britain have a complex but well-established and embedded history in British representations of Irishness. This history has in turn had a significant effect upon the Irishness of the Irish in Britain.

A more unreserved derogatory commentary on Ireland was made in 1985 by then editor of the Daily Express, Sir John Junor (the latest in a series of such comments). Junor's remark provoked the following comment from an observer of Irish affairs:

> John Junor's remark that he would rather go looking for worms in a dunghill than visit Ireland is but one example of a quite unrepentant anti-Irishness of so much of the Tory press.[25]

Reviewing the London Finsbury Park Fleadh (music festival) for a London newspaper in 1990, Stan Gebler Davies wrote that, 'the easiest way to learn Gaelic is to murder someone for the IRA'. The implication being that the subsequent period spent in the Maze/Long Kesh prison would enable a prisoner to learn the Irish language amongst those incarcerated for similar crimes, a well-established practice for the prison's Republican inmates.26

A regular columnist in the most popular broadsheet in Scotland, The Herald, has a long history of invoking of the British social, cultural and political construction of a 'thick Paddy' cultural stereotype, a refinement illustrated in the contemporary Irish joke. Writing of a 'bright young colleen' looking for some information regarding an enquiry from a Scot working in Dublin, the 'colleen' admitted there were no rules and regulations regarding the enquiry but would the enquirer like a copy of the 'unwritten laws'. The same journalist also made mention of tickets for an Ireland versus Scotland rugby international which cost ten punts and which he sardonically added 'included admission'.[27] In 1996 the same columnist highlighted a spelling mistake on the part of an advertisement for Jury's Hotel in Glasgow. This columnist's penchant for degrading Ireland and the Irish became more obvious when he told his readers to, 'bear in mind they are an Irish company'.[28]

Celtic Football Club's Irish identity has also been the object of the 'thick Paddy' racialised stereotype found within the media and in other cultural outlets. A newspaper reported that after going through sound checks on the public address system came the following words from Celtic's stadium supervisor: 'if this announcement cannot be heard in your part of the stadium, please contact control'. This was intended as a humorous story that relied significantly on the newspaper readership's understanding and knowledge in recognising and comprehending the article's underlying meaning. The newspaper sarcastically added, just as well for Celtic's 'continuing links with Irish ways'.[29]

For some British media commentators, a meaningful bond between the Catholic faith and the people and country of Ireland, including its diaspora, also provides a means to denigrate Ireland, Irish Catholics and the Catholic faith. In 1996, writing of several recently reported Catholic clerical misdemeanours in the Scottish Daily Mail a journalist stated:

> I have never understood why Roman Catholic clergy, as distinct from their Protestant brethern, are expected to forsake the company of women. Especially since, as anyone who has eavesdropped in an Irish village pub well knows, so many of them don't.[30]

Stereotypes also played a significant role when Observer Scotland profiled new author and soon to be MP, Helen Liddell, who originates from the popularly known 'Catholic Irish' town of Coatbridge. This particular correspondent wrote: 'Sex in Coatbridge, after all, had been traditionally a very straightforward exercise in human reproduction, the result in days gone by of a healthy intake of Guinness at the Labour Club'.[31] The abuse of Ireland's national drink, the stereotyping and demeaning of a town and many of its inhabitants with the biggest percentage per head of people with Irish antecedents in Britain, the sexual morality of Catholic teaching and practice, and the strong links between the Labour Party and Catholics in west-central Scotland, all dovetailed with an ethno-religious typecasting in this report in a considered quality Sunday newspaper. Due to an already established widespread understanding and representation of 'Catholics of Irish descent in Scotland', this article required no further elaboration to explain its underlying message for its readers.

In 1996, the Scottish Daily Mail's Bruce Anderson continued in this vein when he spoke of Irish European Union Commissioner Padraig Flynn. Anderson described Ireland thus:

> As soon as you arrive in Ireland, you leave the modern world. Every mile you travel west of Dublin is also a mile west of the twentieth century. . . This is a pre-twentieth century economy, based on the pig and potato and presided over by the priest.[32]

In 1987 the same writer wrote of Ireland's Sean McBride, winner of the Nobel Peace Prize (1974), the Lenin Peace Prize (1977) as well as the American Medal for Justice among other prestigious tributes.

Anderson determined that McBride had two guiding principles throughout his career, 'the first was hatred of Great Britain, the second was a worship of violence'. Of course, if this was the case McBride would not have received such widespread positive recognition. In this light, in contrast Oliver Tambo, former president of the ANC described McBride as 'a great beacon, guiding and assisting oppressed people to the path of national liberation and self-determination'.[33]

The unacceptability of Irish-Catholics (particularly if born in Scotland) to the Orange community, is one of the most perceptible contemporary manifestations of hostility towards the immigrant diaspora in Scotland.

> Study the [Irish-Catholic] names of some of the 'Labour' candidates elected. . . What do Glasgow's Protestant clergymen think of this situation? What do the genuine patriots in the SNP's rank-and-file, think about it?. . . and how do they relish the thought of their city – the birthplace too of so many famous Scots – being run by a bunch of Roman Catholics of immigrant Eirish stock (that's 'nationalism' not 'racialism') hardly outstanding for their talents, culture, or general education? Some Glasgow Roman Catholics may claim to be 'lapsed' Roman Catholics (who never criticise their Church), but they are never 'lapsed' Eirishmen! There isn't a Scoto-Eirishman in Scotland, a Lally, a Murphy, or a Gaffney, who is not Eirish under his skin. Scratch them and their Eirish bit comes out. That is why their priests are so committed to segregated schooling. To teach them 'history' with a Roman Catholic and Eirish slant. To pump into them whatever politics suits at the time and place. The children leave the Roman Catholic schools in this country semi-prepared or conditioned to vote Labour. . . [34]

Similar sentiments have frequently been expressed by some of the Reformed Churches in Scotland. In 1986, the Moderator of the Free Church of Scotland addressed its annual Assembly. His speech included criticism of the Catholic and Irish nature of those of immigrant extraction:

> In 1755 there were no Roman Catholics in Glasgow, our largest city today. In 1786 there were about seventy and by 1830, they numbered 30,000, with 14,000 in Edinburgh. . . As the Irish came pouring into Scotland friction set in between Protestant and Roman Catholic working classes competing for work and housing. . . In our land the constitutional and institutional arrangements have led us to think that the land was Protestant. . . The 1918 Education Act incorporated all schools into the

> state system, but the State, in effect, had to buy the Catholic schools over. . . The short-sighted Presbyterians had their schools secularised and gained nothing. Educationally this meant that Scotland came to support a huge Irish Catholic educational ghetto, to its own future detriment. . . Today the Roman Catholic system is virtually triumphant in Scotland. Being allowed by its constitution to lie and cheat as long as its own ends are realised, its close organisation and its intelligence set-up has enabled it to infiltrate the whole educational framework of the land.[35]

The nature of some of the antagonism towards Irishness in Scotland also emerged from a writer to The Herald newspaper in 1990.

> I suggest that, when the flag of a foreign and frequently hostile state, whose constitution impudently claims sovereignty over part of the United Kingdom, and whose land and people the present pope has declared to be 'Mary's Dowry', no longer flies from the mast-head of 'Paradise', there may be, I say only may be, less 'bigoting' in the stands of Ibrox.[36]

The foreign state is the Republic of Ireland, Mary is the Virgin Mary and Paradise is the colloquial name for Celtic Park. Ibrox is the home of Glasgow Rangers Football Club. Another correspondent argued:

> The problem with the west of Scotland is the RC Irish descendants still hang on to their Irish roots – flying a tricolour at Celtic Park is like a red rag to a bull where Scots are concerned. . . If I love my native land more than the one that gave me a living, I would move back to that country. . . Before you write me off as a bluenose, I have a daughter married to a Catholic, and when we lived in the Canadian Arctic I played the organ in the RC mission in the morning and the organ in the Anglican mission in the afternoon.[37]

This particular writer 'establishes' his own self-defined 'neutral' and 'non-sectarian' credentials after demonstrating a hostility that in fact might militate against any evidence of such credentials. The writer also suggests that affinity for Ireland – 'disloyality' – on the part of the Irish diaspora in Scotland should mean a kind of repatriation. Again there is a claim to 'neutrality' in this matter, while in fact this writer contributes to and sustains a recurrent and widespread ideological polemic against public manifestations of Irishness and Catholicism. In such views, religion, politics and sport are compounded thus demonstrating their relevance for ongoing social relations in Scotland.

Versions of national and cultural identity emerge to dominate in most if not all societies. Such processes are reflected in the histories of the formation of states and countries. Nevertheless, dominant narratives and representations of Ireland and Irishness assist in the pursuit of cultural homogenisation in Scottish society, driving the seemingly centrifugal tendencies of Scottishness and its primacy at the expense of other cultures and identities. In this context, the essentially minority Irish identity is either omitted or misrepresented while Scottishness becomes the 'natural' and 'common-sense' identity. Significantly, Maley adds that the Scottish media has persisted in its refusal to stand up to the realities of anti-Irish racism.

> Scotland is a country which does not respect cultural difference. Only the cloistered academics and other privileged professionals, cushioned from the vicissitudes of economic deprivation could fail to see that sectarianism rather than religious bigotry is the product of national and social discrimination.[38]

The notion of how sport is, 'enmeshed in the media's reproduction and transmission of ideological themes and values which are dominant in society', is reflected in the print media comments evident in relation to Irishness as well as Gaelic football in Scotland.[39]

The comments of O'Hagan and Devine link with this encounter in terms of the struggle of Irishness to be recognised in Scottish society. Such dominance is widespread, frequent and characterises numerous elements of the Scottish media. Blain and Boyle report on the capacity of the Scottish print media to actively construct national characteristics through reporting on Scottish football, emphasising the hegemonic capacity of popular sources of information, values and cultural practices.[40]

Talking about Celtic's supporters, a popular and former 'Young Scottish Journalist of the Year', criticised them for seeing:

> No inconsistency in packing their ground to wave the flag of another country. They flap the Irish tricolour and sing sad Irish songs and roar of the Irish struggle. There's a country called Ireland for goodness sake, why don't they go and live there?[41]

With reference to the Irishness of Celtic's Scottish-born second, third and fourth generation Irish diasporic fanbase and his perceptions of what Scotland should represent to them, another journalist expressed the view that:

> there is a section of the Celtic support, in particular, who turn my stomach with their allegiance to the Republic of Ireland in preference to the nation of their birth.[42]

Such privileged, frequently repeated and widely accepted narratives, have served to undermine and marginalise Irishness in Scotland and those who constitute part of the worldwide Irish diaspora. They have assisted in distorting and shaping public perceptions of Irishness while offering little opportunity for Scotland to build a society equal in its respect and recognition for the numerous peoples that constitute Scottish society in the early twenty first century. In Gaelic sporting terms, such diminished and marginalised Irishness has exacted not only a toll on the maintenance, promotion, sustenance, confidence, articulation and celebration of Irishness in Scotland, but also on the capacity of Gaelic sport to become a significant aspect of Irish ethnic and cultural distinctiveness in Scotland.

1. Out of the Ghetto? The Catholic Community in Modern Scotland, Conference, University of Stirling, 24/1/97.
2. As is evidenced throughout this work such discourses characterise much Scottish press reporting regarding matters connected to the Irish in Scotland.
3. Devine, 1991 introduction.
4. M Tierney on Andrew O'Hagan in 'Leaving Caledonia', The Herald Magazine, 9/10/99.
5. Interview Mark Burke, Naomh Padraig Celtic Supporters Club, Dublin, 3/12/99
6. T Devine, The Herald, 'Scotland's Dark Trade in Slavery', 18/10/03.
7. MacMillan, 'Scotland's Shame' in Scotland's Shame', Edt T Devine, 2000, pp13-24.
8. The Times, 11/9/06, reported that 'Coatbridge in Lanarkshire is the least Scottish town in the country according to research which suggests just 39 per cent of residents have names considered to be historically Scottish. This compares with 85 per cent in the Hebridean island of Barra. Coatbridge's figure may be explained by its high level of Irish immigrants'.
9. Monkland's Official Guide, published by Ed J Burrow & Co Limited, London, 1989.
10. Glasgow Herald, Weekender, 29/6/91.

11. See B Walter,S Morgan, M J Hickman and J M Bradley, Family Stories, public silence: Irish identity construction amongst the second-generation Irish in England, Scottish Geographical Journal, Special Edition on 'The Fate of 'Nations' in a Globalised World', Vol 118, No 3, pp.201-218, 2002.
12. M Hickman, 1990 & 1995. Much history teaching in Scotland has been traditionally been centred on British and English characters and events.
13. Ibid.
14. This project was financed by the Government sponsored Economic and Social Research Council in 2001/02 and essentially looked at questions and issues of identity focusing on people born in Britain of at least one Irish-born parent or grandparent. Interviewees have been given pseudonyms for the purpose of reporting findings. The work was carried out by Dr J Bradley, Dr S Morgan, Prof M Hickman & Prof B Walter. For further references see http://www.anglia.ac.uk/geography/progress/irish2/
15. For reference see Hickman, 1998.
16. Airdrie and Coatbridge Advertiser, 12/3/03.
17. Ibid.
18. Ibid, 19/3/03.
19. Ibid.
20. Sunday Mail, August 1954.
21. Sunday Scot, 23/6/1991.
22. Jack McLean in The Herald 'Sport', 25/3/1996.
23. The Glasgow Herald, September 1996.
24. Reported in the Irish Post, 27/2/1993.
25. Reported by Donal MacAmhlaigh, Ireland's Own 5/7/85.
26. Irish Post 25/8/90.
27. Tom Shields, The Herald 17/1/96 p. 15.
28. The Herald 9/1/96, p. 21.
29. The Herald 9/2/96, p. 21.
30. Keith Waterhouse, Scottish Daily Mail 23/9/96 p. 12.
31. Observer 'Scotland', 10/6/90, p. 8.
32. Scottish Daily Mail 1/11/96 p. 8.
33. Irish Post 9/11/95 p. 8.
34. Orange Torch, June 1984.
35. Moderator's address to the Church Assembly, Church Records, July/August 1986.
36. Dr B C Campbell, letter to the Glasgow Herald, 6/5/89.
37. The Sunday Mail, letters, 27/4/03.
38. Maley, Glasgow Herald, 29/6/91.
39. Hargreaves & McDonald, 2000.
40. Blain & Boyle, 1994.
41. J MacLeod, The Herald, 18/2/02.
42. R Travers, Scotland on Sunday, Sport, 9/11/97.

Chapter 13

Political echoes: Ireland

CULTURAL, NATIONALIST AND PATRIOTIC IDENTITIES: IRELAND

Modern Irish history reflects a society where religion, nationality, culture and politics have been significant, defining and contested. In this context, as an inherently counter hegemonic body born from and into this environment, Irishness and Irish nationalism are the most important of the defining pillars on which the G.A.A. stands.

Nevertheless, although nationalist and political in organisational and ideological terms, the G.A.A. has always included, accommodated, and indeed, embraced many people from numerous backgrounds, regardless of attitudes to the national question, political affiliation or Irishness. Although retaining a considerable political character and identity, historically the G.A.A. has steered clear of overt political agitation, allowing many shades of Irish Ireland, nationalist as well as patriotic and non-patriotic identities, to collaborate through sport and culture.

In addition, the significance and salience of the formative political, social and cultural environment and experiences of the G.A.A. have changed a great deal since the late nineteenth and early twentieth centuries. This means that as society and national politics in Ireland have changed, so also has the Gaelic Athletic Association. As with other social and cultural manifestations, the G.A.A. continues to reflect change in local and national cultures, attitudes, identities and experiences.

However, as a result of its historical development and the perceived unresolved national question, whereby the island of Ireland remains divided because of the machinations and intrigues of its former colonial ruler, politics continues to have an influence upon the G.A.A. So long as there is a division of the 'north' from the 'south' and sustained British hegemony and neo-colonial influence, as a national organisation which commands allegiance throughout the island on the basis of ignoring many partitionist aspects of life in Ireland, the G.A.A. is not only a national body but, also nationalist.

> That the G.A.A. is national, and that the G.A.A. is involved – has always been involved – in the mainstream of Irish nationalism, is not in dispute. . . from the outset the social, cultural and national aspirations of so many of our people were embodied within the G.A.A. ethos. It was a national fusion, and, indeed it was as inevitable as it was desirable. . .This modern Association remains the product of a people's determination to pursue the Gaelic, the national tradition of these times. To promote the games, and, through the games, to work towards the national ideal was the Association founded. That role has been constant through the years. Today the Gaelic Athletic Association finds itself not the captive but rather the proud custodian of that tradition, that ideal. and is compelled by history to the continuing pursuit of the G.A.A. and the national ideal. . . In a word, in 1984 as in 1884, Nationalism and the Gaelic Athletic Association are indivisible.[1]

> To the youth of Ireland, a knowledge of the circumstances in which the G.A.A. was founded, of the part it played in the years before the Rising of 1916, of the share its members had in the fight for freedom, is merely knowledge of their own inheritance and shall not be held from them. Such knowledge would mark out the native games as more than mere games and would show that the Association which promotes them has had, and still has, a strong influence for National good.[2]

The history of the G.A.A. mirrors that of the complexity of Irish nationalism: like other nationalisms it has been multi-dimensional and has often been conditioned by the peculiarities of context and the vicissitudes of British colonialism and domination in Ireland. For Humphries:

> ties between Irish nationalism and the playing of Gaelic games have never been severed. Nor will they be. As the sharp political edge of Irish nationalism recedes and is replaced by a softer but equally intense interest in the culture and language, the games of hurling and football

> are increasingly cherished as part of the national character. They come as part-and-parcel of a less threatening nationalism. As every yard of fibre optic cable and every bounced satellite beam shrinks the world, a small place without a vigorous language of its own can be pervious to every form of global blandness. Hurling and football are elements in which we preserve the root of ourselves.[3]

In the north of Ireland the G.A.A. is bound to the community in the same way it is to its membership on the rest of the island and beyond. However, the differing circumstances in the 'separated' and up until recently war-torn six counties has given rise to differing consequences and the character of northern Irish nationalism and patriotism means that the significance of the political edge of the G.A.A. is often retained there because it is viewed as directly relevant, indeed, is less idealistic or romantic and more of an ongoing experience and everyday reality.

Focusing on St Gall's Gaelic club in Belfast, Humphries captures some of the reality of that club's character during 'the troubles'.

> St Gall's for instance, isn't composed of a group of people who have chosen Gaelic games from an extensive menu of leisure pursuits available to them. St Gall's, the club, the colours, the teams, represent a community, an area. Generations pass the club on to each other. What affects the community, affects the club.[4]

Likewise, during the course of the recent troubles in 'Northern Ireland', a particularly stressful period for the Association, many clubs in the North assisted in caring materially for members who were drawn into the armed constituent of the conflict and were imprisoned. Much of this assistance was by way of helping to look after a member's family. This action was often spurred on by local loyalty, family and community, rather than for any wish to attract to the Association undue hostility by appearing to favour 'armed struggle'. Although, undoubtedly some, even many, members supported this dimension of their war of liberation, or at least viewed it in a radically different way from much of British and even 'southern' Irish opinion, as an organisation the G.A.A. did not support armed struggle. Indeed, like much opinion in Ireland it was generally against the pursuit of this strategy in the national conflict. Reflecting the Association's attitude towards armed struggle, for one Republican inmate of Long Kesh/The Maze prison:

> Contrary to what people think, Republicans don't have a great opinion of the G.A.A. and what it has done nationally over the troubles. Clubs and families have been tight, but nationally the G.A.A. has been as apathetic as anyone else.[5]

Nonetheless, the nature of the Association means the overlap between culture and Irish history, past and present perceptions and reality, means that the politics of transformation and cultural resistance is inseparable.

In the six counties of Northern Ireland, among many in the unionist population, Irishness has long been generally detested or at least held as alien, treated with scorn and viewed as inhibiting and threatening due to its perceived Catholic connotations. Although many British observers, and indeed many unionists/loyalists in Northern Ireland, have often viewed G.A.A. members as potential revolutionaries or terrorists awaiting the call of battle, Flanagan argues that:

> this narrow-minded vision of the organisation, resulted in victimisation of the Association, its players and spectators by non-association members which has continued through the decades into Northern Ireland in the 1990s'.[6]

In County Down clubhouses in Loughlinisland and Bryansford were burned down whilst clubs such as Bellaghy in County Derry had similar experiences during the troubles. In Crossmaglen County Armagh, throughout much of the troubles period and until the first years in the new millennium, the British Army occupied the local Rangers club's ground for use as a helicopter landing pad. This was the most well known example of how the G.A.A. has been a significant focus in the conflict between Irish and British identities in the North of Ireland.[7] After winning the All-Ireland minor competition of 1987 at Croke Park the Down team passed through Clough where the bus was stoned by Loyalists on its way to Downpatrick. When the senior team passed through with the Sam Maguire four years later, as a matter of precaution all lights were dimmed in the team bus and in the town.

In 1991, despite large attendances and as the only major field sports during the summer months, a Unionist councillor complained to the press there was 'too much Gaelic football being shown by the British

Broadcasting Corporation' in Northern Ireland. Clubrooms at Ballycran in County Down were burned to the ground whilst North Down Borough Council voted not to send a letter of congratulations to Ulster Champions Down who had won the All-Ireland for the first time since 1968.[8] During May of 1997 the chairman of a County Antrim Gaelic club was tortured and killed by loyalist paramilitaries, while in December of the same year the manager of a Gaelic football club in north Belfast was killed.[9]

Hassan reports how in 1999 Sean Bradley, chairman of the Wolfhounds Club in Limivady, County Derry, informed him of some of the problems his club encountered at the hands of loyalist paramilitaries.

> The goalposts were cut down, so we put them up again. They were actually cut down five times. The pitch was strewn with broken glass. They [loyalists] sprayed the pitch with chemicals to make a large union jack in the middle of the pitch. There were various threats against individuals. I would have received telephone calls saying that I would be shot dead. On adjoining land a new [Roman Catholic] chapel was being built and on one November night it was blown up. The UDA placed statements in the newspapers at the time claiming the reason why the chapel had been blown up was because the catholic authorities had given the GAA a pitch to play on.[10]

Historically, sporting conflict, or sport's links with wider elements of hostilities in Ireland, has not been confined to a cleavage between Irish and British identities as typified in Gaelic sporting traditions. Many other sports have also been characterised or influenced by religious, cultural and political considerations. For example, Sugden and Bairner show this in relation to soccer and rugby, the latter having a 'pre-political cultural impact similar to the G.A.A., but operating in the opposite direction'. Likewise, the complex political situation in Northern Ireland means that the political dimensions of sport, 'varies from sport to sport, from level to level and from one region to another'.

> Sport in itself is neutral, but because it can never be divorced from the politics of its players, administrators and supporters, it necessarily responds to the political currents of the habitat within which it thrives.[11]

Talking specifically about the G.A.A. in Northern Ireland, the same authors state:

> It would be a mistake to over-emphasise its formal political role, but, in a context where tradition and imagery are paramount, its potency both as a rallying point for Irish Catholics and a symbol of alien culture to northern Protestants is of great indirect political importance.[12]

In celebrating Irishness, Gaelic sport has an inherent capacity to attract hostility from those who are repulsed by such expressions.

Over the course of its history, the G.A.A. has been an important component of Irishness as well as nationalist identity. Historically, with the entire country embroiled in turmoil and conflict, the Association could not remain aloof from this. Indeed, it can be argued that historically, this conflict made the G.A.A. into a significant body in Irish life. After all, it was a perception of the clash between oppressed and oppressor, between native and usurper, between colonist and colonised, which led to its foundation. In that experience, the Association's nationalist involvement, and many of its members' participation in 'rebellious' activities that resulted from and produced a mixture of ideology and reaction to circumstances, has meant that the G.A.A. has been viewed as a focus for cultural and political resistance.

Nevertheless, even if many aspects of culture in Ireland have been significantly politicised, it would be a narrow assessment to conclude that the present Gaelic Athletic Association is simply a rallying point for Irish nationalism. Irish nationalism is multi-faceted and the Association has managed to transcend many of the distinctions, tensions and divisions within it. The G.A.A. reflects the island of Ireland and its many shades of green. As the G.A.A. Official Guide states:

> The Association is a national organisation which has as its basic aim the strengthening of National identity in a 32 county Ireland through the preservation and promotion of Gaelic games and pastimes.[13]

Although deeply embedded in Irish culture and a bastion of Irishness in the Republic of Ireland, there G.A.A. members have existed relatively untouched by many of the considerations that have endured in modern Northern Ireland. In the north of Ireland in particular, where the situation and context of everyday life is affected to a greater or lesser degree by religious, cultural and political cleavage, the Association continues to perform:

> a general and complex political function, as an advocate of Irish independence and national unity, as a symbol of Gaelic separateness and as an open forum for the allegiances of all factions of nationalist persuasion.[14]

As symbols and expressions of Irishness, the G.A.A. and its membership are viewed with deep hostility by many in the unionist population. This has to be viewed in the context of the historical conflict between 'gael' and 'planter' and 'native' and 'colonist', a factor that has determined distinctions throughout much of northern Irish life. Even where Nationalist and Unionist, Catholic and Protestant share cultural forms, division and conflict also have a role. Within soccer and rugby for example, allegiances and participation are frequently informed by ethno-religious and political factors. The G.A.A. in Ireland has historically intertwined with and become part of this larger depiction.

In recent decades some historical, political and journalistic observers have condemned the G.A.A. denying it a role in contributing positively to modern Irish identities and arguing that it has failed to 'respond to the forces of modernism and revisionism'.[15] Such arguments frequently posit political argument under the guise of revisionist academic research. They can often also ignore the reality of the experience and perceptions of many people, particularly those in the conflict-ridden north.

Although a unique sport amongst the Irish and their offspring, many G.A.A. people also participate and contribute to activities beyond the confines of the specifics attached to Gaelic sports. Despite being 'peculiarly Irish', involvement with and support for the G.A.A. cannot simply be taken as an indication of either a parochial or worldly view. Revisionism is essential in historical debate, but negates itself as academic when carried in the guise of 'neutrality' only to be sophistically construed as political and cultural opposition. Schlessinger makes the important point that:

> to assert that national cultures might, indeed, do, exist does not by any means exclude the reality of there being a transnational or global culture as well. We need to think in terms of the simultaneous interaction and parallelism of different cultural levels within given social formations. To insist upon 'either. . . or' makes for good polemics or political sloganeering but poor analysis.[16]

In Ireland, although historical circumstances have meant culture can also be politics in its broadest sense, and therefore also a means to make a political statement, the majority of G.A.A. members are not immediately concerned with political issues. As with any sport, the glories of achievement, especially in individual, parish and county terms, predominate. In some parts of Ireland the G.A.A.'s membership is politically conscious, and involvement with the Association is additionally an underlying though varying, cultural and political statement. Although the pursuit of human achievement, accomplished for individuals, family or locale, is a major driving force for many enthusiasts, within the G.A.A., ethnic origin, region, locale, religion, nationalism, politics, culture and even class, all within a context of 'Irishness', have and continue to make, a significant contribution to Gaelic sporting identities. Though few can detach themselves from the central tenets and symbols of the G.A.A., it can be a variety of things to different people. It can be a way of life, a statement, a badge, whilst it can also be simply games. For one of Ireland's most successful Gaelic football players of the 1990s:

> There's nothing better than seeing the basic skills performed well. . . blocking, catching and kicking. The game in its purest form.[17]

Likewise for a prominent and successful hurling manager of the 1990s:

> Living in the present of Ireland rather than trying to live in the past. I find that bigotry disgraceful, and distasteful and disgusting'. I don't care which side it's on. Nationalism is fine, but I'm living it. We're really living it.[18]

The Association has been faced with problems regarding the most recent 'nationalist' para-military campaign: a para-military campaign that has been portrayed by much of the media, and some politicians in Britain (as well as in Ireland), as encapsulating the essence of the Association as well as the ideals of Irish nationalism. As the media has frequently shaped the discussion of the Northern Ireland troubles around a question of nationalist violence, support for Irish nationalism is often popularly viewed solely in this context. This constructed perception has become a tool in the British propaganda war against Irish nationalism. The basic premise of this propaganda assault has been that the more simply portrayed and one dimensional (as terrorists and Godfathers) this war and its Irish nationalist adherents are presented, the less likely they are to win support and their ideology to attract credibility. However, this has been shown to be just one of many strategies used by the British to win its struggle against Irish nationalism. This strategy has also delayed the possibility of peace and the evolution of a penetrating alternative analysis and solution to the conflict.

Therefore, people who are seen to support an Irish nationalist agenda have become demonised and marginalised within British and some parts of Irish societies. Public opinion is often dominated by a popular assumption that support for Irish independence and unity, or Irish nationalism, as well as criticism of Britain's role in Ireland, equates with support for or ambiguity towards violent atrocities. This is an assumption that is misinformed, superficial and lacks moral reflection, despite its capacity to pretend otherwise. This perspective is also one that creates difficulty for the G.A.A. in Ireland and amongst the Irish diaspora, including the community in Scotland. Although the Association can be characterised as patriotic and nationalist, it is inaccurate to view it as actively seeking the unity of the island. Such matters are left to politicians, because any party or factional advantage or domination within the G.A.A. could prove to be its undoing.

Although political strength, intensity, activism or identity within a particular G.A.A. club might be significant in some areas, G.A.A. activities are pursued as sports, and the political dimension is more characterised as national and patriotic symbolism and tokenism. It is something that is intuitively part of the G.A.A., rather than the G.A.A. being part of it. For other individuals and communities who would not countenance armed struggle in the 'cause of Ireland', the G.A.A. is an agency for expression: a peaceful means to express their historic Irish identity that has been unable to escape, or has only partly emancipated itself, from British domination and influence. Likewise, for many G.A.A. members particularly those in the North, until its removal from the rule book 'Rule 21' which disbarred members of the 'Crown Forces' from being members of the Association, was not a weapon 'but a shield, a comfort, not an insult'.[19]

1. Padraig Uasal O'Bogaigh, Uachtaran of the G.A.A., in Gaelic Athletic Association: a century of service, 1984-1994, 1984, p.7.
2. Padraig O Fainin, in Gaelic Athletic Association: a century of service, 1984-1994, 1984, pp.28-29.
3. Humphries, 1996, p.5.
4. Ibid, p.105.
5. Ibid, p.129.
6. Flanagan, 1991, p.46.
7. G.A.A grounds in Cork and Limerick were amongst the first to experience this in 1914.
8. Quinn. 1993, p.91.
9. Scotland on Sunday, 7/12/97.
10. Hassan, 2003, p.101.
11. Sugden and Bairner, in Allison, 1986, pp.90-117.
12. Ibid.
13. The Gaelic Athletic Association: The Official Guide, Croke Park, Dublin, 1980.
14. Sugden and Bairner, in Allison, 1986, pp.90-117.
15. For example see Cronin, 1996.
16. 1991, p.305.
17. Quinn, 1993, p.305.
18. Liam Griffin, manager of 1996 All-Ireland hurling champions Wexford, in Scotland on Sunday, Sport, 1/9/96.
19. Humphries, 1996, p.130. Rule 21 has of course been disgarded from the G.A.A. Rulebook.

Chapter 14

Political echoes: Scotland

CULTURAL, NATIONALIST AND PATRIOTIC IDENTITIES: SCOTLAND

British colonialism in Ireland has meant that like other cultural associations and organisations, the evolution of the G.A.A. has been strongly influenced by issues connected to the (Irish) national question as well as the struggle of Irishness to survive in the face of British hegemony. The consequences of British colonialism contributed significantly to the creation of waves of migration from Ireland in the nineteenth and twentieth centuries and the legacies of Irish-British conflict have, to a greater or lesser extent, been manifest and have found expression wherever the Irish have settled. This has often meant that the centuries-long conflict has been expressed in differentiated forms amidst the Irish diaspora, amongst subsequent generations of Irish offspring and, particularly in areas of settlement such as Britain, the eastern seaboard of the USA and in former British colonies. These legacies have also been manifest in Scotland, where a significant number of Irish Catholics and their offspring settled in the nineteenth and twentieth centuries, from where a majority of British colonists journeyed to settle Ulster in the seventeenth century and, where a strong anti-Catholic culture and identity has existed since the sixteenth century Protestant Reformation. From the sixteenth and seventeenth centuries this anti-Catholic culture extended to the rest of Britain as Protestantism and anti-Catholicism became integral pillars in the construction of British, as well as English and Scottish, national identities.

One aspect of cultural and political assertion that has been a symbol of resistance and expression of opposition against colonisation, imperialist ideology, dominance and anti-Irish expression has been the counter hegemonic custom of naming a Gaelic club after a national, nationalist or patriotic figure. Many Gaelic clubs have been named after Catholic parishes, Christian saints or Irish symbols, but a high proportion are also called after individuals or groups who are discerned as having spent much or some of their lives working on behalf of the people of Ireland or who have given their lives for causes linked to the national question and Irish liberation. According to Dr Douglas Hyde:

> Our games were in a most grievous condition until the brave and patriotic men who started the Gaelic Athletic Association took their revival in hand. . . Besides reviving our national sports, the G.A.A. has also revived national memories, the names of its clubs perpetuating the memory of many great and good Irishmen.[3]

The Pre-match Irish News, Guinness-sponsored souvenir paper, contained a half page of 'best wishes' for the County Tyrone team which was about to participate in the 1995 All-Ireland Final. All the county's famous clubs contributed. They included Coalisland Fianna, Tomas Clarkes, Pomeroy Plunketts, Galbally Pearses, Derrylaughan Kevin Barrys, Aughabrack O'Connells, Drumragh Sarsfields, Kildress Wolfe Tones, Eoghain Rua Ui Neill, Ardboe O'Donovan, Cogher Eire Og: all names which have broadly defined 'nationalist' connotations. They include Tom Clarke, Joseph Plunkett and Padraic Pearse, three of the leaders of the 1916 Uprising, Wolfe Tone, a Protestant and the considered father of contemporary Irish republicanism, as well as Patrick Sarsfield, who led Irish armies against the Crown forces of King William in the seventeenth century.

Amongst the British-based Gaelic matches reported by The Irish Post (an Irish newspaper catering for the Irish community in Britain) in July 2006 were games involving Shalloe Pearses versus St Anthonys, Roger Casements versus Naomh Padraig, Erin go Bragh versus Sean McDermotts, St Colmcilles versus Cambridge Parnells, Robert Emmets versus Thomas McCurtains, Sean Treacys versus Fr Murphy, St Brendans versus Moindearh and Bros Pearse versus Granuaile. All of these names embrace the memory and commemoration of the perceived cause of

Irish liberation or are called after Christian saints.[4] At half time in the 2006 All-Ireland Football Final held at Croke Park in front of over 80,000 people, including the President of Ireland, the Taoiseach, numerous members of the Catholic hierarchy and watched on television and heard on radio by millions across the globe, the entertainment was partly provided (as it is traditionally) by the Artane Boys Band. Amongst the tunes played by the band was 'On the One Road', a song celebrating the Irish nationalist vision of everyone in Ireland supporting a united Ireland and 'God Save Ireland', a 'rebel' song commemorating the Manchester Martyrs, Allen, Larkin and O'Brien, who were hanged for the same Irish cause in Manchester in 1867.

Within many Irish immigrant communities in the early twentieth century the practice of calling an organisation in memory of a perceived patriot was commonplace. In Scotland, this is reflected in the names of National Foresters friendly society branches: Kevin Barry (Edinburgh), Thomas Meaghar (Motherwell), Owen Roe O'Neill (Greenock), Michael Davitt (Coatbridge), Charles Kickham (Glasgow), Young Ireland (Springburn) and Robert Emmet (Falkirk). During the early twentieth century, other branches as well as additional Irish organisations in Scotland such as the Gaelic League included Shamrocks and O'Connells and priests and Irish saints as their branch names. Such names are exclusively Irish and reflect a distinctive view: a view at variance with those that have traditionally dominated in Britain in relation to Ireland's history, particularly those conflictual aspects in terms of its near neighbour.

A number of Gaelic clubs in Scotland have followed suit during the course of G.A.A. history. The first club in Scotland was of course Red Hugh O'Neills founded in 1897. In the 1920s Patrick Sarsfield had two clubs named after him in Coatbridge and Greenock, the 1940s witnessed the Thomas Davis Club in Motherwell, Padraic Pearses in the south side of Glasgow, Fintan Lalors from Govan Glasgow, Roger Casements in Clydebank and South O'Hanlons based at Eastfield Cambuslang Glasgow in the 1960s. Since the early 1980s a number of G.A.A. clubs have emerged in Scotland that have chosen names reflecting Ireland's history and admiration for people who are perceived as having given their lives for the cause of Irish liberation. However, with violence and civil conflict again erupting in Ireland from the late 1960s, and such names having a contemporary as well as historical relevance, this has resulted in a tendentious journey for several clubs in Scotland.

Pearse Harps, based at Pearse Park in the Cambuslang area of Glasgow, originally found itself without a name as it was about to engage in its first competitive encounter in March 1985. Before the game a handful of the club's players met in the antiquated dressing rooms at the park and decided to link the new team with their home ground. Those who choose the name of the club were mindful of the link with the Rising in Dublin in 1916, Padraic Pearse being one of the prime movers in that event. Nonetheless, there was no conscious desire to connect the new club with an ideology of militant republicanism or the more recent troubles in the north of Ireland. Pearse, a poet, educationalist and revolutionary, who almost certainly never fired a shot during the Rising, has also been commemorated and celebrated during the twentieth century alongside the evolution of the Irish state. This has included numerous streets and estates in various towns in Ireland and a main railway station in Dublin being named after Pearse as well as his commemoration through the issue of a special postage stamp by 'an Post' on the centenary of his birth in 1979. Numerous Gaelic clubs are called after Pearse and calling a Gaelic football team after him in Scotland continued this tradition. For the new Pearse club this was in imitation of a custom practiced amongst many people not only involved with the G.A.A., but elsewhere in Irish society.

Founded in 1988 it would seem logical that in Edinburgh, a city where another of the leaders of the Irish Rising of 1916 was born, a new Irish Gaelic football team would consider naming the club after James Connolly. However, during the same period of the development of Gaelic football in the area there was also a growth of Republican demonstrations in the city and corresponding opposition from loyalists and others. The Republican organisation in Edinburgh was known as the James Connolly Society. As a result of these events and primarily through negative representations in the Scottish media, the name of James Connolly has become synonymous with the political and bigotted skirmishing that initially characterised these parades. Some of the first members of the new Gaelic club were associated with the James Connolly

Society. However, after a few seasons the club became more influenced and indeed sustained by students from Ireland who attended courses in the city's local Edinburgh and Heriot Watt Universities. By the mid 1990s all of the clubs original players had departed the football scene and the team was comprised almost entirely of young men originally from Ireland who worked and lived in Edinburgh, many with a number of financial institutions. By 2007 almost all of the club's players were Irish-born living, working or studying in the Edinburgh area. In 1996 discussions took place at the club with regards changing its name because the members had become aware of 'outside' perceptions, hostility and suspicions. A decision was made to abide by the club's name and trust that 'people could see beyond the prevalent sectarian perceptions which dominated'.[5]

Although Dundee Dalriada arose from a name that connected the north east of Ireland with the west coast of Scotland, the first choice of the club's members was to name the team Dundee na Fianna. This name evokes the sagas of Cuchulain and others of early Ireland. Na Fianna also translates as Fenians, the revolutionary body of Irishmen who engaged in military conflict with the British during the mid to late nineteenth century. It is also the name adopted by the most successful political party in modern Ireland, Fianna Fail. Nonetheless Tayprint, the first sponsors of the Dundee club, was reluctant to be seen to associate itself with such a label if it became a contentious issue. As a result the name was changed to Dalriada.

Another short-lived club in Scotland was that of Saltcoats Gaels. Based at Jack's Road in Saltcoats, and initially announced as 'The Invincibles', the club made its debut in senior football during season 1990. Although the name seemed appropriate for a competitive sports team, this was also the name of a tiny republican body who in 1892 assassinated T H Burke and Lord Frederick Cavendish, the newly appointed chief secretary for Ireland. Eventually the team's founder John McCreadie, reacted to warnings of potential criticism by renaming the club Saltcoats Gaels.

One of the most significant Irish nationalist leaders of the late nineteenth century was Michael Davitt. Davitt was convicted of Fenian involvement in 1870, was imprisoned by the British, became a member of the Irish Republican Brotherhood, was an Irish Land Leaguer, a human rights activist and later one of the foremost leaders of the Irish Home Rule movement. Davitt subsequently decided against using military means to liberate his country though he declared that Britain was the root cause of all of Ireland's social, economic and political problems. He had a deep influence on both the political ideas and activities of the 'Parnell era' in the late nineteenth century. Davitt also supported the Land League in north-west Scotland and was an important patron of Celtic Football Club in Glasgow. As far as some G.A.A. activists were concerned his name was thought worthy of a new club that began to be formed in Glasgow around 1995. However, despite a few active members and the involvement of a number of youths in the fledgling Davitt club, a competitive side failed to evolve in the same area of Glasgow that had produced the first Gaelic Athletic club in 1897.

BOBBY SANDS AND TERENCE MACSWINEY

> The greatest love a person can have for his friends
> is to give his life for them. (John 15:13)

It is said we live in modern times,
In the civilised year of 'seventy-nine'
But when I look around, all I see,
is modern torture, pain, and hypocrisy.

In modern times little children die,
They starve to death, but who dares ask why?
And little girls without attire,
Run screaming, napalmed, through the night fire.

And while fat dictators sit upon their thrones,
Young children bury their parents' bones,
And secret police in the dead of night,
Electrocute the naked woman out of sight.

In the gutter lies the black man, dead,
And where the oil flows blackest, the street runs red,
And there was He who was born and came to be,
But lived and died without liberty.

> As the bureaucrats, speculators and Presidents alike,
> Pin on their dirty, stinking, happy smiles tonight,
> This lonely prisoner will cry out from within his tomb,
> And tomorrow's wretch will leave its Mother's womb.[1]
>
> Bobby Sands

> "I wish to point out again the secret of our strength and assurance of our final victory. This contest of ours is not on our side a rivalry of vengeance, but one of endurance – it is not they who inflict the most, but those who can suffer the most, who will conquer – though we do not abrogate our function to demand and see that evil doers and murderers are punished for their crimes. . . Those whose faith is strong will endure to the end and triumph."[2]
>
> Terence MacSwiney

In the mid 1980s Coatbridge-based Gaelic football club Sands MacSwineys developed from Pearse Harps in Cambuslang. For one former club member of Sands, its name was chosen to reflect the aspiration of an independent and united Ireland, 'just like that of the G.A.A. itself'.[6] It was a name chosen in a context when Sands' sacrifice had been a major news story and when many of the first players connected to the club had been emotionally influenced by his death. It was also a name that was believed to reflect admiration for the sacrifice endured by Bobby Sands.

Although the initiators of the club were aware of the possible misinterpretation and misrepresentation that could arise from the name, its founders were also convinced that it was erroneous to think that it should be taken as an indication of support for nationalism pursued by military means. Indeed those who shared this consciousness of such things were determined to face down what they interpreted as the ignorance and prejudice of their potential opposition. With this awareness in mind, why might the club's initiators call the team after Bobby Sands and Terence MacSwiney? Indeed, why might any G.A.A. club call themselves after such figures?

In fact, Sands and MacSwiney are two of the most significant figures in modern Irish history. Although sixty years separates their experiences, in the last years of their lives both individuals encountered remarkably similar circumstances. Despite a variety of political opinion and historical interpretation characterising the Irish over the course of the seminal periods which surrounded the lives of Sands and MacSwiney, a review of both individuals and the events which gave them a significant place in twentieth century Irish history adds insight into the choice of such names on the part of many thousands of Gaelic clubs since the founding of Red Hugh O'Neills in Glasgow and Tuam Kruger's in Galway in the late nineteenth century and, since Smith O'Brien's (Killaloe) became the first hurling team to represent County Clare in the 1887 All-Ireland series, just three years after the establishment of the Gaelic Athletic Association.

At the time of the Irish War of Independence, Terence MacSwiney was an educationalist, cultural activist, T.D. (member of the Irish Parliament) for mid-Cork, Lord Mayor of the City and Commandant of the Cork No. 1 Brigade of the Irish Republican Army, then fighting a War of Independence. In the two last posts, MacSwiney had replaced his friend and colleague Tomas MacCurtain, who was the victim of a premeditated execution by British Crown forces in March 1920.[7] Similar to the thoughts of Patrick Pearse before him, MacSwiney believed that 'a man must be prepared to labour for an end that may be reached only in yet another generation'.[8] Several decades later Nelson Mandela expressed a similar response to his incarceration and the plight of his people.

> I have fought against white domination, and I have fought against black domination. I have cherished the ideal of a democratic and free society in which all persons live together in harmony and with equal opportunities. It is an ideal which I hope to live for and to achieve. But if needs be, it is an ideal for which I am prepared to die.[9]

Poignantly, these sentiments were also to be shared with Bobby Sands sixty years after the life of Terence MacSwiney. For Costello:

> The story of Terence MacSwiney's life is more than the story of a heroic and tragic hunger strike which would unsettle the mightiest empire of its time. . . teacher, playright, propagandist, soldier, elected official, husband, father and Catholic mystic – which combined to produce a man of considerable complexity.[10]

The events that immediately led to MacSwiney enduring a hunger strike were as a result of him showing himself to being:

> a particularly dangerous man in the eyes of the British government. His multiplicity of Republican activities, together with the platform he occupied as Lord mayor of Cork, had contributed greatly to the breakdown of the King's writ in Cork and in the country at large, which was now a hotbed of rebellion.[11]

As a result of opinion that viewed the Cork republican as dangerous, MacSwiney was arrested for possession of a R.I.C. cipher code and other subversive documents. In protest at his imprisonment and British rule in Ireland, at a time when such men believed that the Irish Republic was a living reality, MacSwiney commenced a hunger strike. He believed that no British court should be able to pass judgement within an Irish jurisdiction.

> Thus had began the battle of wills that would soon command worldwide attention, pitting a determined individual against the greatest empire of its time.[12]

MacSwiney's capacity to suffer for the cause of Irish liberation was clear in his writings prior to the events that led to his hunger strike. In a collection of essays, one entitled 'Principles of Freedom', MacSwiney argued:

> Now, and in every phase of the coming struggle, the strong mind is a greater need than the strong hand. . . In the aberrations of the weak mind decrying resistance, let us not lose our balance and defy brute strength. . . To the man whose mind is true and resolute ultimate victory is assured. No sophistry can sap his resistance; no weakness can tempt him to savage reprisals. He will neither abandon his heritage nor poison his nature.[13]

MacSwiney was a particularly devout religious man. Six weeks after the commencement of his hunger strike, and contrary to his own expectations that his hunger strike could last so long, MacSwiney released a public statement:

> I attribute this to the spiritual strength which I receive from Daily Communion bringing me bodily strength assisted by a world of prayers, of which the intensity is so apparent. My comrades, who are fasting two days longer than I, are clearly sustained in like manner. I believe God has directly intervened to stay the tragedy for a while for a Divine

> purpose of his own: I believe he has intervened not solely for our sakes. We have laid our offering at his feet to be accepted or not, according to his Divine Will.[14]

There is little doubt concerning the degree of suffering encountered when the human body is starved of food.

> Every expenditure of energy is subservient to the greater need, to keep the brain going via the heart and liver. Metabolism is reduced, the body shuts down on unnecessary physical activity. This produces the familiar signs of lethargy. Apathy is not just a description, it is a recognised medical symptom of starvation. The onset of protein loss is quite quick.

When the body is already weak due to prior poor conditions, such as living in a poverty stricken African country or being imprisoned in Brixton Prison or Long Kesh/The Maze 'On the Blanket', the onset of protein loss is quick,

> the guts atrophy, vital organs are reduced in size, vitamin deficiency increases, raising the apathy. Victims begins to lose any desire to move.

Further, the skin stops repairing itself and immune responses are greatly weakened. Gradually, or sometimes suddenly, the human body dies.[15]

Terence MacSwiney suffered for seventy-four days on hunger strike. Two of MacSwiney's sayings remain significant for Irish nationalism:

> 'If I die I know the fruit will exceed the cost a thousand fold. The thought makes me happy. I thank God for it'.[16]

> 'This contest is one of endurance, and it is not those who inflict most, but those who can suffer most, who will conquer'.[17]

During MacSwiney's hunger strike in Brixton Prison, both Cork and Tipperary G.A.A. called off most playing activities in a gesture of solidarity. The Munster hurling final was cancelled, a time when virtually the whole of Munster (apart from Waterford) was under military rule. After his death on the 25th October 1920, Central Council of the G.A.A. made a special announcement:

> Provincial Councils, County boards, League and Tournament Committees are hereby requested to make next Sunday, 31 October, a closed date all over Ireland so as to record the sympathy of the Gaelic Athletic

> Association with the Lady Mayoress of Cork in her great bereavement, our admiration for the Lord Mayor's heroic sacrifice and to mark the Association's protest against the inhuman treatment meted out to the Lord Mayor of Cork by the British Government.[18]

Like Tom Ashe, who in 1917 had died as a result of forced feeding during hunger strike, for many Irish people MacSwiney's death became a symbol of Irish resistance. Notably, Ashe was also a leading G.A.A figure in county Dublin before the Rising of 1916.

Tens of thousands of people attended MacSwiney's funeral along with thousands of Association members. Pope Benedict XV sent an Apostolic Blessing, showing how deeply his sacrifice had impressed beyond the shores of Ireland and Britain.[19] For supporters and sympathetic observers, MacSwiney embodied the ideal of sacrifice that has characterised many struggles compelled by a perception of injustice. The struggles of Mahatma Ghandi in India and the suffragettes in Britain are two other such examples around which the British Government was also involved during the early twentieth century.

Although not an active G.A.A. member, MacSwiney shared the ideals of many of the founders and supporters of the Association. In similar style to Archbishop Croke, Douglas Hyde, Patrick Nally and other nationalists of the time, he spoke of:

> the hellish materialistic Power that has fastened itself on this our country by trickery and treachery; that had rooted one half of the people from the land and was stifling the soul of the other half; and had now stationed amongst us barracks and garrisons like the fang of some devilish ogre that we might not rush upon and struggle forever.[20]

In an open letter to the Cork Examiner, Bishop Cohalan of Cork stated that:

> I ask the favour of a little space to welcome home to the city he laboured for so zealously the hallowed remains of Lord Mayor Terence MacSwiney. For the moment, it might appear that he has died in defeat. This might be conceded if there were questions merely of the individual, but it is not true when the resolve of the nation is considered. Was Lord Edward Fitzgerald's death in vain? Was Robert Emmet's death in vain? Did Pearse and the other martyrs for the cause of Irish freedom die in vain? We are the weaker nation in the combat. . . Special questions such

> as the questions of the land, of local government, of housing, or education, for a time engage our whole attention. But periodically the memory of the martyr's death will remind a young generation of the fundamental question of the freedom of Ireland. . . Terence MacSwiney's takes his place among the martyrs in the sacred cause of the freedom of Ireland. . . We bow in respect before his heroic sacrifice. We pray the Lord may have mercy on his soul.[21]

Originating from the pen of a well-known anti-Republican, Cohalan's letter reflects the effect upon Ireland's struggle that perceived sacrifices of men such as MacSwiney has had. In such contexts, there can be a heightened awareness of Irish history amongst Irish people, which in turn often encourages G.A.A. members to name a club after an Irish patriot. Six decades after the death of MacSwiney a similar struggle once again elevated the historical conflict involving Ireland and Britain in popular consciousness.

Like MacSwiney, Bobby Sands was a hunger striker. However, his death took place during the most recent phase of Ireland's troubles and for Gaelic sports clubs whose members and founders lived in the same era as Sands, selecting his name could be construed as more subversive, more militant, than that of using MacSwineys, who many people would be unaware of and, who may simply be viewed as another figure from the distant pantheons of Irish martyrdom.

Although not involved in G.A.A. matters to the extent of other hunger strikers like Kevin Lynch, who had captained a Derry minor team to all-Ireland hurling victory in the mid 1970s, Sands did play some Gaelic football (his main field sport being soccer) in Belfast during his youth. Caught up in 'the Troubles', before joining the I.R.A. Sands had been stabbed in a sectarian assault, intimidated at gunpoint from his employment and his family had been driven from its home by Loyalist intimidation.[22] These confrontations with those he perceived as his oppressors led to his joining the I.R.A. and ultimately to his arrest.

O'Hearn charts Sands rapid education and politicisation in prison and his maturing as a thoughtful and well-organised soldier and political activist.[23] The struggle of Republican prisoners resulted in their 'Blanket-No-Wash' protest that developed steadily as a result of conflict with the

British Government and prison authorities. For Sands and the other strategists within the prison system,

> They [republican activists] were fighting for social recognition and they were a political army, resisting injustice and fighting for a new and better society. Thus, they had to win their struggle not primarily for themselves but to validate the right of oppressed people to resist.[24]

By 1981 Bobby Sands was the Officer in Command of Republican prisoners in the H-Blocks of Long Kesh/The Maze Prison, having taken over from Brendan Hughes who had led a failed hunger strike in late 1980. In the wake of being deceived by the British Government in its dealings with that hunger strike, and beginning on 1st March of the following year, on the initiative of the prisoners and against the wishes of Republicans on the outside of the prison, Sands led another hunger strike. The broad Republican movement on the outside of the prisons was adamant that such a clash inside would 'divert resources from armed struggle into a prison support campaign'. This opinion also reflected the fact that Sinn Féin, the political arm of the Republican Movement, was so underdeveloped and did not have the capacity to run a protest campaign.[25] It is in this light that the actions of Sands and his fellow prisoners on hunger strike can be seen to have greatly affected the shift in the Republican movement that precipitated and prepared for a more politicised campaign and direction than previously. This strategy was also one of the main contributors to the development of the Peace Process of the 1990s and beyond.

In his later communiqués from prison Sands clarified his thinking on the morality of the struggle to remove the British military and governmental presence from his country. Sands said he was sorry that people had lost their lives, but,

> The British created the climate for political violence. . . their actions created the IRA. . . I don't want to see anyone hurt or dying but so long as injustice reigns in this country I feel it is my duty to fight it whatever way I can. [26]

Sands also demonstrated his capacity for thinking about political developments beyond Ireland. During his period on hunger strike he wrote of current events.

> I am abreast with the news and view with utter disgust and anger the Reagan/Thatcher plot. It seems quite clear that they intend to counteract Russian expansionism with imperialist expansionism, to protect their vital interests they say. What they mean is they covet other nations' resources. They want to steal what they haven't got and do so (as the future may unfortunately prove) they will murder oppressed people and deny them their sovereignty as nations. No doubt Mr Haughey will toe the line in Ireland when Thatcher so demands.[27]

As political proceedings conspired to cajole the prisoners towards hunger strike Sands thinking was also clear. He told a journalist about the conditions in the H-Blocks and explained why they were protesting . . . there were daily beatings and many prisoners were sick. Several had worms from eating their food with contaminated hands. One man, he said, had been taken to hospital after spending the day vomiting hundreds of worms.

> If one of us doesn't die through starvation and disease in this place. . . we'll die from the beatings we get. . . I admit that I am afraid. . . I lie in my cell and wonder if the footsteps I hear will stop at my door and it will be my turn next. . . I know I am dying. I'm prepared to die on the blanket. I will never, never accept criminal status. All the prisoners have the same determination as myself, and we never give up.[28]

Cardinal Tomas O'Fiaich, the Catholic Primate of Ireland, visited Sands and others in the H-Blocks. His description of his visit was to unsettle and counter much of the propaganda that had until then dominated on the part of the British authorities.

> I was shocked at the inhuman conditions prevailing in H-Blocks 3, 4, and 5, where over 300 prisoners were incarcerated. One would hardly allow an animal to remain in such conditions, let alone a human being. The nearest approach to it I have seen was the spectacle of the hundreds of homeless people living in sewer pipes in the slums of Calcutta. . . I was surprised that the morale of the prisoners was high. From talking to them it is evident that they intend to continue their protest indefinitely and it seems they prefer to face death rather than submit to being classed as criminals. Anyone with the least knowledge of Irish history knows how deeply rooted this attitude is in our country's past.[29]

Linking with the sentiments of O'Fiaich, while on hunger strike Sands stated:

> I am a political prisoner. I am a political prisoner because I am a casualty of a perennial war that is being fought between the oppressed Irish people and an alien, oppressive, unwanted regime that refuses to withdraw from our land. . . I am dying not just to attempt to end the barbarity of the H-Block, or to gain the rightful recognition of a political prisoner, but primarily because what is lost here is lost for the republic and those wretched oppressed whom I am deeply proud to know as the 'risen people'. [30]

Sands thoughts on his own possible death from hunger strike resonate with those of MacSwiney and many of the deeper issues that have evolved during centuries of conflict as a result of British colonialism in Ireland. Sands wrote, 'My dear father and mother':

> It is no joy to any one of us here to have to embark upon another hunger-strike. All of us realise and understand too well the consequences involved and torment endured by all the families but we have no alternative. . . Last Christmas was my ninth Christmas here in prison. I've lost because of it, including the wife I love and the son I love. Even so I would go back again tomorrow and fight because I'm not foolish, I'm not wild. I'm intelligent, responsible and hold ideals that generations have died for. I do not enjoy prison. I do not enjoy the thought of death. . . [31]

As Sands entered his hunger strike he embarked on maintaining a diary, the first entry of which read:

> I am standing on the threshold of another trembling world. May God have mercy on my soul. My heart is very sore because I know that I have broken my poor mother's heart and my home is struck with unbearable anxiety. But I have considered all the arguments and tried every means to avoid what has become the unavoidable.[32]

Standing as an 'anti-H-Block' candidate, in April 1981 Bobby Sands was elected Member of Parliament for Fermanagh/South Tyrone with 30,492 votes cast for him – ironically more than British Prime Minister Margaret Thatcher won in her Finchley constituency. Indeed, it is pertinent that amongst Mrs Thatcher's most famous words, those stating that 'economics are the method; the object is to change the soul' appear very different from those of Sands with regard to political change.[33]

During the hunger strike, G.A.A. matches all over Ulster were cancelled:

> The intensity of support for the prisoners and prisoners' rights, was expressed by individual clubs throughout the area and votes of sympathy were unanimously passed on the death of the hunger strikers, many of whom were G.A.A. members.[34]

As with the Catholic Church in much of Ireland, in 'the south' the G.A.A. refused to become overtly embroiled in this aspect of the conflict though invariably many of its membership did participate to a greater or lesser extent. Nonetheless, many of the relevant statements emanating from the Church reflected a perception of the British Government as inhuman in its treatment of the striking prisoners and of generally mishandling the conflict in the North. For Cardinal Tomas O'Fiaich, the British government was in danger of incurring the wrath of the whole nationalist population if its rigid stance was not modified.[35]

After sixty-six days on hunger strike, Bobby Sands died on May 5th 1981. Around one hundred thousand people attended his funeral in Belfast: not overtly and necessarily in support of the military campaign of the I.R.A., but within the complexity of Irish nationalism, to be seen as expressing solidarity with a perceived patriot who had reflected what they viewed as their centuries-old suffering and struggle. Many people supported this current of Irish nationalism and many others supported those who were on hunger strike at the time. However, to view such expressions as uncritical or unquestioning support for armed struggle is to misjudge the complexities of not only related moral questions, but also of Irish nationalism and much of Irish history. Nevertheless such simplistic perceptions have been constructed to such an extent that they dominate within the British media.

In most British political and journalistic circles as well as in popular ones, the argument was that Sands death was suicide: he was forced to die on the orders of the murderous, terrorist organisation to which he belonged. The Daily Express declared a common sentiment:

> Why do young men like Robert Sands commit suicide for such a cause? Because they follow darkness, believing it to be a romantic dream. Hatred is their goal.[36]

Despite this dominant view within the British media and general populace, the last part of this particular assertion seems at odds with

Sands' own frequently quoted words, 'Our revenge will be the laughter of our children'.[37]

Outside of Britain and the Unionist community in Northern Ireland, many perceptions of events like the hunger strike of 1981 and of the death of Bobby Sands were radically different from British views. In Poland, Solidarity organiser and future political leader of the country Lech Walesa, considered Sands 'a great man who sacrificed his life for his struggle'. Walesa sent his deepest sympathy to Sands' family on behalf of Poland's Solidarity movement. The East German Government ordered its Ambassador in London to the Foreign Office to protest and hand in a note that compared the situation in Northern Ireland with that in South Africa.[38] Around five thousand people demonstrated in Sands' favour in Milan. The Portuguese Parliament observed a minute's silence and sixty MPs signed a document denouncing British intransigence during the Hunger Strike. In the European Parliament, the one hundred and twenty strong Socialist group sent a protest telegram to Margaret Thatcher. In the United States dockers rebuffed British ships for twenty-four hours while there were pro-Sands marches in many of the country's major cities. The Michigan State legislature passed a resolution ordering the eviction of the British Consulate in Detroit 'because of the inhuman treatment of Irish Hunger-Striker Bobby Sands'. Other US state legislatures carried out similar resolutions. Several thouand people marched on the British Embassy in Paris in support of Sands. There were comparable demonstrations in Norway, Spain, Holland and Greece.

The Indonesian Observer contained the headline, 'Bobby Sands, a Modern Martyr'. In India, prior to his death, Prime Minister Indira Ghandi sent a message to Margaret Thatcher attempting to intercede on Sands' behalf. In the Indian Upper House, there were tributes to him 'of a kind normally reserved for dead head of states'. In Tehran the British Embassy now sits on Bobby Sands Street.[39]

> In Cuernavaca, Flora Guerrero Goff and hundreds of supporters behind a banner that read 'Bobby Sands, viviras para siempre' (Bobby Sands, you will live forever) blockaded a major British exhibit that was to be inaugurated by the British ambassador to Mexico, causing its cancellation. Sixteen organisations and over two hundred individuals

> from Cuernavaca sent a telegram and letter to Rosaleen Sands [his mother), expressing solidarity and citing the parallels between U.S. policies in Mexico and British policies in Ireland. . . On Robben Island, Nelson Mandela joined a group of young prisoners from Umkhonto we Sizwe (ANC) on a hunger strike that was directly inspired by Bobby Sands. . . Twenty years later in Turkey, when hundreds of political prisoners went on hunger strike, they too, sent secret messages planning their action and their campaign. The code word in their secret communications for the coming hunger strike was simple and appropriate: Bobby Sands.[40]

In response to these kind of events, the editor of Britain's Sunday Telegraph newspaper wrote, 'How strange, then, that she (Britain) should be left to stand alone against the tide of hostile opinion from all quarters of the globe'.[41] Such support and admiration for Sands and the other Hunger Strikers, as well as positive recognition of other figures involved over centuries on the Irish side in the conflict with Britain, are often at variance with dominant perceptions in Britain. However, it is only in such views and in learning – in more scholarly and less one-dimensional crude terms – about the centuries-long cultural, economic, social, religious and political struggle many Irish people have engaged upon to liberate their island from British hegemony, that we can begin to develop an understanding of the causes and the manifestations, as well as the possible solutions, to the conflict.

Such knowledge is also required if one is to begin to discern not only the views of many Irish, but also to begin to understand why Gaelic sports clubs, as well as many other Irish organisations and associations, are called after people like Terrence MacSwiney and Bobby Sands, in addition to many hundreds more icons and patriotic figures. This knowledge is also required to comprehend that remembrance of these people in such a way constitutes admiration, pride, recognition, reverence, affection and inspiration, and that this is not necessarily or inevitably connected to support for or belief in, armed struggle. Indeed, such admiration can transpire within a context of disagreeing with, or at least not supporting armed struggle, while simultaneously recognising the sense of self-sacrifice that such a strategy often entails on the part of many of those who engage it.

The use of such names by Irish organisations and associations, including those amongst the diaspora, clearly also pertains to disagreeing with and opposing the historical British conquest of Ireland. The rationale for opposing, or at least not uncomplicatedly accepting violence from one's 'own side' in such a dispute, is partly reflected in the words and actions of Cardinal Tomas O'Fiaich, the Catholic Primate of Ireland who demonstrated support for Irish political prisoners in their plight while on protest in the H-Blocks of Long Kesh/The Maze. In face of much opposition in Britain, O'Fiaich also supported the McBride principles that opposed discrimination against Catholics in the workplace in the north of Ireland, opposed extradition of Irish political prisoners from the USA to Britain, refused to encourage Catholics to join the Royal Ulster Constabulary, declined to abide by Garrett Fitgerald's (Irish Premier in the 1980s) request to say that voting Sinn Féin was wrong and was a supporter of Irish reunification and British withdrawal from the north of Ireland. Importantly, and also perhaps revealingly for people in Britain with little knowledge but ill-informed opinion concerning the Irish-British conflict, O'Fiaich was also against Irish nationalist and republican violence. However, reflecting his Christian approach to these issues, O'Fiaich was also against violence from any relevant source, not only Irish nationalist, but also Loyalist-Unionist or British Imperial Forces.[42]

It is in this light that the tradition of naming Gaelic clubs after Irish patriots also requires to be understood. In this context there is broad recognition of the rightousness of the cause of Irish liberation against British imperialism in Ireland and admiration, pride, recognition, reverence, affection and inspiration for many of those who have sacrificed their lives and have been prepared to die for this sense of liberation. One of the most recent clubs founded within the G.A.A. that uses a name linked to the 'Troubles' and the national struggle has been the U.S. Boston-based Gaelic football club, 'Aidan McAnespie'. The club website explains the rationale for its name.

> On Saturday, February twenty first, 1988 the 23 year old Aughnacloy footballer walked to see his Gaelic football team play a match on a field close to the border. As he approached the checkpoint, a British Army soldier fired his weapon, piercing the man in the back, killing him. The official reason for the alleged accident is that a British soldier's wet

> hand slipped as he was cleaning his gun, causing him to release the trigger, discharging three rounds. One of which ricocheted off the road, striking McAnespie in the back. The soldier responsible was never prosecuted. He was subsequently charged with manslaughter, but the charges were dropped. The McAnespie family, friends, and colleagues believe it was premeditated and intentional because he was one of the few Catholic men in the area to go back and forth on a regular basis. This case just adds to the list of victims of the security force. Killings and injustices that every family and persons had to endure and make part of everyday life in the north before peace proceedings commenced. Aidan McAnespie will never be forgotten in the border towns of County Tyrone. A memorial marker has been erected at the spot where Aidan was shot at the border. In Boston, his memory has been continued with this football club bearing his full name, established in November 1995. The Club has come a long way in the past few years by being one of the most competitive and widely supported clubs in Boston.[43]

Such a perspective on the killing of McAnespie can of course be considered political, but it is also cultural and communal as well as spiritually 'Catholic'. It is related to and reflective of, the history of the Gaelic Athletic Association, colonial and anti-colonial struggle and, one of the consequences of that history and environment: in this instance, the killing and loss of a G.A.A. member walking to his local park to play football. Calling a sports club after such a person or incident in Britain is unheard of because the circumstances have not existed that might create a similar outcome.

From an Irish nationalist perspective, it could be argued that Sands and MacSwiney personify the centuries-old dreams of thousands of dead patriots. Their vision also characterised many G.A.A. founders and members throughout the late nineteenth, twentieth and into the twenty first centuries. Although the perspective amongst the Unionist community of Northern Ireland and amongst many people in Britain is often not only different, but fundamentally opposed to these ideals, calling a club after these individuals has been characteristic of not only the G.A.A., but for hundreds of years, this has been the tradition of numerous other Irish organisations; sporting, cultural and political.

For one member of the current Sands MacSwineys Gaelic football club, he concludes:

> I've never known any of our members to be involved in politics of any kind – except for one who's a member of the local Labour Party. Gaelic football and promoting our Irish identity is what Sands is about.

Other members expressed their views:

> As long as players want to play Gaelic football and understand our links to Ireland, there's no reason for a problem. Some people have had the wrong impression regarding our team's name. There's no way I support violence: Irish or British.
>
> Our origins are different from the majority community in Scotland. We might be born here but people like Sands and MacSwiney are part of our history. They symbolise opposition to Britain's poisonous role in Irish affairs and the assertion of Ireland's right to self-determination. We're born and live in Britain as a result of this history. They're our heroes. Britain and Scotland have theirs.[44]

In Britain soccer clubs and other sports bodies are generally not called after significant figures. However, streets, squares, days, train stations and other focal points are called after Scottish, English and British historical figures and events; Trafalgar, Wellington, Churchill, Wallace, Burns, Bannockburn, Hume, Haig, etc. In Glasgow, streets around the city centre are often called after people who made their money from Britian's slave trade and Empire. Like many other nations and countries, Britain/Scotland is no different in remembering its 'heroes' and iconic figures. One of the most significant modern occasions where this practice took place was when Glasgow City Council renamed St George's Place, the location of the South African consulate, Nelson Mandela Place, in his honour. Mandela was at that time the imprisoned leader of the African National Congress, a banned militant body that was at the forefront of a popular uprising against a racist regime that held power in South Africa. In addition Mandela, whose organisation pursued a course of armed struggle as well as various other means, was considered a 'terrorist' in the eyes of British premier Margaret Thatcher. Mandela was eventually released in 1990 and became his country's first democratically elected president in 1994. Naming an area in Glasgow after such an iconic figure as Mandela, especially one who was incarcerated at the time and who was reviled by the British political establishment, is reminiscent of the authorities in Iran naming the street in which the British Embassy was located after Bobby Sands.

Selecting such names for Gaelic football clubs in Ireland and amongst the diaspora undoubtedly assist in the construction of what Cronin considers an 'identity which stresses and publicises their links as sports [people] to the nationalist mission, the embrace of things Irish and the rejection of West Britonism'.[45] Significantly, such names are also local, family and community as well as cultural, historical and ethnic markers. Further, they are distinctive, in that they are not Scottish or British, something that all of the founders of the Association or the initiators of clubs and grounds desired. Indeed, they are also not German, Mexican or Japanese or of any other country or nation: they are specifically 'Irish'. In that sense, as they would be in any other country, state or nation, they are also 'nationalist'. The orginators of the G.A.A. as well as many subsequent activists and members have overtly or subtly rejected and resisted British hegemony, whether this has been perceived in a national, linguistical, cultural, musical, sporting, class or ethnic fashion.

In essence, various Irish historical events, as well as personalities who have come to the fore as a result of British colonialism in Ireland, are remembered through the naming of G.A.A. clubs, sports grounds and stadiums. This has been the practice of not only the Gaelic Athletic Association and its various component parts since 1884, but for hundreds of years, other Irish cultural, sports, political, historical, educational, musical and national bodies, organisations and associations.

Naming associations, organisations, streets and sports clubs after patriots, national icons and political, military, religious and cultural activists and leaders is not limited to the Irish in Ireland or the Irish diaspora. As the British examples demonstrate most countries similarly utilise and commemorate national icons and events, especially in relation to those seen as important in the path of national liberation, independence, unification, or as in some cases, in support of expansion, dominance and imperialism. This is seen as important in that these people are not forgotten, are viewed as important by way of their teachings, are considered partly as role models and, for the construction of memory and national identity, are recognised as important so that future generations have an understanding and awareness of why they are where they are and who has influenced the historical events that has assisted them become whatever they imagine themselves to be.

1. From 'The Writings of Bobby Sands', Sinn Fein POW Department, Dublin, 1981.

2. Costello, 1995, p.115.

3. Douglas Hyde speaking in November 1892, from Purcell, 1982, p.236. Notably in relation to British shaped perceptions of its 'Irish' problem, Hyde was a Protestant who was born in County Roscommon and educated in Trinity College Dublin. A scholar, he won prizes for English verse and prose as well as gaining fluency in Latin, Greek, Hebrew, French, German and Irish. The Irish language and the folklore of the west of Ireland captivated him and he penned many books of collected verses and folk-tales, such as Beside the Fire (1889) and Love Songs of Connacht (1893). Hyde was one of the main founders of Conradh na Gaeilge and became its first president in 1893. He became the first professor of Modern Irish in University College Dublin in 1909 and held the chair until his retirement in 1932. He ended his distinguished career by being unanimously appointed first President of Ireland in 1937 and remained in office until his term was finished in 1945.

4 The Irish Post, 29/7/06, pp.58-60.

5. Interview Dunedin Connollys official.

6. Interview Sands MacSwineys official.

7. Costello, 1995, p.117.

8. Ibid, p.13.

9. Mandela, 1994, p.322.

10. Costello, p.13.

11. Ibid, p.145.

12. Ibid, p.150.

13. Terrence MacSwiney, Principles of Freedom, Dublin, 1921.

14. Ibid, p.181.

15. Observer Sunday, 23/12/90, 'A child quietly starves to death'.

16. Costello, p.150.

17. Ibid, p.115.

18. Purcell, 1982, p.180.

19. Beresford, 1987, p.18.

20. Costello, 1995, pp.24-25.

21. Ibid, pp.230-231.

22. Feehan, 1984, p.76.
23. O'Hearn, 2006.
24. Ibid, p.227.
25. Ibid, p.228.
26. Ibid. p.251.
27. Ibid. p.340.
28. Ibid. p.251.
29. Ibid. p.201.
30. Ibid. p.335.
31. Feehan, pp116-117.
32. Ibid, p.118.
33. Flanagan, 1991, pp.55-56.
34 'The Gods of the Copybooks Headings', website, http://godscopybook.blogs.com/gpb/2004/10/quotes_from_a_w.html.
35. Irish News, 22/5/1981.
36. Feehan, 1984, p.22.
37. Belfast Wall Mural.
38. Feehan, p.21.
39. Frank Dolan, The Irish Post, 11/5/91, p.8.
40. O'Hearn, pp.377-378.
41. Frank Dolan, The Irish Post, 11/5/91, p.8.
42. Ibid, 2/6/90, p.8.
43. http://www.aidanmcanespiegfcboston.com/
44. Interviews with Sands MacSwineys members, June 1997 & October 2006.
45. Cronin, 1998, p.96.

Chapter 15

Disputing Irishness in Scotland

OPPOSITION

As Irishness and Gaelic sports activities are so intertwined, events, personalities, perceptions, as well as the discourses that directly or indirectly influence or reflect upon the Association's life in Scotland, can extend our knowledge and understanding of the Irish there. Although there is an enormous range of positive experiences attached to the story of the Irish in Scotland, there are also an overwhelming variety of narratives that indicate that hostility, maltreatment, insult and prejudice have been intrinsic to shaping the encounter faced by the Irish and their offspring in Scotland. Indeed, it might be argued that these have largely defined and characterised their overall experience.

Conroy suggests that for Catholics in Scotland (who are mainly of Irish descent), 'keeping one's head down and appearing 'normal' may actually be quite important'.[1] The idea of keeping one's head down was indirectly referred to by a Glasgow-born second generation Irishman, Johnny Kiernan, an interviewee on the Irish 2 Project, when he spoke of how in the early 1970s his school headmaster advised job seekers not to enter St Patrick's High School (Dumbarton) on their application forms but instead write Dumbarton High on the basis that not to identify themselves as Catholic might help them gain employment.[2] Another interviewee explained how a friend changed their Irish Catholic name to a more Scottish or neutral sounding one in an effort to acquire suitable employment.[3]

In similar fashion, an obituary in The Herald in 2000 told how a Glasgow-born Irishman called Sean changed his 'public' name to John when he entered the labour market, realising that it denoted his Catholic background and this might create prejudice against him.[4] That this has been common, and indeed is still practised, is evident in relation to ongoing research amongst Catholics of Irish descent in Scotland.[5] A woman respondent at a relevant group discussion regarding an Irish cultural issue offered the view that, 'we know we're Irish but we should keep it in our hearts'. This assertion was an implicit recognision that the privatisation, disguising or concealment of Irishness, is the best way to negotiate social progress and a peaceful social existence in Scotland.[6]

Murray notes the disguising of Irish-related Catholic identity (and vice versa) in terms of the finals of the Scottish Schools Cup seven-a-side competition in 1996. That year the finals were played at Glasgow Rangers Ibrox Stadium in front of 50,000 people during the half-time period of the crucial 'league decider' versus Aberdeen.

> The winning team was Christ the King Primary School from Holytown, but they did not play under their own name, being called 'the red team' instead. . . the decision to label the teams by colour rather than by their real names was taken when the finalist became known: in addition to the winning team, the losing semi-finalists were St Bridget's of Baillieston and St Flannan's of Kirkintilloch. In explanation, it was pointed out that the organisers wanted the boys to enjoy themselves without a section of the crowd turning against them.[7]

The case of third generation Irish Celtic soccer player Aiden McGeady also highlights how a statement of Irishness in Scotland can attract opprobrium and marginalisation. In the case of McGeady, the choice was not to dilute his Irishness and this has resulted in hostility becoming publicly manifest. The denial and rejection of Irishness in Scotland can be partly examined through reflection on McGeady, one of a number of third generation Irish players at Celtic Football Club. Such a reflection allows us to see intolerance towards Irishness in Scotland in a sporting and cultural form, but more significantly, also offers a minor insight into this kind of prejudice in terms of the attitudes that can inform economic and cultural life styles and opportunities.

In 2004 McGeady chose to play senior international football for Ireland, thus representing his family and migrating community's country of origin, rather that Scotland, his country of birth and upbringing. The popular and media reaction that surrounded his decision is a pertinent illustration of the denigration, denial and rejection of the Irishness of the Irish diaspora in Scotland. The reactions to McGeady's decision personifies, embodies and reflects much of Scotland's problematising of the Irish diaspora in Scottish society at a time that coincides with the Scottish Executives multi-culturalism campaign, One Scotland, Many Cultures.[8]

The public airing of McGeady's decision was met with a great deal of negative media comment as well as abuse from the opposition fans of almost every team in the Scottish Premier League during the football season 2004-05 and thereafter. At Celtic Park in August 2004, the visiting Motherwell fans abused McGeady and subsequently sang the popular Scottish anthem 'Flower of Scotland'. At Tynecastle, the home of Edinburgh-based Hearts, in April of the same year a BBC Scotland football commentator stated that he was to interview McGeady after the match, adding: 'I'll need to take down a bottle of whisky and some shortbread to Scottify him'. This commentator's fellow broadcaster, himself a former professional footballer, denied and rejected the player's ethnic, national and cultural identity, as well as that of others like him in Scotland. He argued that McGeady was not Irish but Scottish:

> He may well have chosen to play for Ireland, as far as I'm concerned the boy was born in Scotland and that makes him Scottish and that's the end of the matter.[9]

Leaving aside this former player's ignorance of the complexity of national and cultural identity and citizenship and how this is manifest in sport, there are other elements of discourse worth examining in relation to anti-Irish racism in Scotland. Hearts supporters' abuse of McGeady during the match was viewed as legitimate, acceptable and understandable, as far as one football commentator and newspaper columnist was concerned. He believed that McGeady had turned his back on Scotland, showed a lack of patriotism (despite his patriotism in choosing Ireland) and he was disloyal to Scotland. He further hoped that McGeady has a miserable career as an Irish internationalist.[10] A Scottish football fan agreed stating:

> It's a disgraceful situation. McGeady has chosen to play for a foreign country rather than represent Scotland. He's getting stick for it and rightly so.[11]

A Daily Record sports writer also supported the abuse of McGeady believing that:

> This isn't about sectarianism, this is about being Scottish and proud of it. McGeady has been educated here, used our health service and learned all his football in Glasgow. But thanks to his mum, he has now chosen to play for the Irish national team. It's heartbreaking. It's time all Scottish Celtic fans got over their obsession with Ireland. The fact that Glasgow sports shops sell as many Ireland football tops as Scotland football tops is both pathetic and ultimately unhelpful.[12]

Another Record reporter stated:

> Celtic's new boy wonder insisted he would prefer to play for the Republic of Ireland, his grandfather's birthplace, ahead of his own country [and] that has been met with widespread fury from some Scottish football fans and could result in him being the target of abuse.[13]

Neither of these reporters contemplated the possibility of their own prejudicial or racist mindsets and their capacity for creating, sustaining and inflaming such attitudes in others. Their lack of education and knowledge in matters ethnic in multicultural Scotland is therefore exposed in a blatant fashion. During the same period, complaints regarding McGeady dominated on radio phone-ins and on many Scottish football websites, widely used and accessed forms of modern football supporter communication in Scotland. On the Glasgow Rangers fanzine/website, Follow Follow, one of Britain's most significant and popular football websites, many fans reiterated the abuse of McGeady.

> A wee traitor of the highest order. Should be booed at every ground he appears at.

> Sums up the mentality of the Fenian player. Rather ditch his roots to pick up tatties in terrorist country instead.

> He honed his skills dodging police whilst shopping.

> I can only assume that the Republic of Ireland will be sending over the dole money to pay for him and his like minded friends not to mention the contribution for their schooling et al.[14]

A Scotland on Sunday broadsheet sports writer discussed McGeady's choice to play for Ireland suggesting the young player might have a twisted streak in relation to not choosing to play international football for the country both he and his parents were born and bred in.[15] One of Scottish football's most well-known media commentators, who hosts a BBC radio phone in, appears on Scottish Television's football programmes and writes several football columns, also contributed to the debate surrounding the player. This Daily Record sports writer frequently conveys negativity towards the Irish diaspora in Scotland expressing Irishness within football culture as well as other related matters. The tone of this narrative is consistent with many others throughout the Scottish football media and beyond. Its hostile and disapproving tenor states that expressions of Irishness in football in Scotland are wrong. In one column, this commentator attempted to pre-empt accusations of ignorance, prejudice and racism by stating that his hostility was not based on an anti-Irish agenda, only that he was a proud Scot who made:

> No apologies for that and this fixation with Ireland which so many Scots have makes my blood boil.[16]

In a further dimension of this dominant popular discourse, those who publicly supported McGeady's choice were also criticised. Celtic footballer, Neil Lennon, who had defended McGeady's choice in international football was criticised by The People columnist who stated:

> Lennon's reasoning if such it was that McGeady will incite the wrath of Scottish football fans because the Glasgow youngster has snubbed the land of his birth to play instead for the Republic of Ireland, for whom he qualifies as his dad is Oirish.[17]

The use of the word Oirish by this columnist is particularly revealing and may be considered racist, the term used frequently by people being derogatory towards Irishness, especially in hostile football websites, fanzines and other outlets. As with a number of other sports columnists this particular writer expressed concern over the possibility of Jim

O'Brien, a young third generation Irish Celtic footballer, playing for Ireland in international soccer and accused Ireland of being a 'foreign power'. In an article indicatively titled, 'Why O Bro do people suffer a national id crisis', the writer criticised both O'Brien and McGeady. The columnist opined that:

> What is puzzling is the current trend of some Scots, born and bred here, who want to pledge their allegiance to a foreign power.[18]

These articles reflect a dominant narrative that is hostile, demeaning, prejudiced and accusatory towards Irishness in Scotland while they also link ideologically with the comments of others, including those to be found on the Follow Follow website.

Indicatively, given the widespread commentary regarding McGeady's Irishness, the booing and verbal abuse of the player has been generally ignored by the media when reporting Celtic games, despite this (to a greater or lesser degree) taking place at almost every match McGeady has played for Celtic in Scotland.

This silence also extended to a prominent sports writer on Scotland's biggest selling broadsheet, The Herald: a columnist who frequently addresses controversial subjects in Scottish football, including sectarianism and racism. In terms of the issues surrounding McGeady, strikingly, this journalist only briefly remarked that:

> McGeady is a single-minded young man, as made evident in his bold and controversial decision to play for Ireland instead of Scotland.[19]

Revealingly, at a lecture in 2005 this journalist stated that with regards Celtic and its fanbase, he found the Irish-Catholic thing too difficult to address though ironically this did not preclude him having a hostile attitude towards the 'Irish-Catholic thing' when he stated that this:

> over-egging of we're Irish and, these third and fourth generations . . . I can't help feeling uncomfortable with this overemphasis on Irishness.[20]

On reviewing a book by Celtic supporters, some of whom purposefully addressed this subject, the journalist declared that the book contained too many examples of 'drooling, dripping Irishness'. He believed that Celtic fans expressing these significant aspects of their history, experience, culture and identity was upsetting because in the book,

> I find people who were born in Scotland, who live in Glasgow, and who support the world-famous Glasgow Celtic, yet for whom being Scottish is just about the last thing they desire.[21]

The journalist later admitted to reading only three of twenty-one chapters, equating to approximately ten per cent of the book. Of the chapters missed he had ignored the first third of the book written by the editor which contextualised the work of the Celtic supporting contributors who were Catholic, Protestant, non-'believers', as well as from North America, Germany, Ireland and Scotland. In his review, this leading sports journalist demonstrated a lack of knowledge about, and acquaintance with, immigrant life in Scotland as well as ethnicity, Irishness, community and cultural identities. He reproduced a standard interpretation of seeing Irishness as the opposite of, or, as being opposed to Scottishness, but not as an identity in its own right.

Such views raise questions regarding the roots, origins and nature of prejudicial perspectives especially those passed as objective and neutral commentary but which manifest themselves as racist and prejudicial views and opinions. They also invite an important question regarding a similar book that might purport, through the window of sporting activity and culture, to explore the offspring of Asians in Scotland, Scots in Canada or Turks in Germany. Would those books have been criticised for drooling with Asianness, Afro-Caribbeaness, Scottishness or Turkishness? Or would those descriptions have invited accusations of racism by the journalist?

Problems and hostility arising from Irish differentiation in Scotland reflect an inability to use reflective, accommodating and positive language in describing the Irishness of the Irish diaspora in Scotland. Reflecting aspects of the hostility and confusion over how to describe a Scots-born Irishman, or even criticise the abuse he attracted, an Express sports writer called McGeady 'an Irish kid',[22] while a Herald sports columnist called him 'a Scot.[23] A Sunday Herald writer referred to McGeady as 'being as Scottish as the rest, even if he seems to think otherwise', while a Sun columnist stated that McGeady was '100 per cent Scottish. . . but the bad news is that he is just about to turn Irish'.[24] In the latter descriptions identity is imposed and constructed through discourse upon someone who is not what most of these writers negatively, aggressively and thoughtlessly or deliberately assert. McGeady's assumed, experienced and chosen Irish identity is ignored and little or no reference is made (apart from negatively in the wider discourses) to how he actually sees himself and how he values and imagines his country of origin.

Despite this hostility towards diasporic Irishness, the print media in Scotland is not unfamiliar with the concept of having a national or cultural identity that reflects family and community origins rather than those of country of birth. This partly indicates that it is Irishness in Scotland that invites particular opprobrium. In 2005, The Herald described a person as a Nigerian, born in London.[25] A Herald writer described US-born actor and singer Frank Sinatra as a skinny little Italian boy in his younger days[26] and announced that Coatbridge-born and bred Ayesha Hazarika, a second generation Indian comedian, had become young achiever of the year at the Asian Women of Achievement Awards in London.[27] The same newspaper described boxer Michael Gomez as a Dublin-born Englishman[28] and London-born singer Rod Stewart as a veteran Scottish rocker.[29] The Herald also spoke of Eric Liddell (Chariots of Fire) as Scotland's best-known athlete and as having always remained in his nation's heart when referring to his place in the Scottish Sports Hall of Fame. Scotsman Liddell was of course born in Northern China of Scottish-born parents.[30]

Scottish tabloids have also been able to extend themselves conceptually in relation to questions of national and cultural identity and sport. The Daily Record's sister paper, the Sunday Mail described former Celtic footballer Mike Galloway as an English-born Scot[31] while throughout the 1970s and 1980s, Scottish international footballers Richard Gough (born in Sweden and brought up in South Africa from mixed nationality parentage) and Stuart McCall, Andy Goram and Bruce Rioch were almost always individually or collectively referred to as Scots although all were born in England or elsewhere. Likewise, the same language was used to describe John Beattie of British and Irish Lions rugby fame, though Beattie was born in Asia and spent the first twelve years of his childhood in Borneo before returning to Scotland with his family.[32]

The widespread opprobrium that ensued in the wake of McGeady's decision is significant because it partly reveals how embedded and tolerated this is within Scottish football and, to a degree, wider Scottish society. Attitudes towards McGeady, as well as Celtic and its fanbase generally, are specific in that these can only be understood in their historical and cultural contexts, which offer meaning to contemporary identities, attitudes, affinities and prejudices. This is of course, partly what the Scottish Executive website maintains in its anti-racist educational role in reflecting on the development and evolution of white on non-white racism in Scottish society. However, no such context is utilised to explain anti-Irish hostility in Scotland, the longest established of Scotland's racisms. Indeed, it is clear that such racism is barely mentioned, if at all. Key to understanding this omission is the fact that the Irish diaspora does not experience any substantial or positive public recognition in Scottish society. The case of Aiden McGeady is but one example of this.

The perceived hostility towards the Irish in Scotland during the nineteenth and twentieth centuries has necessitated the use of a variety of strategies by those of Irish descent to negotiate social life in Scotland. For some immigrants and their offspring, this has resulted in a negation of their Irishness in an attempt to acquire the cultural capital perceived as necessary to achieve acceptance and positive recognition.

The Irish 2 Project interviewees in Scotland narrate how people of Irish Catholic status and descent negotiate many of the social, economic, political and cultural barriers they believe they are faced with. The case of Aiden McGeady reveals aspects of this experience in a very public manner.

Significantly in terms of popular football and newspaper reading cultures, media commentary surrounding McGeady constructs a prism through which Irishness in Scotland is viewed as a disloyal, malevolent, irrational and divisive presence. Paradoxically, at the same time the Irishness of those born in Scotland is seen as not real or genuine. This prism dominates in Scotland when Irishness is addressed. In the eyes of some of the newspapers quoted, 'the Irish in Scotland should do us all a favour and relocate to Dublin, there's a country called Ireland for goodness sake, why don't they go and live there'? and, 'its time all Scottish Celtic fans got over their obsession with Ireland'. Such sentiments are mirrored by Aberdeen fans that deride Celtic supporters with the cry of 'you're in the wrong country'. A similar attitude was expressed by Glasgow Rangers fans in a match versus Celtic in December 2006 when a number of them held up banners stating, 'This is our city. Where in Ireland is Glasgow'.[33]

Several choices seem to dominate for those in Scotland who esteem or give cultural precedence to their Irish origins, history, community, symbols and identity; return to the land they have a strong affinity for, privatise their Irishness to such an extent that they do not publicly display it or, be socially reconstructed as Scottish to become more acceptable to the wider Scottish society. This is important to understanding past and present Irish identities in Scotland while such hostility towards Irishness also links to Hickman's thesis on the denationalising of Irish people and their offspring in Britain. Revealingly, in terms of anti-racist drives in Scotland, the Scottish Executive's own One Scotland Many Cultures campaign almost completely omits anti-Irishness from its popular campaign while the anti-racist website associated with the project includes little or no recognition of the Irish diaspora as the longest established, numerically most significant, ethnic group in the country.

The Irishness of the offspring of Scotland's Irish immigrant population is an area of much social, cultural and political dispute and contestation. The experience of McGeady and others as evidenced in the Irish 2 Project has also been reflected within G.A.A. circles in Scotland in the latter twentieth and into the twenty first centuries.

Many members of the G.A.A. in Scotland believe they have to be vigilent in seeking to promote Gaelic games as well as the Irishness that often parallels Gaelic sport. This has meant that hostility from outwith the community, as well as from within, can be a barrier to the sport's advancement. With little acknowledgement of Scotland's Irishness within the Scottish education system, academia or journalism, and with little public recognition of the social, economic, cultural, political, indeed sporting, contribution the Irish and their offspring have made to modern Scottish society. Gaelic sports, like other manifestations of Irishness in Scotland, exist in a context substantially defined by the historical colonial relationship between Ireland and Britain, and therefore, also between Irishness and Britishness.[34] In this context in Scotland, for those of the Irish diaspora who wish to celebrate Irishness, this is undertaken in circumstances where Irishness is almost totally omitted from positive representation in Scottish public life and where it is also maliciously misrepresented and socially and culturally denigrated and marginalized. In recent decades this has been significantly manifest politically as well, particularly in relation to the 'Troubles' in Northern Ireland.

The historical context of Ireland's centuries-long domination by Britain is important in considering the position of Irishness in modern Scotland as well understanding discourses of so called 'sectarianism'. This is particularly evident in relation to how domination has diminished and undermined Irishness, the most obvious example being the virtual destruction of the use of the Irish language and other cultural distinctions.

In its historical context the marginalisation of Irishness has been a long historical process linked with British colonisation. This is partly evidenced in a quote from Sir William Parsons about the Irish in 1625, a statement that invokes connotations of contemporary arguments about Irishness in Scotland. For Parsons, only the depreciation and destruction of Ireland's cultural traits and identities could result in the Irish being absorbed into the Crown's realm:

> We must change their course of government, apparel, manner of holding land, their language and habit of life'.[35]

For Parsons and his fellow colonists over a number of centuries, manifestations of Irishness were unacceptable in British conquered Ireland. A perception on the part of British colonists was that the Irish were required to change if Ireland and its people were to be shaped in the interests of the British Crown. For contemporary Irishness in Scotland, the process encouraged by Ireland's colonial administrator

Parsons, is ongoing in a different time, place and space, thus constituting a metaphorical, though no less real, colonisation of Irishness and its reproduction as cultural and national identity.

The rigours of a perceived struggle, to be accepted and not viewed with hostility by the wider society, is an important part of the story of the Irish in Scotland. It is also one that has resonance with the origins and history of the Gaelic Athletic Association in Ireland and is part of the context for understanding Irishness, Gaelic sport and the G.A.A. in Scotland.

1. J Conroy, 2003.
2. Interview Johnny Kiernan, Irish 2 Project, ESRC.
3. Interview, focus group, Irish 2 Project, ESRC.
4. The Herald, Obituary for Sean Tierney, 22/4/00.
5. Research ongoing.
6. Contribution made by parishioner to discussion on location and erection of Irish National Famine Monument in Scotland, 11/11/99.
7. Murray, 2003.
8. See Bradley, 2006.
9. G Smith, BBC, Radio Scotland, 25/ 4/04.
10. S Cosgrove.
11. The Daily Record, 31/12/04.
12. J McKie, The Daily Record, 1/1/05.
13. The Daily Record, 2/5/04.
14. Follow Follow, Glasgow Rangers supporter website, 26/4/05.
15. A Smith, Scotland on Sunday, 2/5/04.
16. J Traynor, The Daily Record, 2/5/05.
17. D Leggat, The People, 26/12/04.

18. D Leggat, The People, 8/5/05. The same columnist has written numerous similar items including a denunciation in 2005 on SPL sponsor Irish company Setanta Sports (The People, 9/10/05, p15) using descriptions like 'the Irish TV company', 'same tricks', 'sitting in their boardroom in the Irish Republic', 'Irish TV paymasters', 'murkier agenda', 'the same Irishmen', 'Setanta's Blarney Bhoys', 'Who are their SPL scared of. Their Setanta Paymasters in Ireland? Celtic?' 'Setanta, an Irish organisation'.

19. G Spiers, The Herald, 11/12/04.

20. G Spiers, Newman Lecture, University of Glasgow, 17/3/05.

21. G Spiers, The Herald, Arts, Books and Cinema, 1/5/06.

22. I MacFarlane, The Scottish Daily Express, 8/12/04.

23. D Broadfoot, The Herald, Sport, 2/8/04.

24. M Grant, The Sunday Herald, Sport, 9/1/05 & R Grieve, The Sun (Scottish Edition), 21/9/02.

25. The Herald, 12/7/05.

26. 5/8/05.

27. The Herald, 27/5/05.

28. The Herald, 3/1/05.

29. The Herald, 2/5/05.

30. The Herald, Sport, 27/8/05.

31. The Sunday Mail, 28/11/99.

32. See Boyle and Lynch, 1998, p.108.

33. The Herald, Sport, 18/12/06.

34. See Bradley, 1995.

35. The Irish Post, 8/12/90.

Chapter 16

Gaelic sport in Scotland and faces of hostility

THE FEAR WITHIN: BORN FROM WITHOUT

Since the nineteenth century the social, cultural and political environment in Scotland has traditionally been hostile to expressions and celebrations of Irishness. As an aspect of this experience, the cultural and political nature of the G.A.A. and its membership has also attracted negative attention on the part of anti-Catholic and anti-Irish organisations and individuals in Scotland. Since the 1990s, several incidents as well as various media discourses have reflected some of the contestations that have evolved as a result of the Irish presence in Scotland.

This hostile atmosphere has also meant that a strand of thought has developed within the G.A.A. which has taken a view that if it is arduous to exhibit Irishness in Scotland, on this basis the Association must endeavour to deflect and dissuade unwanted disapproving attention and comment. In turn, this has resulted in contestation 'within' Irish and Gaelic Athletic circles as to the path best thread to avoid such denunciation and criticism.

The perceived risks of being associated with the G.A.A. has been reflected in Orange and Loyalist literature that has sought to depreciate Irish cultural activities and identity in Scotland. Some of the disparaging comment and criticism relates to the G.A.A. generally but also to the names of some Gaelic clubs as well as references to the rules within the G.A.A. that banned British military personnel from membership. In addition, significant reference has also been made to the alleged 'genuine' Irishness of the Irish in Scotland, thus echoing some of the disapproving sentiments expressed by many people in Scotland towards Aiden McGeady.

> Loyalists may be surprised to learn that this Ayrshire coast town [Saltcoats] is the venue for frequent activity of an entirely different nature. The town's Laigh Dyke Park frequently hosts contests between teams of the Gaelic Athletic Association (G.A.A.) which is, of course, the sporting wing of the I.R.A. . . [1]

> Under the guise of culture a time bomb of sectarianism and political extremism is now in place in Scotland. It is hidden behind a spokescreen of sport and blarney. . . Rule 20 of the G.A.A. handbook prohibits any member of our fine Scottish regiments, the K.O.S.B., Gordons, Black Watch etc from playing this game in Pearse Park or anywhere else for that matter. . . The Irish have the same rights as every other group in this country to enjoy cultural activities. . . But it did seem strange for this promotion to be taking place in 1993, when the genuine Irish in Scotland seem to be fewer than they have ever been. . . [2]

As a result of such discourses the Invincibles Club in Saltcoats did of course change its name to one viewed as 'less contentious'. The Ayrshire team and its manager, County secretary John McCreadie, experienced what they viewed as intimidation because of the club's presence on the Gaelic scene. The club's football park and meeting place was noted in this Loyalist literature with a view to them being subjected to pressure to desist from playing.

As County secretary, McCreadie also pursued a Scotland G.A.A. application to join the Scottish Sports Council in the early 1990s: membership potentially leading to grant applications and greater recognition. This was hampered, ostensibly because of a perceived lack of a Scotland-wide spread within the G.A.A., despite clubs in Edinburgh, Dundee, Ayrshire, Lanarkshire, Glasgow and Dumbarton. However, McCreadie believed that the presence of a former police chief constable on the Council was significant in causing the application to be rejected on the basis of his interpretation of the G.A.A.'s policy with regards members of the 'Crown forces'. When it transpired that such a rule had an historic and contemporary relevance in Ireland and that the Clan na Gael Club in Hamilton could in fact be contacted using the phone number of a police officer in a local station who played with the team, McCreadie believes some attitudes 'softened'. A defence of the G.A.A. was also conducted by former Glasgow M.P., Mike Watson, who met with the UK Sports Council in response to his discovering the problems encountered by some of his local constituents. The G.A.A. was eventually advised that individual clubs could apply for funding. In all, the application took approximately thirty months to evolve to a stage where clubs could apply as individual bodies.[3]

Although much less significant in media, cultural or political terms, as in Northern Ireland, the G.A.A. in Scotland has faced other opposition. In the early 1990s a cross errected to the memory of Padraic Pearse at Pearse Park was vandalised and destroyed. The Glasgow field has also attracted the attentions of organisations like the British National Party and Loyalist paramilitary support groups.[4] On several occasions Sands MacSwineys found its council owned pitch strewn with broken glass stamped into the ground while staff in a local sports shop were intimidated and threatened by local loyalists to desist from selling replica tops of the Coatbridge team. Several other incidents of intimidation have taken place against Sands MacSwineys personel. Generally, Sands members perceive a degree of censorship as well as a racist and bigoted prejudice against the club in local press reports and elsewhere. More widely, similar perceptions also exist within the local Catholic community of Irish descent with regards matters with an Irish ethnic and religious connotation that are also reported in, or indeed, omitted from, the local press.

THE EUROPEAN 'SOCCER' CHAMPIONSHIP

At a more calculated and deep-rooted level other instances demonstrate some of the difficulties Irishness and Gaelic sport in Scotland experience in Scottish (and British) society. For example, early in the new millennium a joint Irish-Scottish bid for the European Football (soccer) Championships of 2008 was manifest. The G.A.A. in Dublin nominally found itself part of this bid despite the fact that it is not a soccer organisation nor had it actually requested or volunteered to be part of the bid. In addition, the G.A.A. also had Rule 42 in its constitution that did not allow soccer and other sports to take place at its Gaelic grounds: a rule that had an historical, cultural and national rationale and context.

One dimension of the attraction for the soccer authorities in Scotland and Ireland who constructed the bid, as well as those politicians who supported it, was the possible availability of the Gaelic Athletic Association's main arena in Dublin, Croke Park, one of the best sports stadiums in Europe. However, as the organisation explained, when asked if there was a possibility of Croke Park being available for such an occasion, the relevant decision could only be made once such a motion had been submitted and had been democratically discussed and voted upon at annual Congress. This is normal procedure for the G.A.A., such a vote involving representation of its membership from all of Ireland's thirty-two counties as well as from its units abroad. However, as the submission was required within a particular time and as no formal request had previously been made to the G.A.A. to become part of the bid, in response to the growing media references to the centrality of Croke Park to the application, the G.A.A. President at the time, Sean McCague, stated that the decision to include Croke Park 'was flawed':

> suggestions that Croke Park will be made available in the next few years are unfounded and mischievous. The FAI have stated that they consider Croke Park unsuitable for soccer games because of the scale and associated atmosphere. . . also, the bid for the 2008 European Championships was made without any consultation with the G.A.A.[5]

> Only Congress can decide. . . it was a flawed situation that Croke Park was included as an anchor stadium for hosting the championships when neither I nor anyone else could guarantee what will happen in the future. . . The bid process was initiated and in the public arena without any consultation with the GAA. . . We did, however, point out when the bid was made that our rules exclude us from leasing or letting the ground to others and it would take a Congress decision to change that.[6]

In response to the perceived difficulties in 'acquiring' Croke Park for the Championships, a spokesperson for the Tartan Army, Scotland's national soccer team supporters, was reported as saying,

> This is shocking news. . . it looks as though this will wreck the bid. I can't believe the Irish have thrown this spanner into the works at such a late date. It's a disgrace.[7]

Much media commentary in Scotland was disparaging of the Irish side of the bid, but especially so of the Gaelic Athletic Association. This included blaming it for the weakness of the application (in that the G.A.A. was being blamed for Ireland – and Scotland – not having the required stadiums to validate the bid). However, the Scottish media and the vast majority of the public in Scotland know little about the Association including about its amateur and democratic nature. The criticism disregarded the fact that it is an association that virtually every family on the island of Ireland, outside of the north's Unionist/Loyalist community, is connected to. Indeed, the G.A.A. has a membership of around three-quarters of a million people. This means that per head of population it is one of the biggest sports associations in the world with a corresponding cultural significance. In this sense it is an independent body with its own sports to oversee and does not by nature promote or protect other sports.

However, the main focus of disparaging commentary was in representing the G.A.A. as a body 'stuck in the past', of being 'intransigent', being an advocate of an 'ancient law' and being trapped by an 'ideological hurdle'.[8] In almost no journalistic 'observation' was any aspect of the history of the G.A.A. mentioned; its amateur and volunteer status, its huge successes in Ireland and beyond in the diaspora, the nature of its rules and regulations with regards meetings, accountability and voting rights, its eminence throughout much of the island as a sporting and cultural body (with less of a commercial raison d'étre than other comparable bodies), the history of the Association as an expression of resistance towards, and a counter to, British colonialism and hegemony in Ireland, its anguish and distress as a result of the northern 'troubles' and the related widely existent perceptions of Ireland as a British partitioned country. In addition, no explanation was offered of the 'ideas' utilised in such commentary, particularly those relating to degradation of the 'past', although it was clearly taken for granted that something in the 'past' did not represent modern and progressive thinking as perceived therein. The use of such terms is of course also partly ideological.

In fact the G.A.A. never 'closed the Croke Park door' on the bid and had accommodated UEFA officials who wished to inspect the stadium. One significant factor also remained virtually unmentioned in the British media during the debate: the fact that important games in the G.A.A.'s own hurling and football championship calendar were to be played at Croke Park during the period of the suggested UEFA tournament. Playing another sport at Croke Park during the summer would present a considerable problem for the G.A.A. if the Association 'opened its doors' at this time of year.

Of course, offering such background or explanatory information in the media, particularly in the tabloid media, would be unusual in most journalistic articles and is not limited by considerations that are particularly Irish or concerned with the G.A.A. Nevertheless, this cannot be taken as an explanation for portrayals and representations that ignore environment, background and context and which lead to, sustain and create intolerance and prejudice with regards the G.A.A. and its membership.

A Scotsman journalist stated that it would be:

> a setback if the most suitable Irish stadium in the bid was removed from the equation by the apparent intransigence of the G.A.A.[9]

A reporter with The Sun opined that,

> The G.A.A. last night slammed the door shut on Ireland's joint bid with Scotland for the Euro 2008 soccer championships.[10]

The Sunday Times reported:

> The Gaelic Athletic Association has started to move with the times. Yesterday's decision to give the G.A.A.'s central council the power to decide whether Croke Park should be made available temporarily to the Irish rugby and football teams represents a significant step forward for the organisation.[11]

The Times report continued to focus on what that newspaper believed to be 'the traditional faultlines that run through the G.A.A.':

> It is deeply disturbing that, after a decade of peace in Nothern Ireland, the northern counties should vote unanimously in favour of the status quo. Their refusal to countenance change demonstrates how far the peace process has still to travel if it is to decommission mindsets as well as illegal arms. Cork, too, fell on the wrong side of the faultline, a clear example of a county orgnisation that has lost touch with its members. . . The G.A.A. has now taken a step into a brighter future, one that will no

> longer be tainted by the suspicion of bigotry and sectarianism that has always lurked beneath the surface of its refusal to share its facilities. . . it was time for the organsation to recognise that Ireland has moved on.[12]

News of the World's Scottish columnist, Gerry McNee, spoke of the 'ideological hurdles dating back to 1916 and beyond',[13] while Stephen Halliday in The Scotsman, referred to:

> The Gaelic Athletic Association, owners of the 80,000-capacity Dublin stadium, had been thought to be ready to relax their ancient law preventing its use for anything other than Gaelic football or hurling.[14]

At one stage The Sun described the bid as 'alive and kicking – despite the GAA's stance on Croke Park'.[15] Scotland's main Sunday tabloid, The Sunday Mail, reported that:

> Scotland's Euro 2008 bid could be killed off by a primary school headmaster Sean McCague. . . He is President of Ireland's Gaelic Athletic Association, which owns Dublin's 80,000 capacity Croke Park stadium.[16]

In this short report, that invokes a banner headline, McCague's position is demeaned by his seemingly low status in 'only' being a 'primary school headmaster'. This is despite the fact that his social and cultural position as 'an Uachtarán' and President of the Association, and the only status actually relevant to the debate, is a democratically elected one and is regarded as a station of noteworthy prestige by many people in Irish society. Besides, not only do the G.A.A. 'own Croke Park', but over many decades its members raised the money to build it and numerous other G.A.A. stadiums around the country. Despite the G.A.A. being blamed for the probable failure of the tender the newspaper report contains no information and exhibits no understanding of the context or the history of the G.A.A. as well as the fact that the G.A.A., as a non-soccer body, had no actual role or desire to be part of the bid.

Part of the context for understanding such discourses is the lack of regular references – particularly positive – to Ireland within the Scottish media, except in terms of the northern conflict. Another factor is the virtual public invisibility and lack of affirmative acknowledgment, historical, social and political, of the Irishness of the Irish diaspora in Scotland.[17]

Gaelic sport in Ireland receives no mainstream media coverage in Scotland, except through a small number of references in the Irish ethnic and Catholic religious press due in the main to the efforts of Gaelic activists themselves. These Gaelic sports advocates in Scotland are also acutely aware of their sport's omission in the mainstream media or, how negatively Gaelic sport and their Irishness, can be constructed and portrayed in the media. One pertinent example of how Gaelic sports are ignored in Scotland was reflected in the sports section of the Sunday Herald in 2007. This significant broadsheet prints a calendar of major sports events and dates from various countries in January each year. Included is American Football, Athletics, Badminton, Basketball, Bowls, Cricket, Curling, Cycling, Darts, Equestrian, Soccer, Formula One, Golf, Hockey, Judo, Motogp, Racing, Rallying, Rowing, Rugby, Skiing, Snooker, Squash, Superbikes, Swimming, Table Tennis, Tennis, Touring Cars, Triathlon and Weightlifting. Some of these are principal world sports, others are important to Scotland: some or many are neither. Each year the calendar is published there is no mention of either the Gaelic Football or Hurling Finals that take place in Dublin every September.[18]

IGNORANCE, MALEVOLENCE, PREJUDICE AND SAM MAGUIRE

This perception of being excluded, as well as unfair and negatively discriminatory attention, was highlighted in early 2006 when Football Champions Tyrone visited Glasgow to display the All-Ireland Trophy the Sam Maguire to the crowd at a Celtic Football Club league match. As the soccer team of the Irish in Scotland and of the worldwide Irish diaspora, such a visit seemed appropriate to Celtic, its supporters, County Tyrone, as well as the G.A.A.

The parading of the All-Ireland is part of the duties and course of events for every County that wins the trophy in September each year: the cup usually travelling around clubs, counties as well as several countries where there is a G.A.A. presence, including in the USA, Britain and beyond. This is not viewed by G.A.A. members or supporters as controversial and is uncontested within or by any country where it is displayed: it is in fact a widely perceived cultural norm, indeed honour.

Nonetheless, although Kerry, Galway and Armagh had since the 1990s visited Celtic Park with the All-Ireland trophy, on the occasion of Tyrone's visit with 'Sam' to Glasgow, publicity followed that left the authorities at Croke Park as well as others in Ireland bemused.

That displaying the All-Ireland trophy was completely uncontroversial and usually uncomplicated was reflected in a standard and straightforward report in the Irish edition of The Mirror on January 6th 2006: Sam Maguire was to,

> be paraded in front of an anticipated 60,000 soccer fans in Glasgow. . . a delegation of Tyrone players and county board officials are planning to take the All-Ireland trophy to Celtic Park in Glasgow, prior to the clash between Celtic and Dundee United on January 29th.[19]

However Scotland's Mail on Sunday had a different perspective on the visit of 'Sam' to Glasgow. It's sensationalist headline read, 'Parading of IRA trophy puts pressure on Celtic'. The report continued:

> Celtic Football Club was yesterday facing fresh controversy over alleged links between its fans and the IRA. . . the club was at the centre of the storm after agreeing to allow a football trophy named after an IRA intelligence chief to be paraded around Celtic Park. . . All-Ireland champions Tyrone have been allowed to take the Sam Maguire on a lap of honour. Club captain Neil Lennon played Gaelic football for the Armagh team in his youth. However, Sam Maguire was head of IRA operations around the time of the Easter Rising in 1916. . . Maguire is a revered figure in Republican circles, having sworn in Michael Collins to the Irish Republican Brotherhood in 1909. . . The disclosure will come as a major embarrassment for Celtic chief executive Peter Lawwell. . . No one from the club was available for comment yesterday.[20]

The Sun newspaper picked up on the story and stated that:

> Celtic were blasted by a Glasgow MSP last night for allowing an Irish football cup named after an IRA legend to be paraded at Parkhead. Tory Bill Aitken said it was 'unfortunate' Irish champs Tyrone would do a lap of honour. . . He added: While I appreciate Celtic have an Irish background, they are a Scottish club. I do not see what relevance the activities of Tyrone have. It is time all of this baggage was put behind us. . . Maguire was head of IRA operations in London at the time of the Easter Rising, and is said to have ordered the 1922 murder of a Tory MP. Celtic refused to comment on the controversy.[21]

A few days later The Sun spoke of:

> . . . revelations that Parkhead chiefs will allow the parading of a Gaelic Football trophy named after a terrorist.[22]

Such sensationalist reporting links directly to and reinforces and sustains many British people's 'lack' of knowledge and awareness about affairs Irish, including history, culture and politics. It also connects to dominant notions of what pertains in relation to the historical British-Irish and more recent northern Irish conflict, including what constitutes 'terrorism', 'murder' the reasons and rationale for the conflict, including Britain's crucial role as an instigator of and significant participant in the conflict, as well as related moral issues and questions. Such reporting reflects some of the propaganda war engaged in between Nationalists/Republicans and British/Unionists/Loyalists, as well a widespread lack of basic knowledge in Scotland regarding historical events in Ireland and between Ireland and Britain.[23]

These articles and comments originate from people who had not previously commented upon Gaelic sports affairs and had little obvious acquaintance with Ireland or Irishness – often important in terms of basic knowledge and awareness. Further, the relevant articles are also written in a cultural context whereby numerous newspapers and columnists have previously been seen to make comment recogised as anti-Irish as well as anti-Celtic Football Club. For example, The Sun's Bill Leckie frequently comments on Celtic and its supporters' Irishness. Previously this sports columnist referred to the Irish diaspora in Scotland within the Celtic football support as the 'pseudo-Irish' who have a penchant for 'diddly-dee music'.[24] A Herald newspaper columnist agreed:

> especially coming from the musical equivalent of Darby McGill [O Gill?] and the Little People with their 'Have A Potato' style of hokey Irishness.[25]

In terms of the visit of Sam Maguire to Glasgow, Conservative MP Bill Aitken's deprecating comments concerning Celtic's Irishness are familiar in terms of conventional and analogous comment towards Irishness within the sports (and wider) media in Scotland. Celtic and its fanbase are regularly criticised for their Irishness, the repeated mechanism and discourse behind notions such as 'sectarianism', 'baggage', 'the past', 'I can't see the relevance' and 'I don't understand', reflecting Irishness as a contested identity. Here, those in Scotland of Irish descent, who esteem this, are constantly instructed that they are 'not Irish but Scottish', or alternatively, they are advised to 'get back to Ireland'. Aitken's comment that 'while I appreciate Celtic have an Irish background, they are a Scottish club' is a common one. In 2003 as Celtic participated in the UEFA Cup Final in Spain, the Daily Record's lead sports writer stated that,

> Celtic, a Scottish team whether some of their fans are willing to admit it or not. . . Celtic ARE Scottish so they belong to more than the supporters who follow them week in, week out. . . This is Scotland against Portugal. . . right now Celtic, albeit unwittingly, are flying our flag. . . [26]

A number of other commentators and letter writers to newspapers agreed.

> I was absolutely appalled and disgusted when watching the UEFA Cup Final. I am sure I am not the only non-Celtic supporter who was urged to 'get behind' the Scottish team. How many Scottish flags were in the stadium? I counted one but maybe I couldn't see the others due to the sea of Irish Republican flags in display. Isn't it about time that people like this decided which nationality they are? [27]

> I could have sworn the UEFA Cup Final in Seville was between teams from Scotland and Portugal, but judging by the flags in the stadium I think it was actually Ireland against Portugal; there were more American, Canadian, or Australian flags than Scottish. How do you expect neutral football fans to support their Scottish team when the fans make it very clear that they have no loyalty to Scotland and where their true allegiance lies? I can't imagine what the rest of the world thought as they watched this disgraceful sight which was attended by some of our politicians who supposedly abhor this type of behaviour. This was not a good reflection on our culture and a bad night for Scottish sport.[28]

Another columnist, who criticised the G.A.A. on the Irish-Scottish European Championships bid has, in his various roles in the Scottish sports media, repeatedly referred negatively to the Irishness of the Celtic support. In 2006, on Scottish Television's flagship football programme,

Scotsport, he called for an end to 'all this Irish tosh'[29] while in his News Of The World column he considered Celtic Park to be full of:

> Plastic Irishmen and women who drink in plastic Irish pubs and don't know their Athenry from their Antrim when it comes to Irish history or politics. . . Celtic must stop. . . flashing their Irishness. . . if Celtic are so keen to flaunt their Irishness perhaps they could do us all a favour and relocate to Dublin.[30]

These are similar comments to those of the former 'Young Scottish Journalist of the Year', who stated his thoughts on Celtic supporters in The Herald, Scotland's biggest selling broadsheet newspaper:

> There's a country called Ireland for goodness sake, why don't they go and live there?[31]

With regards the invective visited upon Celtic, its supporters, Irishness in Scotland, the G.A.A. and the Sam Maguire trophy, Irish Post journalist Joe Horgan noted:

> Most recently the anti-Irishness surfaced again when the Mail on Sunday equated parading the Sam Maguire Cup at Celtic Park with support for the IRA. Ireland on Sunday thought it best not to include the same story in its edition.[32]

A subsequent communication from Croke Park revealed the astonishment of the G.A.A. at such a turn of events as well as an understanding and perception of Irish history and society seemingly beyond the consideration of many Scottish and British commentators. The communication also revealed part of the thinking behind the cultural distinctiveness in naming not only cups, but parks, stadiums, clubs, streets and public buildings after such figures.

> The Sam Maguire Cup was named in honour of the man's sterling work as secretary of the London County Board and not for anything he did for the cause of national independence (however worthy). The implied suggestions of sectarianism don't tally with the fact that Maguire was a Protestant. He was involved in the War of Independence but then so too were the likes of future Prime Ministers of the country such as Eamonn De Valera, Sean Lemas and President Sean T O'Ceallaigh, not to mention Nobel Peace Prize winner Sean McBride. . . Every country has a history and any country that gained its independence generally did so by force of arms. You only have to consider George Washington's contribution to

> the American War of Independence, and it is unlikely [the journalist] Mr Drury would object to a trophy in his honour being paraded at Parkhead. Sam Maguire is no different. Indeed, as you know many famous Irish streets, housing estates, buildings, train stations etc are named after those who fought in the War of Independence – it is not unusual and never before has this issue been raised in such a mischievous context. Incidentally, the Nelson Mandela Cup is the name of the trophy presented to the winners of the annual tri-nations clash in rugby between Australia and South Africa – there would have been a time when Mandela was viewed as a subversive by his own state and indeed was imprisoned on this basis. I mention this to highlight the importance of context around such issues. . . this is a disgraceful piece of mischief making by an individual who it appears must have an agenda against Celtic and the GAA and has no understanding whatsoever of the complexities of Irish politics and the National question.[33]

The minor media furore regarding the visit of the All-Ireland trophy to Celtic Park replicates and mirrors many other similar commotions. These include examples with regards Irishness as well as those pertaining to the G.A.A membership in Scotland. It is but one small instance of the way the media distorts, shapes, determines and represents Irishness, Ireland, Irish politics and the 'troubles', as well as matters to do with Celtic or other concerns that have an Irish dimension in Scotland.

THE SHAPING OF IDENTITY: RE-CONSTRUCTION FROM WITHIN

The external environment experienced by Irishness in Scotland has also prompted an internal contestation within Irish, Catholic, as well as G.A.A., circles, on how to endure, promote and celebrate Irishness within a Scottish context. Distinct even from the patriotic or political nature of the G.A.A., and although the Association in Scotland has traditionally been a forum for Irish identity, some members have regarded Irishness in contemporary Scottish society as burdensome. For example, during the post-1980s revival in Scotland, representatives of Dumbarton's Saint Patrick's club continually stressed a perceived need to curtail and dilute displays of Irishness while emphasising Scottishness.[34] This was a recurring argument used by an Irish-born founding member of Saint Patrick's who stated at the County's 1996 convention that with regards the expansion of Gaelic football amongst children in the west of Scotland, 'we are not here to turn out little Irishmen'.[35] This opinion is of course contrary to the raison d'étre, history, several objectives, purposes and rules of the G.A.A, as an organisation that seeks to preserve, sustain, celebrate and promote Irishness as well as the island of Ireland as one unit in national, cultural and sporting terms.[36] Although the argument of the St Patricks representative is a minority position within the G.A.A., it is a manifestation of some of the dilemmas faced by people of Irish antecedents who wish to preserve Irishness in Scotland.

During the late 1980s and 1990s a series of incidents and controversies further enveloped St Patricks. A number of these referred to the Irishness of the G.A.A and its membership in Scotland as well as how this might be perceived beyond the confines of the sport. The debates concerning the Irishness of the Association within the organisation is evidence of some aspects of the contested nature of Irish identity in Scotland.

Several G.A.A. players in Scotland have relayed how they were a focus of or overheard instances of what they perceived as anti-Irish comment directed towards players visiting Dumbarton. On one occasion a second generation Irish St Patricks official expressed a view from the side of the pitch that, 'I thought all the Paddys had stopped coming here cause the Famine was over'.[37]

For several years St Patricks officials expressed reservations over the perceived 'overt' Irish nature of other clubs as well as the County Board. This extended to disapproval of some club names, criticism of the flying of the Irish national flag at matches, disagreeing with the playing of the Irish national anthem before a Championship Final and, believing it wrong that an Irish marching band should parade around the pitch before a Championship Final (as was the custom in Ireland and indeed at most Championship finals around the world where G.A.A games are played).

One of the most controversial arguments introduced by St Patricks was in raising the topic of 'sectarianism', with the accusation that some other clubs 'were all Catholic'. Clubs in Scotland strenuously denied that this was accurate, stating that although the vast majority of their membership were Catholic (ironically this was also the case with St Patricks, an unsurprising fact in relation to the sport being born and sustained amongst Catholic Irish migrants to Scotland) all clubs had or contained players who were not Catholic or who were not from an Irish background. In several interviews, Scotland-based G.A.A. activists stated that this had not been an issue for clubs and that St Patricks had introduced it as a matter for discussion and was the sole body where this was seemingly part of a club discourse. In addition, during the 1980s and 1990s several policemen played Gaelic football in Scotland as well at least one 'territorial' part-time member of the British Army, all during the period of G.A.A bans on such membership. At least one player with Sands MacSwineys and another with now defunct Beltane Shamrocks from Wishaw also trained at these Clubs wearing the outfit of Glasgow Rangers: for many individuals involved with the G.A.A in Scotland, a soccer club with a history of an anti-Irish and anti-Catholic identity.[38] In response to these and other controversies in the mid 1990s several Board and Club members attempted to involve G.A.A officials from Croke Park to settle what they viewed as an anti-Irish stance by St Patricks: the accusation in turn being rejected by St Patricks who declined the mediation of Croke Park officialdom to resolve the disputes.

Any attempt to understand this conflict between County, several other Clubs, individual members of the G.A.A in Scotland and the St Patricks Club is fraught with difficulty. Numerous interviewees linked to the G.A.A. have stressed the contentiousness of various personal relationships within G.A.A circles in Scotland as well as how these personalities have shaped the internal politics of the Association (this being a replication of some of the Association's problems elsewhere). Some of the difficulties faced within the G.A.A. in Scotland have partly been a result of these problems. In addition, one interviewee suggested that elements of the difficulty that St Patricks perceived with other clubs was the semi-regular practice of some using players from Ireland who had not been officially transferred. This has caused periodic problems for G.A.A activities in not only Scotland but in other diasporic counties such as New York, London and Lancashire.

Nonetheless, in as much as relations between Catholics and

Protestants are mentioned and in terms of discussions and debates concerning the Irishness of the organisation and its clubs in Scotland, St Patricks stands alone: no other club in Scotland has been distinguished by such discourses. As a result, at a specially arranged meeting held in Edinburgh in 1999 a number of clubs in Scotland discussed their concerns regarding St Patricks, including perceived 'mild but pertinent sectarian and anti-Irish' abuse on the part of St Patricks. A complaint to Provincial Council led to a meeting arranged in Glasgow to discuss these issues and although the meeting failed to address or resolve the relevant issues (including others unconnected to 'sectarian' or racial discourses) by early 2002 due to a range of unrelated reasons, the St Patricks club played its last competitive match and subsequently ended its participation in Gaelic sports.[39] St Patricks finally went the way of many previous clubs in Scotland as its playing and managerial base aged and was not substituted by more youthful volunteer replacements.

In terms of the identity of the Association and Irishness in Scotland, the most remarkable aspect of the issues involving St Patricks is the Irish in Scotland dimension. An interviewee with one club representative and former County official reveals some of the dominant perceptions of the Dumbarton club.

> . . . in some ways it's like an Uncle Tom situation, it's like them saying that the only way we can survive is to dis-associate ourselves from our Irishness. I believe that club's problems came from only one or two sources in actual fact. They started off as a young team and were cautious how they progressed and how they were seen in their local area. These people influenced the young players into thinking that Irishness was similar to an embarrassment and had to be kept away from public display or the club would suffer. St Patricks disowned their Irishness and seemed to want the rest of us to do so as well. We all know the G.A.A in Scotland has a low profile but St Pat's took this to extremes and in some ways even became anti-Irish themselves. The County Board didn't really confront this hostility. I suppose that's what happens with a small organisation but they [St Patricks] certainly made for some unpleasant experiences.[40]

Ironically, bearing in mind media representations arising from events such as those surrounding the Irish-Scottish European Championship bid and the visit of the Sam Maguire to Celtic Park, amongst other such episodes, another interviewee stated,

> Given the nature of Scottish society and the G.A.A in Scotland means that the movement aspect rather than the purely sporting aspect attracts attention that it does not in Ireland. I think this might have been at the heart of St Pat's stance. St Pat's to me almost crusaded against the cultural and national side of the G.A.A.[41]

In the context of the perceived racism and sectarianism experienced by the Irish in Scotland, the G.A.A has traditionally seen itself as enduring media disparagement, a lack of public recognition, a lack of funding and occasional physical damage carried out on its facilities in Glasgow and other venues.[42] The contested nature of Irish identity, as demonstrated in the experience surrounding the St Patricks Club, is reflective of how the externally perceived anti-Irish and anti-Catholic environment impacts upon the internal in-group discourses and politics and the paths seen as requiring to be tread in the wider society. This is an area of in-group and out-group social relations relatively unknown outside the Catholic community of Irish descent in Scotland. As the events and discourses surrounding the G.A.A – St Patricks context partly reveals, Irishness in third millennium Scotland remains contested, not only 'externally' for the Irish diaspora in Scotland, but also, and partly as a result of a history of negative experiences and tensions over manifestations of Irish identity, within the community itself.[43]

1. Red Hand, a Scottish loyalist publication, issue 9, 1991.
2. Orange Torch, March, 1993.
3. Interview, John McCreadie. It should also be noted that applications can often take a long time with such public bodies regardless of any ethnic or religious context.
4. G.A.A. members believe members of these groups smashed the Padraic Pearse memorial cross at Pearse Park in the early 1990s.
5. The Sun, 11/9/02.
6. The Scotsman, 16/8/02.
7. Ibid.

8. Partly relative to this debate, Hassan also notes an enthusiastic revisionist grouping in the Republic of Ireland, 'which disparages the G.A.A. and other Irish Ireland bodies, cultural groups and varying political aspirations, which desires a more secular, pluralist and liberal state and which questions Irish nationhood'. Hassan argues that this grouping is in fact guilty of that which they accuse others of being, advocating a 'one-sided, narrow view of pluralism: in other words, a vociferous neo-unionist alliance'. See Hassan, 2003, pp.92-110.

9. S Halliday, The Scotsman, 16/8/02.

10. A Milton, The Sun, 26/10/02.

11. The Times, Eire News, 17/4/06.

12. Ibid.

13. 24/11/02.

14. 18/8/02.

15. 22/11/02.

16. 3/3/02.

17. See Bradley, 'Celtic Minded' 2004 and 'Celtic Minded 2' 2006.

18. The Sunday Herald, Sport, 7/1/07.

19. The Mirror, Eire edition, 6/1/06.

20. Mail on Sunday, 15/1/06.

21. The Sun, 16/1/06.

22. The Sun, 20/1/06.

23. The propaganda war has been acknowledged and reflected upon in the following books among many; 'The Long War', B O'Brien, O'Brien Press, Dublin, 1993, 'The SAS in Ireland', R Murray, The Mercier Press, Dublin, 1990, 'Ireland the Propaganda War', L Curtis, Sasta, Belfast, 1998, 'British Intelligence and Covert Action', J Bloch and P Fitzgerald, Brandon, Kerry, 1983.

24. The Sun, 8/4/02.

25. E Grahame, The Herald, 8/4/02.

26. J Traynor, The Daily Record, 19/5/03.

27. Daily Star, letters, 25/5/03.

28. The Herald, 23/5/03.

29. Scottish Television, Scotsport, 20/11/06.

30. G McNee, News of the World, 6/5/01 & 7/10/01.

31. J MacLeod, The Herald, 18/2/02.

32. The Irish Post, 25/2/06.

33. Copy of e-mail communication from Croke Park.

34. The use of the Irish national flag (which the G.A.A. requires to be flown at all games in Ireland and important games in Britain) as well as Irish marching bands on the occasions of championship finals were repeatedly a focus for criticism during the 1980s and 1990s on the part of Dumbarton's Saint Patrick's delegates at County Board meetings.

35. Eamon Cullen at minor County Board meeting and annual convention both 1996.

36. See Handbook and rules of Gaelic Athletic Association.

37. Interview with priest who overheard this remark.

38. See Murray, 1984, 1988 & 2003.

39. Versus Sands MacSwineys in March 2002.

40. Interview, G.A.A club activist and member of the Scotland County Board 1995-2000.

41. Interview, former member of Sands MacSwineys GFC.

42. There are several accounts of G.A.A. pitches being damaged, especially prior to major matches that have been advertised in the press.

43. The author is currently working in this under-researched area of Catholic community life in Scotland.

Part 3
Historical and Social Perspectives

Chapter 17
The G.A.A. and Irishness in Scottish society

MAINTAINING COMMUNITY AND THE SEARCH FOR DISTINCTIVENESS

By the new millennium, the G.A.A. in Ireland has become a modern and relatively wealthy organisation. In 2006 a G.A.A. 'Strategic Review' estimated that its grounds portfolio was worth approximately six and a half billion euros (around five billion pounds): this amounting to more than the assets of several English Premier League soccer clubs combined. By this time the G.A.A. owned at least ten grounds across Ireland which could hold more than 35,000 people. Although remaining amateur, the clubs and the Association attract major sponsorship as well as massive media coverage. This has also been important for the Gaelic sporting diaspora in Britain where there has been coverage of Irish sport, particularly by Channel 4 during the 1990s and Sky and Setanta satellite TV since the mid-1990s, covering annual activities in hurling and football All-Ireland competitions.

Gaelic sports training and coaching have become more intense and sophisticated and sports medicine and psychology are seen as increasingly important within elite Gaelic sport. Although it took many decades for the Association to establish itself and become the foremost cultural body in Ireland, and despite a variety of financial, social and political pressures against expansion of the institution, over two thousand clubs involving thousands of football, hurling and camogie teams for multiple age groups now exist across Ireland and many have their own grounds, pitches and clubhouses. Gaelic sport is part of the curriculum in Irish schools. The infrastructure of the G.A.A. is constantly being updated and modernised. The headquarters of the G.A.A. in Dublin, Croke Park, is one of the best sports stadiums in Europe, with all the corporate and visitor facilities now integral to sports stadia.

For many Irish people, Ireland has 'substantially' or 'partly' acquired one of its historical aspirations in taking 'its place amongst the nations of the earth'.[1] For others too, in recent decades the intensity, relevance and context of the historical Irish-British conflict has changed, indeed much diminished since the founding years of the G.A.A. This conflict and the northern 'troubles' have been experienced and perceived differently across the island, and these differences are partly reflected amongst the Irish diaspora. Irish nationalism has varied in response to a changing economic, social and political environment within which it exists. As an organisation the G.A.A. has become less important in the politics of the island. With regards Irish nationalism, changes within that identity and ideology link with contemporary social and cultural theory that contends:

> nationalism is not fixed, but is a process contoured by the changing political, cultural and economic forces in specific social systems.[2]

Study of sporting institutions, activity and participation, has been well established as important to developing more credible and accurate assessments of society. In modern societies, it is virtually impossible for significant sports to develop or exist without a relationship with culture, politics and identity.[3] Using the example of soccer, Finn has helped establish that many clubs in present-day Scotland have religious and political origins and roots.[4] Such evidence also shows that Celtic Football Club, an institution that evolved from and continues to draw the vast majority of its support from offspring of the Irish Catholic immigrant population in Scotland, is not unique in religion or nationality being an important factor in its roots and character. Clubs such as Glasgow Rangers, Queens Park, Moffat, Larkhall Royal Albert and many others have been shown by Finn to have been given birth within a context of religious or political backgrounds. Examples from other countries also reflect that sport, soccer in particular, can have a socio-political, national or ethnic context which provides a basis for development and success, as well as a distinct raison d'étre.

Over the course of the twentieth century, sport has contributed to war and peace, status and ideology, as well as art, health and personal, community, ethnic and national relationships. In the latter part of the century, economics, wealth and commercialisation have had an increasingly significant impact on the direction and shape of modern sporting activity, especially at an elite level. Sport is largely inseparable from these features of human existence. Indeed, at an elite level, and in terms of major sporting clubs and countries, despite the often heard argument that 'sport and politics shouldn't mix', and notwithstanding sport's often inherent physical and artistic qualities, sport is frequently not only social assertion and culture, but politics by other means.

Reflection on just a few past events demonstrate this; the black athletes at the Mexican Olympics of 1968 who raised their fists to highlight amongst other things the lack of human rights for non-whites in the USA; the refusal of both the USA and former Soviet Union to participate in Olympic Games during the 1980s; the significance of any sporting game played between Iran and the USA; even Celtic Football Club refusing to travel to Czechoslovakia in 1968 because of the Soviet Union's invasion of that country.

Other examples of how sport is but an extension of relevant social and political features of everyday life can be found in numerous societies. In Spain, soccer has become synonymous with regional and ethnic identities. In the USA events in 1997 meant that in winning the US Masters Tournament, subsequent negative reports of the experiences of black golfing hero, Tiger Woods, demonstrated to the world that racism does not simply take place in Holywood films and television dramas which have black ghettos as a part of their backdrop. Media reports of the experiences of Woods reflect that racism against blacks has been all-pervading and continues to affect many areas of life in the USA. Sport in the USA reflects this reality. In a Scottish context, Jarvie and Walker believe that:

> sport and in particular, football, is a central arena for the expression of

a range of Scottish national identities in both domestic and international contexts.[5]

To say that sport can be or is 'political' is to stress politics broadly defined as a forum to re-live power relationships, engage in and settle conflicts, discord and antagonisms, as well as raise consciousness and vitality in relation to the things which give meaning to peoples lives.

Although the G.A.A. can be viewed as distinctive in a sporting context, it is not unique. The G.A.A. is but one example of a sporting body or vehicle that has its origins, links and meaning, closely associated with culture, nationalism and patriotism. The case of the G.A.A. has a number of parallels and close relations in other countries. Sport involves multi-dimensional relationships between individual, community and national identity. Such associations are intrinsic to the Gaelic Athletic Association: a considerable sporting body that remains uniquely amateur. Perceptions of the G.A.A. vary though the links between sport, nationalism and religion in Ireland remain significant and, are particularly strong in Northern Ireland where the Association is broadly nationalist, but factionally neutral.

Political, cultural and social contexts and circumstances vary enormously within and between Ireland and Scotland. Nonetheless, historically and in relation to narratives of Irishness, the G.A.A. has been important among sections of the Irish community in Scotland, particularly in the west of the country. The G.A.A. promotes a sense of Irishness in its island of Ireland and diasporic contexts. It represents a direct link to Ireland in terms of history, heritage, ethnicity, politics, family, counties, nationality, culturally, spiritually, communally and symbolically. The sense of Irishness that is reflected through attachment to Gaelic sports and the G.A.A. can be intense and profound. These attributes can be singular and collective and they can fluctuate, become circumstantial, transitory, or they can be lifelong characteristics.

PATTERNS OF MIGRATION AND THE G.A.A.

In relation to the Gaelic Athletic Association and the sporting options and choices available to the migrants and their offspring in Scotland, these were largely determined by the society they entered. Crucially for most Irish migrants, these options and choices were also fashioned by factors of simple survival, the most important feature of their lives. As with many other economic refugees in other countries at other times, regular employment, shelter, social welfare and education were the main concerns and pre-occupations for the vast majority of Irish Catholic immigrants and their offspring for much if not all of their lives in Scotland.

In terms of sport, although many Irish migrants originated from the southern half of Ireland where Gaelic sports had become steadily better organised over the course of the late nineteenth and early twentieth centuries, much of this phase of immigration to Scotland took place before or during the period of the effective organising of the G.A.A. in Ireland.

Vast numbers of Irish arrived in Scotland during the second half of the nineteenth century and had a significant presence in Scotland before the Gaelic Athletic Association in Ireland was founded and, before it had become established, revered and esteemed so widely in Irish society. This is crucial to understanding why it was soccer that many Irish in Scotland turned to for expressing themselves culturally, especially through sport.

Darby's research in Boston serves as a poignant example of how the G.A.A. has largely depended on Irish born migrants giving life to Gaelic sports amongst the diaspora. He notes that after 'the disruption of the Great War of 1914-18 brought a temporary halt to the development of Gaelic football and hurling in Boston', during the 1920s,

> Gaelic sports once again began to cater for the sporting, recreational and cultural needs of Boston's Irish community. . . between 1927 and 1929 nine hurling and 15 football teams had affiliated to the Massachusetts G.A.A.[6]

Related to this development Darby also reveals Gaelic games becoming 'a more central aspect of the lives of increasing numbers of Irish immigrants' to Boston. His point on 'rising' numbers of Irish migrants to Boston is key to understanding some of the variations in the development and sustenance of Gaelic sport in Scotland compared to Boston and other diasporic settings.

This is important to understanding the development of Gaelic games in Scotland because despite later significant smaller waves of movement, the bulk of Irish migration to Scotland had taken place prior to 1920. Although Scotland was possibly numerically and proportionately the most important location for Irish migration from the time of the Great Famine until the early twentieth century, Irish migration to Scotland was finished as a mass phenomenon by the time of World War I and this meant that these migrants had departed Ireland before the firm establishment and spread of the G.A.A. in Ireland.

Unlike in Boston and other recipient towns and cities around the world where the Irish settled, after World War I there was no substantial 'increase' in Irish migration to Scotland. Apart from being a period of heightened anti-Irish and anti-Catholic activity and attitudes in Scotland, British society during this time experienced economic depression and social and political upheaval. For potential Irish emigrants looking to improve their lives, the pull factors that had traditionally existed in Scotland had, for the time being, ceased to exist.

In turn, the depth of knowledge, playing experience, the organisational skills and the growing appreciation of how important Gaelic sport was to a developing sense of Irishness and Irish national identity, which were all required to invigorate Gaelic games, did not migrate with a new wave of Irish migrants to Scottish shores. As far as Scotland was concerned, the majority of Irish to arrive in Scotland were already in Scotland as of course were their offspring.

Therefore, historically much of the explanation for the erratic successes of the G.A.A. in Scotland can be evidenced through a closer inspection of Irish migration patterns. The Association's relative strength in Scotland in the first decade of the twentieth century was similar to the strength of the G.A.A. in Boston in the 1920s. In Scotland, Gaelic sports also expanded in response to increased Irish migration. This is particularly evident in the years of the Association's revival that took place after World War II, when a new wave of migrants from Ireland, chiefly from Ulster, and particularly from Donegal, reinvigorated Gaelic sports in Scotland. However, although significant, this wave was not a reproduction of the mass waves of migration prior to 1920. As a consequence of the varied pattern of Irish immigration, the Association in Scotland 'never' experienced a suitable, sizeable and timely wave of migrants, who had a Gaelic sports background and experience and who were capable of giving life to a vibrant Association in Scotland.

Generally, it is the case that wherever Gaelic sport has been inaugurated, sustained or revived, regardless of the willingness or otherwise of second, third and fourth generation immigrants to take up Gaelic games, it is Irish-born migrants who create the impetus required to establish or re-establish the sport. In this sense a strong association with an Irish-based 'home' G.A.A. club or county is often the predetermined requirement for inauguration, sustenance or revival to take place. The requirement for a 'suitable, sizeable and timely wave of migrants' to give birth and life to Gaelic sports in the diaspora is substantiated by Darby who notes,

> The profile and development of Gaelic sports in the United States has been dependent on the pendulum of migration.[7]

The fact that in relation to the development of the G.A.A., this 'suitable, sizeable and timely wave of migrants' did not arrive in Scotland from Ireland has further significance. As with many 'chain migrations', various towns and villages in Scotland sometimes received a large number of Irish immigrants from one particular area in Ireland. So for example Gorbals in Glasgow was a recipient of many of its migrants from Donegal. Glenboig, a village outside the town of Coatbridge, attracted a significant number of people from counties in the Irish east and central midlands such as Offaly, Westmeath, Carlow and Wicklow. Other towns and villages in Scotland experienced a similar story. However, although all counties are represented among Irish immigrants coming to Scotland, a majority originated from the nine counties of Ulster, north Leinster, and from the likes of Mayo, Leitrim and Sligo. This is also relevant to the strength of the G.A.A. in Scotland in that many of these were the same areas in which the Association struggled most in Ireland. In Connacht and Ulster organised Gaelic activities were often weak and the Gaelic Athletic Association took many years to become established there. This is especially true with regards Gaelic football. De Burca notes that in 1889 many Ulster counties either did not have a functioning Association or were severely weak; in Monaghan, Derry, Antrim and Down, insufficient clubs existed to form a county committee, whilst in Donegal, Fermanagh and Tyrone, there is little if any record of organised Gaelic sports activity at this time. By 1891, there was not a single club in Louth, Monaghan and Tyrone, whilst Mayo had only three and Clare one.[8] By 1900, Connacht and Ulster remained almost entirely outside the G.A.A., though Gaelic games were played there in an unorganised and random fashion.

Despite initial progress in some areas of Ireland, in other parts the G.A.A. took decades to become established. Codification, organisation, management and effective administration also took years to develop in various counties. Many Gaelic clubs took some time to acquire a sound foundation and stability, some emerging only to demise shortly afterwards. In Ireland, at the 1892 annual convention (held in 1893), just three counties were represented. Only three counties contested the 1893 hurling championship while six competed to become football champions. The attendance figures for Connacht finals during the first thirty years of the Association's existence reflects its weakness in this area. Two thousand five hundred are reported as having attended the 1904 Connacht Final, four thousand at the 1905 match and just over two thousand at the 1906 game between Mayo and Roscommon in Tuam. Even by 1918 the Connacht Final was still not attracting significant crowds, only four thousand five hundred watching that match. It took until 1928 before the figure of ten thousand was matched and began to be surpassed as the 1930s progressed.

Association weaknesses must be viewed in the context of the inchoate nature of the Association during this period. During the troubled times of the Parnell era, World War I, the 1916 Uprising, the Irish War of Independenc, and the period of the Irish Civil War, pastimes and cultural activities were frequently disrupted. In particular, counties where many G.A.A. activists were also volunteers with the nationalist movement often became athletically weak as individuals and communities had little time to pursue recreational activities. By March 1915 for example, both Gaelic codes had almost died out due to activity with the volunteer movement.[9]

Even today, the present hurling core region in Ireland is based largely on Cork, Tipperary and Kilkenny though other counties like Limerick, Clare, Galway, Offaly, Laois, Waterford and Wexford have strong hurling traditions. Nonetheless, even within these counties, the game can be designated by virtue of the local geography: often it is not whole counties but parts of counties in which the game is viewed as fundamental. In parts of Ulster's north-eastern counties of Down and Antrim, hurling is also fundamental to local culture. Despite this, and as already noted, it was the 1930s before the G.A.A. began to have the significance for Irish life in Ulster that it had in the rest of the country.

When considering the history of the G.A.A. in both Ireland and Scotland, in relation to immigration it must further be recognised that historically much of the population of Ireland had been demoralised throughout the years of colonialism and particularly as a consequence of the Great Famine of the nineteenth century. Kinealy believes that the price paid by the Irish for the Famine was: 'privation, disease, emigration, mortality and an enduring legacy of disenchantment'.[10] Dr Douglas Hyde, later to become the first President of Ireland, concluded:

> The Famine destroyed everything. Poetry, music and dancing stopped. Sport and pastimes disappeared. And when times improved, those things never returned as they were.[11]

For Scotland, and as far as other countries that Irish refugees and Famine victims settled, Irish immigrants were often much too concerned with surviving in an alien and hostile environment and of not attracting unwarrented attention to themselves. A majority of Scotland's Irish migrants left Ireland before the G.A.A. had made a significant cultural and national impact and well before a new era of confidence in Irish cultural activities and identities had emerged.

Although it remains an aspect of Irish culture and Irish identity in Scotland, the environment and conditions that gave rise to and sustained the Association in Ireland were not replicated in Scotland. Some conditions were closely related and were fed by similar historical factors and experiences, but Irish life in the diaspora has always been a differing experience from that in Ireland.

Partly linking to Darby's discussion on the G.A.A. in Boston in the USA, although having some vibrancy where Irish immigrants reside in large numbers, the Association encounters difficulty in being seen as a primary focus for Irishness.

> Since American-born Irish have traditionally shown little interest in the games of their fathers, the G.A.A. in America has always depended upon Irish immigrants to keep the games alive. . . As a matter of fact, were it not for Irish students who come to America during the Summer to work and line up with G.A.A. teams in various cities, the games of the Gael would be for all intents and purposes dead in many cities.[12]

Since the period of revival in 1984, clubs such as Glaschu Gaels, Dundee Dalriada and Dunedin Connolly's have been constituted almost entirely by Irish-born players, particularly students coming to Scotland to study, though many of these have later settled into employment and family situations and continued to play Gaelic sport. Connolly's have been less dependent on students and more reliant on young professional men from Ireland working in the financial and building sectors of the Scottish economy. As with the USA and elsewhere, this dependence on an Irish-born base was reflected in the 2006 Scotland Championship Final held at Pearse Park Glasgow, between Dunedin Connolly's and Glaschu Gaels. From sixty-seven players registered by both clubs approximately eight came from outside of Ireland, although these were all (except for one player from Brittany, France) of Irish descent. At least twenty-two of Ireland's thirty-two counties were represented amongst both panels registered for the final with Derry (7), Down (5), Dublin (5), Cork (4), Antrim (4), Donegal (4) best represented.[13]

Distinct from factors involving those who are second, third and fourth generation Irish, the considerable number of Irish-born migrants taking part in this match as well as the high number amongst the wider Gaelic sports fraternity from amongst the contemporary diaspora also reflects the capacity of Gaelic sport to provide important social and economic functions for first generation Irish migrants. The G.A.A. can often be one of the first ports of call for emigrant Irish in an otherwise unfamiliar land. In this way a sense of the familiar is provided and the capacity for a Gaelic sports environment to offer not only friendships, but also an important psychological link with 'home' in Ireland. This is reproduced at multiple levels; including family, townland, village, town, city, county and nation. As such, feelings of dislocation and alienation are all countered through attachment to the G.A.A. in Scotland, Britain, the USA, Australasia or elsewhere.

In Scotland, clubs like Mulroy Gaels, Sands MacSwineys and Tir Conail Harps have varyingly contained between thirty to seventy per cent Irish-born, the rest mainly second, third and fourth generation Irish. For clubs such as Beltane Shamrocks and Shotts Gaels, a majority of players were second, third and fourth generation Irish, with only a few Irish-born players participating with these teams over the course of their existence. For all of these, and other Gaelic clubs in Scotland, they have been founded and sustained by Irish-born or second or third generation migrants. All have either been reared in a Gaelic sports environment in Ireland or, as second and third generation Irish, have embraced a strong sense of cultural and nationalist Irishness.

TRADITIONS

Many of the things that today give life to the G.A.A. in Ireland, especially a sense of identity in the shape of parishes and counties, local tradition, community and national memory, history and bloodlines, added to coaching as a part of the modern educational curriculum, do not exist in Scotland. The cultural context and environment within which Gaelic sports exist in Ireland do not constitute any real influence amongst the diaspora. In its island of Ireland context, for Humphries:

> That the Gaelic Athletic Association succeeded at all is due to the manner in which the fare it offered fitted perfectly within the culture, rituals and aspirations of our society. On an island where native culture had for centuries been subordinated to political imperatives, the games became a passionate and rugged expression of a people's soul. When all other forms of Irishness had been stamped out, the spirit burst out of captivity in the form of play.14

Of course, some Gaelic sports activists have attempted to re-create something of this amongst the diaspora. For example, Frank Sheehan, Chairman of the London County Board in the early 1980s, believed the role of the G.A.A. to be extremely important with regards matters Irish in Britain. Although underestimating other social agents as well as other

Irish identities, Sheehan captured some of the essence of the Association abroad when he stated:

> The G.A.A. has its outpost in London for over eighty years kept going by Irishmen who valued at its true value and worth this great link with home. Today it is strong and flourishing just as the parent body is. In other parts of England too there are G.A.A. strongholds. . . Their simple purpose is to provide Irishmen and their sons with a means of expressing their individuality, of keeping alive that incredibly valuable work of nationality. Those who turn away from such an opportunity will soon be lost in the crowd, nonentities, without anything to distinguish them.[15]

Humphries' second assessment seems to get closer to aspects of the Irish in Scotland experience:

> The culture of Gaelic games has been built upon the Irish need for collective self-expression, the desperate hankering after something indigenous and Irish in a world which formally repressed such forms of articulation, a world which has become increasingly homogenised. . . Our distinctiveness no longer shames us.[16]

Although there are significant and ongoing quandaries in Scotland in maintaining and expressing Irishness, contemporary media accounts, Irish diasporic literature and empirical observations reflect Irishness in Scotland and Britain since the early 1990s as more publicly manifest and confident than at any time since the mid-nineteenth century.[17] This change can be partly seen in the way many second, third and fourth generation Irish in Scotland have celebrated and supported the 1980s and 1990s Republic of Ireland soccer side in European Championships and World Cups: periods marked by the presence of many British-born Irish players as members of the Irish international squads. There has been a rise in the popularity of Irish traditional and popular music, and the growth of the Irish music organisation Comhaltas Ceoltóirí Éireann in Scotland reflects this. There has been a notable increase in the use of Irish forenames for children amongst the Irish diaspora in Scotland. Indeed, this is something akin to the north of Ireland where there has been a similar increase on the part of the Catholic community for the use of native Irish names. The post 1990s expansion of celebrations around St Patrick's Day in Scotland has reached a new high while there is a degree of public acceptability (and sharing) of Irish culture evident in the emergence of the Irish theme pub around Britain, which despite being habitually criticised because of their 'plastic' nature, has also given a further dimension to contemporary Irishness. Significantly, the decline in 'Troubles' related violence and British mis-representations and censorship of this issue, and the development of the peace process in Northern Ireland, have created an improved social context for remembering and celebrating Irishness. Such changes have contributed to Irishness gaining a currency that was largely prohibited by the experience of racist and prejudicial encounters on the part of many immigrants and their offspring in Britain. Although narratives of Irishness in Scotland demonstrate continued problems and contestation, for many people Irish identity has been popularised and refreshed whilst retaining much of what many consider to be the richness of its past.

SOCCER, CELTIC FOOTBALL CLUB AND IRISHNESS IN SCOTLAND

In Scotland, during the latter half of the nineteenth century, a sporting form developed that attracted huge numbers of participants and spectators. Inadvertently, this sporting form was also to provide an obstacle to the uptake of Gaelic sport amongst the Irish and their offspring. Soccer exploded onto the social scene over the course of a number of years and rapidly became the game of the working classes throughout the length and breadth of Britain. It was into this social and cultural environment that many Irish settled. As an accessible inexpensive pastime and leisure activity many Irish took to the developing game of soccer.

From a range of Irish soccer clubs that emerged into this environment including Harps, Emmets and Shamrocks from places like Glasgow, Coatbridge and Carfin, Celtic Football Club in the east end of Glasgow became the most significant and most famous.[18] The origins and development of Celtic are embedded and intertwined with the history and evolution of the Irish Catholic community in Scotland. In Glasgow, Brother Walfrid, a member of the Catholic Marist Order, and some of his Irish-Catholic immigrant compatriots like John Glass and Dr John Conway, saw in the development of the game an opportunity to raise money and feed poor immigrant Irish Catholics in the east end of the city. Brother Walfrid's intention was to keep Catholics within the reaches of the faith (and therefore out of the reaches of proselytism), while also raising the religious, cultural, ethnic and national confidence and morale of that community.

Like other commentators, Campbell and Woods argue that, at the time of Celtic's founding in 1887-88, the words Catholic and Irish were interchangeable in the west of Scotland. All the club's founders were expatriate Irishmen or from Irish stock, and the new club's support was drawn from the swelling Irish community in Glasgow. The donations to charity frequently included some to exclusively Irish causes such as the Evicted Tenant's Fund, then an important feature of Irish nationalist politics. In addition, if as Catholics the members were concerned about the plight of local charities, like many other members of their community, 'as Irishmen, they were also pre-occupied with the perennial question of Irish politics, Home Rule'.[19]

For example, John Glass, President and Director of the club in its foremost years, was an outstanding figure in nationalist circles; he was prominent in the Catholic Union, a founder of the O'Connell branch of the Irish National Foresters and the treasurer of the Home Government Branch of the United Irish League. Another member, William McKillop, became M.P. for North Sligo (holding this constituency for eight years before winning in South Armagh in 1908), whilst Michael Davitt (a former revolutionary/Fenian and founder of the Irish Land League), the celebrated Irish patriot, was one of the club's original patrons. Club officials, players and supporters alike, were often involved in politics; supporting Irish Home Rule, campaigning for the release of Irish political prisoners, opposing what they viewed as British imperialism in the Boer War in South Africa and supporting the contentious Catholic endeavour to have their schools brought within the state-funded system.

The political thrust involved in the establishment of Celtic is emphasised by Wilson who notes that although the decision to form Celtic is rightly identified with the needs of Catholic charity in the east end of Glasgow:

> the early nature of the club, and the direction it pursued, owe at least as much to the influence exercised by the political organisation which spoke for the vast majority of the Irish in Scotland in the 1880s, the Irish National League, and specifically one of its branches in Glasgow, known as the Home Government Branch. Among those involved in setting up Celtic, John Glass, James Quillan, the McKillops and the Murphys were heavily involved in the Home Government Branch. . . The influence which the leading figures in the Home Government Branch exercised in the founding of Celtic ensured that the primary aim would be to create a club that was outward-looking, proudly Irish and excellent. . . [20]

The outward looking nature of this Irish club in Glasgow is further noted by Wilson to be of a strong non-sectarian kind. After all, John Ferguson was a Belfast Protestant who founded the Irish National League in Glasgow in 1871. Amongst his closest colleagues were people like Glass, Murphy and Quillan.[21] Although these men established a symbol of, and representation for, Irish Catholic migrants in the west of Scotland, the club incorporated no notion of excluding anyone on the basis of their religion or ethnic or national origins. The club's subsequent history of inclusion has reflected this ethos and, it might be argued, this also reflects a long history of Protestant involvement in Irish nationalist political struggle.

Apart from Walfrid, the club's first important Catholic patron was Archbishop Charles Eyre of Glasgow. Many cartoons of the time, in both the Catholic and the secular press, 'included sympathetic caricatures of priests among the crowds at Celtic games', whilst Woods states that the Glasgow Observer, a Catholic newspaper catering for the Irish Catholic community, took a keen interest in Celtic's progress. Other Irish football clubs also existed at the same time, in Lanarkshire, Glasgow and Edinburgh, who had the same national and religious make-up as Celtic and who made efforts to establish themselves. However, it was the remarkable competitive successes of the Celtic club, as well as good organisation, an apt location and a supportive community, which enabled it to prosper.[22]

Celtic has been the cultural and symbolic champion of the Irish Catholic community in Scotland and its ethno-religious character, along with its early successes on the football field, initially helped attract crowds to football that had never previously been experienced in Scotland. The club came into existence as the focus for much Catholic and Irish community activity and a setting for that community's broad social, cultural and political aspirations.

It is important in exploring and assessing the story of the Irish in Scotland, as well as the history of sport and particularly that of the Gaelic Athletic Association, that we take cognisance of the fact that soccer has not only been the dominant team sport for over one hundred years, but that it has also become one of the most obvious reflections and mediums of Irishness in Scotland. In similar fashion to clubs in Spain, Germany, Italy and elsewhere, Celtic Football Club possesses an ethnic, cultural, religious and political identity. Ironically, despite the G.A.A.'s historic antagonism towards non-Irish sports, Celtic Football Club's identity has similar features to that of the Association. This, in as much that the club draws mainly on the Irish in Scotland and these members of the diaspora have become amongst the foremost of conveyors of Irishness in Scotland and this links with the G.A.A.'s sporting role as a chief conveyor of Irishness in Ireland.[23]

Irish immigrants and their offspring in Scotland have encountered much opposition.[24] For the most part, hostility has revolved around their religious, ethnic, cultural, national as well as political character which has frequently been distinctive from those that have been dominant in Scottish and British societies. Overall, Irish and Catholic immigrant identities have been considered pernicious and deviant influences. In the face of the antipathy towards Irish immigrants and their offspring in Scotland, for many Catholics of Irish descent, Celtic has provided an environment in which to communicate otherwise invisible, repressed or unarticulated political attitudes, cultural affinities and national allegiances.

As an Irish football club and a Scottish institution, Celtic has allowed for the participation of the immigrant Catholic community in a popular facet of the larger society. Football and Celtic became avenues for interaction and integration with the host community, despite the ethnic competitiveness of the game itself. For many members of the consciously Irish Catholic community,[25] and for the offspring of the immigrant community who retain a sense of 'Irishness', Celtic is the greatest single 'ethno-cultural focus'. Celtic partly provides the social setting and process through which the community's sense of its own identity and distinctiveness from the indigenous community is sustained and celebrated through a set of symbolic processes and representations. In becoming a focus for displaying Irishness Celtic have also become a unique football club in world football. Many emotions that might have been displayed elsewhere, or indeed were diminished in other contexts, became central to the character of the Celtic support. For many Irish immigrants in Scotland, supporting Celtic has been, 'a powerful strategy of identity building' as well as a vital symbol for the maintenance and celebration of Irishness.[26]

In Scotland, soccer has enjoyed unrivalled success since the late nineteenth century. Many Celtic fans in Scotland have little knowledge of the historic conflict between soccer and Gaelic sports in Ireland. Others note with pride that a number of Celtic's Irish-born star players of recent decades, including Pat Bonner and Anton Rogan, played top class Gaelic football in Ireland as did manager Martin O'Neill in the late 1960s and early 1970s. A Kildare correspondent to the Celtic club newspaper noted:

> the myriad of soccer shirts worn by G.A.A. players at training sessions; the fact that many Gaelic football teams play soccer matches as part of their training routines; the fact that so many G.A.A. clubs have opened their club houses and held social events in conjunction with Irish international soccer matches. . . [as well as] the array of G.A.A. shirts on view around Celtic Park on match days.[27]

Considering that the popularisation of wearing replica sports jerseys in the post 1970s era has meant numerous Celtic supporters sporting G.A.A shirts on match days, it seems that the historical conflict between Gaelic sports and soccer has been ignored (largely through a lack of awareness) in its Scottish context. This is partly reciprocated and highlighted by the many Celtic replica soccer jerseys on view amongst spectators at Gaelic matches all over Ireland, particularly in Ulster where the nationalist perspective has been at its sharpest since at least the late 1960s and were supporting Celtic has been a more central part of Catholic, Irish and nationalist identity. For a number of G.A.A. and soccer enthusiasts in Ireland and Scotland, Celtic is in fact a point of cultural and symbolic convergence, the Irishness of these institutions being the most significant factor common to both.

This is particularly reflected in the attitudes and identities of G.A.A. people who have little if any affinity for soccer, but who retain an empathy or passion for Celtic Football Club. For example, until his death in 2005, like many G.A.A. members of his age, one Donegal G.A.A. associate referred to soccer as 'the garrison game'. This G.A.A. supporter was

> a former Marist brother, who dedicated most of his life to the promotion of Irish Culture – whether in terms of the language, Gaelic games or traditional Irish music, song and dance. I suppose in this sense he was a zealot and had no time for soccer whatsoever. Indeed he'd frequently chastise us as children for watching 'the garrison game' and was fully convinced of the G.A.A.'s need to keep their grounds solely for the promotion of Gaelic games. A very proud Donegal man, it would hardly be stretching it to say he was 'anti-soccer' and he certainly saw its influence on the G.A.A. and Irish culture as being a negative one. However, he was also an avid Celtic fan. I often rang him during Celtic games for 'the craic' and he couldn't get off the phone quick enough. As I explained to you, I would ask him when he was watching Celtic why he was watching a soccer match, and he would just say 'Celtic are different'. I suppose ultimately he saw the same basic reasoning behind the existence of Celtic as that which spawned the G.A.A. – the need for a distinct identity, a pride in place for those who were part of it, an expression of Irish culture and an opportunity to mix with others of a similar persuasion.[28]

For many Catholics in Scotland, and in a similar fashion to Raynot's description of Barcelona Football Club as a vehicle for Catalan identity in Spain, Celtic have become a metaphor for many aspects of the Irish and Catholic immigrant tradition.[29] In Scotland, soccer is bound up with the process of individual socialisation and community construction. The history of Irish-British relations has meant that for the Irish in Scotland, as well as for those of an anti-Catholic and anti-Irish disposition, Celtic Football Club has emerged as a definition of Irishness itself.

1. See R Kee, 1976, p. 168, for Robert Emmet quotation before his execution by the British in 1803: '. . . When my country takes its place among the nations of the earth, then and not till then, let my epitaph be written'.
2. Reid, 1997, pp. 147-155.
3. Flanagan, 1991, p. 27.
4. See Finn, 1991.
5. Quoted in Boyle and Hayes, 1996, pp.549-564.
6. Darby, 2005.
7. Ibid.
8. de Burca, 1980, p. 58.
9. Ibid: p. 124.
10. Kinealy, 1994, p.359.
11. The Irish Post, 2/9/95.
12. Patrick Hennessy, in Gaelic Athletic Association: a century of service, 1984-1984, 1984, p. 79).
13. Scotland County Championship Final, Pearse Park, 24/9/06.
14. Humphries, 1992, p. 2.
15. Sheehan, May 1992 from Gallagher, 1993.
16. Humphries, 1996, p. 3.
17. The Irish Post, a newspaper of the Irish community in Britain, has charted this change over the course of the past quarter of a century. Also, from information gathered via ongoing interviews, especially the Irish 2 Project.
18. During the late nineteenth and early twentieth centuries, many other Irish football clubs also existed in Scotland: Edinburgh's Hibernian, and Dundee's Dundee Harp (later to become Dundee United) surviving beyond their early difficulties. Nonetheless, Celtic F.C. remains the only club that can be considered in any way Irish in contemporary Scottish, indeed, British society and beyond the shores of the island of Ireland.
19. Campbell and Woods, 1986, p.18.
20. Ibid, p.13.
21. Wilson, 1988, pp.13-14.
22. Campbell and Woods, 1987, pp.11-26, Handley, 1960.
23. See Bradley, 1996, 2004 and 2006.
24. Ibid.

25. There are of course a number of conceptual problems when viewing the Irish in Scotland. For example, the significant number of marriages across communities invariably affects this concept while there is an ongoing academic debate regarding meanings of the term 'community'. However, for many, particularly in the towns and areas of the west of Scotland, where there are meaningful numbers (almost all who are of the Catholic faith) who owe their descent to Irish-born parents, grandparents and great grandparents, 'Irishness' is a clearly distinguishable culture and identity.

26. Rokkan and Urwin, 1983, p. 89.

27. The Celtic View, 3/2/99.

28. Interview G.A.A. employee 4/7/06.

29. Jay Raynor, The Independent on Sunday, 28/6/1992.

Chapter 18

The G.A.A. in Scotland today

For the G.A.A. in Scotland, a paradox exists in that a 'football' club, playing a sport marginalised and for so long banned by G.A.A. authorities in Ireland and amongst the Gaelic fraternity abroad, has for over one hundred years been a primary cultural vehicle for the Irish in Scotland. Although Irishness is a principal identity of Celtic Football Club and its support, this has been to the dismay of some traditionalists amongst the G.A.A. in Scotland. It might be argued that the culture around supporting Celtic has dominated in terms of Irishness, so much so that other Irish bodies and organisations have suffered numerically and in terms of loyalty, affinity and expression. However, paralleling this line of reasoning, Celtic Football Club has also allowed for the expression of Irish identity in circumstances and in a context where Irishness has been viewed with hostility and opposition. Pride in, as well as the maintenance and celebration of Irishness through Celtic Football Club, has partly allowed for, preserved and contributed to, the defence and creation of a cultural environment that allowed for the re-emergence of Gaelic football in Scotland amongst the second, third and fourth generation Irish during the late twentieth century. The cultural interaction and links between these two expressions of Irishness is demonstrated by the significant number of G.A.A. members in Scotland, including several members of the County Board, who have been, and who are active supporters of Celtic F.C. For G.A.A. members in Scotland who are also Celtic supporters, the views of one seems to capture the essence of what the club means to many of its support: 'Celtic might not play in Ireland, but they play for Ireland.[1]

Although a comparatively weak organisation, the history of the G.A.A. in Scottish society reflects that it has been an important focus of social, cultural and political identity for some of the diaspora in Scotland. The critical factor in the involvement of many of the Irish who have involved themselves with Gaelic sports in Scotland, particularly second, third and fourth generation, and especially those who have become most active, has been in viewing Gaelic sport as an expression of a distinctive Irish identity in Scottish society. Since 1984, the G.A.A. in Scotland has played a small, but notable role in maintaining and introducing ideas and images of Irishness amongst those with Irish antecedents. For some activists, it provides an authentic, incontestable manifestation of their Irishness.

> Those who play Gaelic games and organise its activities see in the G.A.A. a means of consolidating our Irish identity. The games to them are more than games. . . [2]

As in Ireland, Gaelic games for G.A.A. enthusiasts in Scotland:

> . . . epitomise the spirit and the personality and the character of the Irish more than anything. . . [3]

As with the example of Sam Maguire's life in Britain early in the twentieth century, for many G.A.A. activists in Ireland and amongst the diaspora, their's is a cultural and ideological commitment to 'the promotion of a national identity'.[4]

In addition, the purpose of individual involvement in a specific cultural context has been primary in linking current G.A.A. activists in Scotland (and amongst the Irish diaspora generally) with the Association in Ireland: this in a frame of reference that invokes its early years. For the Irish and those of Irish descent who have participated in Gaelic sport, this is evidence for and a manifestation of their Irish presence in Scotland, an Irish existence beyond the island of Ireland. The myths of descent, historical memories, territorial association with Ireland, and a sense of solidarity and community, has provided many G.A.A. activists in Scotland with their cultural and sporting motives. The G.A.A. in Scotland enables Irish ethnic and national consciousness to be maintained and expressed. With three quarters of a million adults in membership within Ireland and the diaspora, thousands of children and many more people tied simply by emotion or occasional sporting experience, the G.A.A. forms an important dimension of the Irish 'family' or diaspora, in addition to old and new conceptions of Irishness. It also helps give Irishness a distinctive and heterogeneous quality and outlook.

As in Ireland, the G.A.A. in Scotland contributes to a distinctive ethnic identity. This distinctiveness is a primary reason for the survival of the Association in Scotland as well as the rationale and motivation for those who maintain its existence as a valuable dimension of Irishness. The G.A.A. in Scotland provides an organisational locale for the idea of common descent, a shared history in Ireland and the perception and expression of common experiences in Scotland. It provides for a concrete link with the country of birth or origin. It is an expression of diversity and a symbol of identity.

In Ireland and elsewhere in the diaspora, the Association in Scotland has always incorporated political elements, facets, groups and individuals. Such politics have been ideological, dominated by Irish national culture and identities, idioms and manifestations. After all, these form the very core of the history and identity of the Gaelic Athletic Association. In this context, for some Gaelic sports activists, the G.A.A. has always provided a means to oppose British hegemony. For others not politically aware, conscious of or attracted by Irishness, political ideology and national, cultural and political identities, these are incidental and have little obvious meaning in relation to 'sport'.

Historically and in its contemporary setting, the culturally active and conscientious element within the G.A.A. membership have been primarily concerned with reawakening elements of the diaspora in Scotland to their Irish heritage, as well as maintaining, expressing and celebrating this. In this sense, apects of the character of the G.A.A. and Irishness in Scotland can be considered anti-racist in their counter-hegemonic purpose and design. The G.A.A. is viewed as a focus for Irishness in a situation where many people of Irish origin view themselves, and their previous generations, as being compelled to see Irishness in a negative light.

Allison notes that:

> sport can be the object of great emotion and that the sentiments which surround it are not necessarily neutral in respect of politics or, even if neutral, certainly not inert.[5]

In a practical sense and distinct from politics and culture, as in Ireland, much Gaelic activity in Scotland is concerned with fixtures, providing transport, coaching activities, methods of raising necessary finances and specifically in Scotland, with a lack of referees. Throughout the period since 1984, many clubs have struggled to meet fixtures and to maintain a cohesive and competitive club unit. Since the organisation's most recent revival in Scotland a number of clubs have quickly or slowly demised due to lack of leadership and difficulty in fielding enough players on a regular basis. A serious practical handicap going against the flourishing of Gaelic sports in Scotland has been in the way that players have been required to also be administrators, fund-raisers, managers, coaches, organisers, county officials and referees. Although this is characteristic of many amateur sports, including at the lower divisions of the G.A.A. in Ireland, the diminutive pool of volunteer activists in Scotland results in an even smaller number of people burdened with an excessive number of roles: an experience that is relatively unknown or is less problematic for those players who have also been soccer players or who have played other sports in Scotland. Irish Gaelic sport in Scotland is a minority sport, even amongst those of Irish descent. Gaelic sports persistently exist at a juncture where they could readily demise: they suffer from being invisible to the vast majority of the Scottish population, including those of Irish descent, and are susceptible to termination due to the departure of key players and activists.

Ironically, since the late 1990s as the G.A.A. in Scotland has also steadily raised its playing standards, including participation in British junior championship finals, players have also faded from football activities due to the increasing demands of more rigorous training and competition. Many such players, attracted to Gaelic football because of its Irishness, have been unable to sustain the athleticism or the required improvement in skills as proficiency and fitness levels have progressed.

The organisation of sport and its functions to society are important in relation to health, fitness and social interaction and these have been important to the G.A.A. in Scotland. Distinct from aspects of Irishness, the organisation of sport and its functions to society are important in relation to health, fitness and social interaction and, as for other sports, these have been important to the modern G.A.A. in Scotland and Gaelic sport generally. In relation to its development in Scotland since the late 1990s, within as well as outwith and beyond the multi-generational Irish diaspora in Scotland, Gaelic football has become one of a range of 'alternative' sports experienced and played in parts of Glasgow and Lanarkshire. In this light, it forms an aspect of a social and community response to the challenges presented by disadvantageous and detrimental lifestyles. The promotion of Gaelic football is one of a number of strategies pursued and used by educationists and social and cultural employees and activists to combat drug and alcohol abuse, promote healthy living and, in the regeneration of community in deprived and fragmented neighbourhoods.

However, at a time in Scotland when many sports appear to be encountering difficulties, including a lack of volunteers, falling particip-ation levels, modern sedentary lifestyles and other cultural changes (for example, drug and alcohol abuse), it is often the case that it is the Irish nature and Irish identities invoked by Gaelic sport which helps maintain its life in Scotland. Absent of images of community and a sense of Irish identity, culture and heritage, the G.A.A. in Scotland would not exist over one hundred years after the founding of the first club in Glasgow in 1897.

Though many individuals have departed the Gaelic sport scene since the 1980s, many thousands have also experienced and contributed to Gaelic games and therefore, to the expression of Irish cultural identity in Scotland in this time. Added to those who have been involved with the G.A.A. for all or periods of the recent revival, are those who have participated with now defunct teams as well as the many thousands of primary level schoolchildren, boys and girls, who Shotts Gaels, Mulroy Gaels, St Patricks, Sands MacSwineys, Beltane Shamrocks and Tir Conail Harps introduced to Gaelic games since the early 1990s. In the generation since the revival of the Gaelic Athletic Association in Glasgow in 1984, as much as twenty thousand individuals, children, adults, male and female, have experienced playing Gaelic sports in Scotland: the majority of whom were born in Scotland of Irish forebears, but also, hundreds of others with little or no ethnic connection to Ireland.

Despite being an historically small organisation in Scotland and, although largely peripheral to the Irishness of the vast majority of those of the immigrant diaspora, the G.A.A. and Gaelic sports have provided an important expression of Irishness for over one hundred years. Gaelic sport in Scotland is important to the history of sport in modern Scotland. Similarly, despite its frequent peripheral status to the wider Irishness of Scotland's Irish-born or Irish-descended community, the history of the G.A.A. is also an essential part the ongoing narrative of the Irish in Scotland.

1. Interview of Celtic supporters in Ireland, 2002.

2. G.A.A. Handbook, 1992.

3. Quoted by Liz Howard, Tipperary County Board, on Shinty: Sport of the Gael, BBC Scotland (television), 1993.

4. The Sam Maguire Cup, 1986.

5. Allison, 1986, pp. 1-26.

Appendix 1

Coiste Albain (Scotland)
Football Club Championship Winners 1985–2006

(formerly Glasgow Championship – beaten finalists in brackets).

1985	Clan na Gael, Hamilton	(Mulroy Gaels)
1986	St Patricks, Dumbarton	(Mulroy Gaels)
1987	St Patricks, Dumbarton	(Sands MacSwineys)
1988	Beltane Shamrocks, Wishaw	(Mulroy Gaels)
1989	Mulroy Gaels, Glasgow	(Sands MacSwineys)
1990	Sands MacSwineys, Coatbridge	(Mulroy Gaels)
1991	Sands MacSwineys, Coatbridge	(Dundee Dalriada)
1992	Dundee Dalriada, Dundee	(Mulroy Gaels)
1993	Dundee Dalriada, Dundee	(St Patricks)
1994	Dunedin Connollys, Edinburgh	(Dundee Dalriada)
1995	Mulroy Gaels, Glasgow	(St Patricks)
1996	St Patricks, Dumbarton	(Sands MacSwineys)
1997	Mulroy Gaels, Glasgow	(St Patricks)
1998	Mulroy Gaels, Glasgow	(Paisley Gaels)
1999	Sands MacSwineys, Coatbridge	(Mulroy Gaels)
2000	Mulroy Gaels, Glasgow	(Sands MacSwineys)
2001	Tir Conail Harps, Glasgow	(Dunedin Connollys)
2002	Glaschu Gaels, Glasgow	(Dunedin Connollys)
2003	Dunedin Connollys, Edinburgh	(Mulroy Gaels)
2004	Dunedin Connollys, Edinburgh	(Glaschu Gaels)
2005	Dunedin Connollys, Edinburgh	(Glaschu Gaels)
2006	Glaschu Gaels, Glasgow	(Dunedin Connollys)

Appendix 2

List of member clubs: Glasgow/Scotland since 1984

Ayrshire Gaels (1989-1990)
The wider cultural pursuits of Irish dancing brought into being the Saltcoats club, formally known as 'The Invincibles'. Following the fortunes of his daughters particip-ation with the Setanta School of Irish Dancing, John McCreadie began socialising in circles frequented by existing members of the G.A.A. The decision to begin a club took place at a St Patricks night function in 1989, the team making its competitive debut the following year.

McCreadie, whose forebears came to Scotland from Antrim and Dublin, along with his cousin, John Toal, Eamon Rankin (Dublin), Noel Hughes (Leix) and Michael McLaughlin (Donegal), gave birth to the new team. Noel Hughes also made his mark as a player with the side along with his sons, Joe and Noel. The playing of Irish-born team members was finally made up by Joe Tevenan (Dublin) and Joe Duffy (Donegal) as well as Tony Keane, a Sacred Heart Father from Dublin, based at his orders house in Kilwinning. On the whole, Saltcoats consisted mainly of Scottish-born Irish as well as a few players who had no Irish connections, including importantly for McCreadie, around four or five players who were not from a Catholic background.

The Ayrshire senior team lasted for one year whilst the minor set-up for around eighteen months. The main reason for the dissolution of the club was the onset of Sunday afternoon live televised soccer. With a majority of Gaels players also Celtic soccer supporters, football matches on Sunday's involving the Glasgow Club steadily eroded attendances at matches on Sundays.

Beltane Shamrocks, Wishaw (1986-1996)
Leading on from his success in Hamilton, Eamonn Sweeney inaugurated another club based around his new parish of St Aidan's, Wishaw, called after a local area in the town. By the end of 1986 Wishaw played a few competitive matches while in 1987 they took part in all competitions.

Father Sweeney provided the Shamrocks with most of its direction. Sweeney's efforts to play and participate to the full reflected his love of the game. It was not unknown for Sweeney to serve 1.45pm Sunday Mass as Catholic chaplain at Law Hospital in Wishaw, then dash to play a game at 3.00pm, often wearing a football strip over his priestly garb, and often to places as far afield as Dumbarton and Edinburgh.

With Sweeney being the club's only Irish-born player, and with ex-professional footballer Eric Rooney training the team, Beltane experienced their most successful ever period during their first season. Players Derek McStay, cousin of the famous Celtic soccer player Paul, Tom Delaney, Paul Toner, Billy Williamson, Tony Hogan, Jim Cusack and James Connolly, assisted the St Aidan's curate, as well as parishioner Brian Brawley, in reaching the Championship final of 1987. Playing the match at Wishaw Sports Centre, Shamrocks found themselves ten points down with five minutes remaining. The game turned around when the Wishaw side drew level to force extra time, subsequently winning convincingly due to superior fitness.

Eamonn Sweeney learned a number of lessons concerning the demise of his previous club in Hamilton. He recognised difficulties relating to player strength, training and finance with most Gaelic clubs. He also believed that he had to inculcate a sense of affinity with Gaelic sports in Ireland. Despite his best efforts, as well as those of such as Brawley and Andy Smith, a local player, and aside from a strong bank balance in place, Beltane Shamrocks also folded after Sweeney left to become parish priest of St Michaels Moodiesburn, to east of Glasgow. Having struggled to field fifteen players for their first match of the season in Coatbridge, Beltane failed to field for the rest of the year. By 1997, it was officially announced that the club had demised.

Clann na Gael, Hamilton (1985-1987)
The driving force behind Gaelic football activities in the 1980s was Ballycroy Mayo priest, Eamonn Sweeney. During his ministry as a curate in St Ninian's Hamilton, Father Sweeney founded a local club to participate in the new Glasgow football league inaugurated in 1985. Matches were played at nearby Strathclyde Park were the pitch was named Loftus Park, after the then president of the G.A.A. in Ireland Sweeney's fellow Mayoman, Mick Loftus.

Made up almost entirely of local players recruited from his parish and nearby Holy Cross School, once again Clan na Gael proved the Scottish-born Irish could excel at Gaelic football. In its first season, Hamilton won its way to the Championship final to become victors in the first such competition held in Scotland for a generation. The Hamilton team celebrated its win with a trip to play in Ireland in September 1995. Challenge matches were held in Achill Island and Dublin whilst the latter location also witnessed the visitors from Scotland attend the All-Ireland final between Kerry and Dublin. Orla O'Hanrahan, third secretary at the Irish Embassy in London, and Tom Walsh, well-known Irish cultural activist from Liverpool, presented the Championship winning trophy to Hamilton at the end of the year. The involvement of such figures reflected the growing profile of the game in Scotland by 1985.

Added to his Gaelic football activities Father Sweeney encouraged a number of Gaelic clubs as well as Catholic parishes to participate in B & I Ferries sponsored 'Its a Knock-out' Festivals of 1985. Clan na Gael won the Scottish regional competition to lose in the finals held at Mossney Holiday Camp in County Louth. During this period the Hamilton team was well served by Paul Gallacher, Mick Cassidy (Mayo) and Kevin Brady.

Despite success, Clan na Gael failed to maintain their status as an active club on the departure of Father Sweeney for a new parish in Wishaw, Lanarkshire. Individuals such as Pat McFadden and Brian Molloy attempted to keep active, but by 1987 the club had become extinct.

Coatbridge Gaels, (1991-1994)
Formed as Sands MacSwineys Boys Club, this minor football team eventually took the name Coatbridge Gaels. Advertising in nearby schools and Catholic Churches, enough interest was generated to introduce hundreds of youngsters to the game during the early 1990s.

The team was coached in the main by senior Sands players Joe Bradley, Peter Elliott and Eddie O'Neil (the latter two also managing the team), who in turn were assisted by Stephen Traquair, Pat McHugh and Joe Fagan. The team entertained clubs from Ireland and visited Skerries in County Dublin as well as Maghera, County Derry: it also visited Ni Pairsaig in Manchester in late 1993. By 1996/97 a number of players who has been introduced to the game in the early 1990s began to break into the Sands MacSwineys team and remained with the club into the new millennium. Sands MacSwineys minor development was reinvigorated in 2004.

Cuchulains, Glasgow (1992-1993)
This short-lived club was set by Tommy Doherty whose family originated from Dungloe, County Donegal. Doherty's son was involved with the ailing Pearse Harps team

when he decided to give birth to another club. Tommy Main and John Nally of the County Board along with Rory Campbell, whose sons also played with Pearse Harps, assisted with the organisation of Cuchulains.

Cuchulains coaches found inspiring a team in Pollock extremely difficult in an exceptionally poor and deprived area of the city where discipline and organisation meant little to many of the children involved with the club.

Although training and coaching began and several matches were played little became of Cuchulains. Much of the club's organisation was handicapped when Doherty decided to return to Donegal. John Nally subsequently moved the team to a more receptive eastern Glasgow base and renamed the new club, Michael Davitts.

Derryvale, Glasgow (1993-1995)
Previously involved with Pearse Harps, Tommy Millar began to organised a youth set under the banner of Derryvale, the club name recognising his roots in Derry. Although operating during a high point in the success of youth football the club was also inhibited by drawing its players from the same area in Glasgow as Tir Conail Harps and Mulroy Gaels.

However, Derryvale made one notable impact on the game in successfully attracting players from the local Asian community while also making its mark in nearby non-denominational schools, thus drawing players from outwith the Irish community in the south side of Glasgow.

Dundee Dalriada (1989)
Initial efforts to begin a Gaelic football team in Dundee were instigated by Peter Mossey from Gortin, County Tyrone, whilst a student at the City's university in the late 1970s and early 1980s. Though failing, due mainly to a lack of oppostion, it was another set of students from Ireland who resurrected the idea and began a club in late 1989: a time when the G.A.A. had re-started in Glasgow and the environment was more favourable to developing the game. Declan Curran from Tyrone, Barry Grimes and Ian Hannon from Armagh canvassed around the university as well as in the Lochee district of the city, an area known locally as 'little Tipperary', due to a high percentage of its inhabitants originating from Ireland, especially in the late nineteenth century.

With some assistance from the university sports council an area of ground at Lochee Park was secured for training and playing. Almost all of the players of the developing club were Irish-born students, with the exception of two former Sands MacSwiney players who had moved to Dundee to work, Paul Lennon and James 'Jinky' Gilmour. 1993 All-Ireland final squad member with Derry, Stephen Mulvenna (formerly Antrim), also played for the team during its formative period. The first match played by the club was a successful challenge match against Beltane Shamrocks in Wishaw.

In January 1990 a meeting was hosted by Father Eugene O'Sullivan at St Francis Friary, Dundee, chaired by Peter Mossey and attended by two other well-known stalwarts of the Irish community in the area, Willie Dowds (Donegal) and John Joe Moran (Kerry) as well as the Dundee students. The new club was formally founded at the meeting. Father O'Sullivan from Kilkenny, also player and founder in 1973 of Tayforth Shinty Club, was elected first president. In February 1990 the club was accepted for membership of the Glasgow County Board.

Until this point in time the club had been known as Dundee Fianna. However, with the latter part of the name meaning soldiers/warriors, some players believed that this could prove contentious due to its possible political connotations by those hostile to things Irish. By a narrow vote the name was changed to the less contentious and Celtic connotive, Dundee Dalriada: Dalriada being the name of the Gaelic tribe who had came to the south west Argyllshire coast of Scotland from Ireland during the 6th century, and, who later contributed to the founding of the Kingdom of Scotland.

Since playing its first competitive match in early 1990, periodically, Dundee proved one of the best sides in Scotland during the early years of the most recent resurgence. However, with a club consisting almost entirely of Irish-born university-based players this also gave those who live in the area numerous problems in sustaining an adequate side throughout the season.

Subsequent to being beaten in the final at Pearse Park by Sands MacSwineys in 1991, Dundee won the County Championship in 1992 and 1993. In 1993, after defeating Birmingham's John Mitchells' and Southern Gaels of Poole, Dundee reached the final of the British Provincial Club Championship, losing 0:15 to 1:10 to one of the best clubs in England during the same period, Tir Conail Gaels of London. For its efforts in becoming the first club from Scotland to win two Provincial matches in recent decades, Dundee were recipients of an Irish Post club award in 1993. Remarkably, the Dalriada panel of that year contained several players from the village of Glin, County Limerick, all students attending University in Dundee. This included two Ryans', two Reidys', O'Connor, Lynch, Healy (RIP) and Currivan.

Since 1997, despite the occasional recruitment of several high profile players through the universities of Dundee and Abertay, in particular Seamus Mulgrew and Declan McCrossan, both of who have since won All-Ireland medals with Tyrone, Dundee did not achieve any further honours. In 2003 the club was unable to field for any matches though it has recently extended its recruitment to include students from Aberdeen and has assisted to a very small extent.

Dunedin Connollys, Edinburgh (1988)
Edinburgh has contained a large immigrant Irish population since the middle of the nineteenth century. However, it took until the late 1980s for this to be reflected in the emergence of a Gaelic football club. The club took its description from the Gaelic name for the city and from one of the leaders of the 1916 Easter Uprising in Ireland, Edinburgh-born of immigrant parents, James Connolly.

During his photographic travels covering Irish events in Scotland, the Irish Post's correspondent in Scotland, Tommy Main, found himself an important link between a number of groups and individuals. Developing an interest in Irish cultural activities, Main was also to promote some of these activities by way of encouragement and publicity: thus emerged Dunedin Connollys. After much prompting, Tony Haughey from Belfast and Benny McGinley began to think seriously about starting a club to compete in the growing Gaelic scene in the west. In 1988, at a regular Irish function held at the St Mary's Star of the Sea Catholic Parish in the Leith area of the city, also attended by Father Sweeney of Beltane Shamrocks and Clan na Gael Gaelic clubs', some of these individuals came together to form the Edinburgh team. Among them was a strong Donegal and Mayo representation. In 1989 the club played its first competitive match.

Most of the original players of the Connollys club lived in the Liberton/ Gilmerton area of the city. However, by 1991/92 the club succeeded in attracting a number of Irish-born players who lived in the city or who attended Edinburgh or Heriot Watt Universities. With a growing Irish-born base, and therefore a more experienced network of Gaelic footballers, in 1991 the club began to emerge from its youthful beginnings. In that season it reached the semi-final of the Championship and rested at fourth in the league competition. Players such as Neal O'Doherty from Kildare, Oliver McKenna, Ciaran McLarnon and Mick Mulvihill all began to make their mark within the game in Scotland. During the same season the club also secured use of a home park in the grounds of St Augustine's School in the Broomhouse area..

In a final played at the home of Beltane Shamrocks in Wishaw in 1992, Connollys won its first trophy, the O'Fiaich Cup, defeating rivals Mulroy Gaels 0:11 to 1:7. During 1993 the club continued to gain a strong current of players through links with Heriot Watt University. A number of former players with the Heriot Watt-based Gaelic football team decided to live and work in the area and the local side reaped the benefits. In 1994 an influx of players made a marked difference to both the depth and quality of the Edinburgh squad. Connollys reached the final of the 1994 Championship and after drawing the first match against Dundee, the Edinburgh side easily won the replay at Pearse Park by 3:10 to 0:5. Connollys also won both the County seven-a-side tournament and the Pearse Cup in 1996.

By 1996 the club contained none of the players or members who had instigated Dunedin Connollys. By then the club had attracted manager Frank Gallagher from St Brendans of London, under his management previously winners of the prestigious London County Championship. Gallagher hailed from Ballyshannon in County Donegal. In the same year, positive relations with Duddingston-based Edinburgh rugby team, Portobello FP, led to the decision to move to that club's large playing area where a pitch was set aside for Gaelic football.

During the period 2001-2006 Dunedin Connollys reached all six Scotland Championship finals loosing to Tir Conail Harps in 2001 and Glasgow Gaels in 2002. Connollys won three in a row between 2003 and 2005 before losing their sixth final to Glaschu Gaels after extra-time in 2006.

In 2004 Dunedin Connollys played St Peters of Manchester in the British Junior Club Final. The game went to extra time twice after both teams could not be separated and only the last kick coming in the 1twentieth minute of the game could separate them, with a final score line of Dunedin Connollys 1:12 St Peters 1:13. A similar story ensued in 2005 when Dunedin Connollys played London's Harlesden Harps in the British Final: Connollys again losing by a single goal.

A Dunedin Connollys women's team was founded by Suzanne and Peter Dillon when they moved from Manchester to Edinburgh in 1998. This team struggled at first to compete against the universities of Aberdeen, and Robert Gordon but with an influx of new players to complement the old they became more competitive and won the Scotland Championship three years in a row.

Glaschu Gaels (1999)

Glaschu Gaels GFC was formed in 1999 after the amalgamation of two local sides, Glencovitt Rovers and Paisley Gaels. The amalgamation was a result of problems with too few players on the part of each club. Matched resources and the energy of G.A.A stalwarts Paul Gallagher, Jimmy Kelly, Michael Hollinger and Charlie McCluskey, saw the new club develop quickly.

Since its foundation Glaschu has been among the most successful clubs in Scotland, winning the County's annual Seven-a-Side tournament, O'Fiaich Cup, Davit

Shield, Pearse/Morkan Cup and the League twice in 2004 and 2005. The Gaels won its first championship in 2002 while it has also featured in several other finals. The club also won the Championsip in 2006 and were beaten in the British Junior Championship at the semi-final stage by eventual winners, Fulham Irish. Glaschu has retained a majority of Irish-born players in its ranks since its foundation, a smaller number being Scottish-born of Irish descent, while the team has also included a handful of players from France and Australia.

The club has taken part in high profile challenge games against the Derry and Down senior county squads and the 'Underdogs' team from Ireland managed by Jarlath Burns. Visits by GAA stalwarts Mickey Moran, Mickey Harte, Peter Canavan, Sean Marty Lockhart and Anthony Tohill, as well as Uachtarans' Sean McCague and Sean Kelly, have also further enhanced the profile of Glaschu Gaels. The establishment of a ladies team in 2006, combined with a strong relationship with Glasgow University men and ladies GFCs has offered the club strong foundations. Glaschu also began a minor development scheme in early 2007.

Glencovitt Rovers, Clydebank (1991-1998)

Former St Patricks player and assistant, Jimmy Kelly, returned from the eastern side of Glasgow to live in the western Glasgow conurbation of Clydebank in the early 1990s. Kelly's roots lay in County Antrim and his return to Clydebank was the catalyst for the re-emergence of Gaelic football in the area in March 1991. Donegal-born players, Danny Friel and Colm Doherty were important as the new club began to recruit and participate in competitions. Locals like Mark Docherty, Stuart McDonald and Mick Timoney were introduced to the game by Kelly and until 1997 remained important players for the club.

Although there had been a G.A.A. club, Roger Casements, in the area a number of decades previously, the current club's name was chosen when Colm Doherty on visiting his home in Donegal, returned with a couple of footballs courtesy of a former schoolmaster. The school was located in Glencovitt, Ballybofey, and that was the name adopted by the new Clydebank team.

After briefly using facilities in the shape of a converted rugby pitch in Dumbarton the council in Clydebank eventually provided local playing facilities at Strauss Avenue. Although facilities were poor and the pitch was extremely small, the club was finally locally based. Glencovitt raised its profile with the visits of, as well as visits to, Dublin-based G.A.A.

club, Good Council of Drimnagh. The Dublin club was subsequently requested to play in a combined rules Hurling/Shinty match to celebrate the centenary of the West Highland Railway Line in Scotland in 1994. Assisted by John Gallagher, during the period 1993-94, Kelly attempted to introduce youth football to the area. Although this was a short venture due to a lack of support, several of the young people involved retained a degree of interest in the sport.

In 1996, amidst local government restructuring, Glencovitt lost its playing facilities. Having no home venue or training facilities proved a major problem for the club. For Kelly, the resultant travel costs and lack of local sponsorship and focal point took a heavy toll on the progress of Gaelic activities in the area. Nonetheless, Glencovitt did manage to win its first trophy in 1996. The 'B' Championship was won using Doherty, Docherty, McDonald and Timoney, as well as others such as Richard Gough (Australia), Ciaran McCrory (Tyrone) and Paddy Keenan (Louth).

Michael Davitts, Glasgow (1993-1996)

Inspired by John Nally, who had previously gained playing and organisational experience with Pearse Harps and Cuchulains, and assisted by Charlie McCluskey and Tim Porter, Davitts emerged in the wake of the demise of Cuchulains in Pollock. As Cuchulains demised their existing resources were transferred to Davitts.

Davitts was an under-age club which participated in primary school competition as well as under-12 football. The club drew substantially from St Anne's Primary School located near Celtic Park, trained at Glasgow Green and played fixtures at a number of venues in the city. The club were noted for the first modern appointment of an Irish language officer in John Lee from Dublin, also sponsor of the team and owner of local Irish bar, The Squirrel.

Mulroy Gaels, Glasgow (1984–2005)

Mulroy were re-invigorated in 1984/85 by Seamus Sweeney, a Glasgow-based contractor who originated from Fanad in County Donegal. The first side was made up of players mainly from Rathmullen and Fanad in Donegal as well as a number of Scottish-born players whose roots lay in the same area of north-west Ireland. Players, Neil Boyle, Liam Sheridan, John Crowe and Mick Shiels remained with Mulroy for most of the period of Glasgow's Gaelic football resurgence.

Former player, Eddie Canning (Donegal) was a significant contributor to Mulroy's youth policy during the first half of the 1990s, although this initiative faded due to a lack of assistance on the part of other adult members of the club. Nonetheless, during this time the club enjoyed success at minor level.

Although having failed in a number of Championships finals and semi-finals, Mulroy proved to be one of the most successful clubs in recent G.A.A. history in Scotland. The club has won every trophy available including the Championship in 1989, 1995, 1997 and 2000, as well as recording a remarkable run of successive league titles between 1985 and 1994. In 1989, Mulroy lost narrowly to St Vincents of Luton in the British Provincial Championship.

Paisley Gaels (1994-1998)
Formed by ex Pearse Harps player Michael Hollinger, Paisley Gaels joined Glencovitt as one of the new teams in the flourishing G.A.A. scene in Scotland of the early 1990s.

Along with Hollinger, underage players Tony McLaughlin, Shane Quinn, Paddy Campbell and Ian McGugan assisted in the launch of the new club. The first chair of the club was the late Rory Campbell and with students from Paisley University, Karl Friel (Tyrone), Declan Bradley (Derry) and John Barrett and Cliff Byrne (Kildare), the club was successfully launched. New additions followed including local brothers Eamon and Martin Brennan, whose family hail from Laois, and Paul Gallagher from Arranmore in County Donegal.

Paisley experienced early success with the winning of the B Leagues and B Championships while several of the squad represented Scotland in the first two International tournaments held at Belfield in Dublin. A highlight for Paisley Gaels came in 1998 when the club won the Pearse Cup.

The loss of several players, a downturn in Irish migration and a detrimental change in local student fees, led to Paisley considering changing its name to Glaschu Gaels in an attempt to survive by attracting more players from a bigger catchment area. This change also resulted in an invite to the management and committee of the recently folded Glencovitt club to amalgamate with Paisley. This move proved to be a positive decision as the new Glaschu side benefited from the new facilities at Paisley University's sports ground at Thornley Park to become one of the best Gaelic football clubs of the new millennium.

Pearse Harps, Glasgow (1985-1993)
Mainly as a result of the efforts of numerous G.A.A officials like Father Eamonn Sweeney who advertised for young potential footballers and Mick Moran who helped train those who went along regularly to Pearse Park on Sunday afternoons, Pearse Harps were constituted as a club during 1984-85. Managed by Joe Bradley the club began competing during the season of revival in 1985. Based at Pearse Park in Cambuslang, Pearse drew its players from various parts of Glasgow as well as having a strong representation from Coatbridge.

Links with games in the 1960s and 1970s came through the efforts of Pat O'Callaghan from Armagh who played football in the area for three decades. O'Callaghan also played beside his son who became one of the most able of the young breed of second-generation Irish playing Gaelic sports while players like Eddie McHugh from Tyrone likewise had participated in earlier decades. Other early stalwarts of Pearse were Frank Farmer, Joe Reilly, George Crawford, Joe Bradley, Jim McInness and Martin Docherty. Pearse became a club that offered solid competition for the other teams. Its greatest moment arriving in season 1986 when the club won the Pearse Cup (formerly Summer Cup) against rivals Mulroy Gaels at Pearse Park, a ground shared by both sides.

During September of 1986 Pearse Harps visited Letterkenny in Donegal, Maghera in Derry, Crossmaglen in Armagh and Ardoyne in Belfast to play local sides. As a result of preparations over several months, on returning to Scotland, the Coatbridge-based players set up another club in their own area: an amicable arrangement in an attempt to develop the game further. Around the same time, a group of young men were motivated to begin football training in the Garngad district of the city. The hope was that they might join with Pearse Harps to form a strong city-based club. A number of these players were drawn towards Gaelic football because of its perceived political connotations. However, after a handful of training sessions only one or two pursued any further contact with Gaelic sports.

Although the departure of Coatbridge players initially had an effect on the numbers involved with Pearse, it maintained its status and enjoyed a presence for a number of years. During the early 1990s the club, influenced by Tommy Main, John Nally, Mick Hollinger and Mick Moran, began a number of minor teams. These sides proved to be successful and attractive in relation to numbers and the game's promotion. However, the ambitions of the minor section were not matched by those at senior level: eventually Pearses minor administrators began to look for other avenues to pursue its potential. This culminated in the evolution of Tir Conail Harps. However, this also had a detrimental effect upon Pearse and by 1993 Pearse Harps found it increasingly difficult to field full strength sides and this led to the club's demise during the season.

Saint Malachys, Chapelhall and Calderbank (1992-1993)

St Malachys were inspired by Armagh man Sean Duffy who was a player in Glasgow during the 1960s and 1970s as well as being Secretary of the County Board of Scotland in the early 1990s. Involving mainly primary school children from the local Corpus Christi and St Aloysius schools in his adopted Chapelhall and Calderbank areas of Lanarkshire, St

Malachys played several challenge and competitive matches. However, the club demised when Duffy departed the County Board in late 1993.

Saint Patricks Dumbarton (1984-2002)

As was the pattern in Glasgow G.A.A. matters, the first games held in 1984 were of a mixed team nature and these games often involved players from Dumbarton. In Dumbarton, schoolteacher Eamonn Cullen started the St Patricks Gaelic football club, taking its name from the town's Catholic school that was to provide the main base for the club's future. Along with fellow St Pat's teachers Donald Hoey, Jimmy Grimes and Gerry Carey, as well as Jimmy Kelly, future founder of Glencovitt in Clydebank, and relying initially on friends from the local Leven Rugby Club, St Patricks began to field a regular side. The first squad of players, almost all Scottish-born of Irish descent, to represent the town in Gaelic football, consisted of:
Steven Mairs, Michael Docherty, Paul Ferguson, Jimmy Grimes, Andy Young, Donald Hoey, Gary Casey, Saul Docherty, Sean McDonald, Gerry Carey, Martin Hannan, Eamonn Cullen, Paul McGrogan, Bobby Neil and Robert Floyd.

By the time the club won the Scotland County championship in 1996 (its last major honour), beating Sands MacSwineys in the final played at Coatbridge, Cullen remained manager, Mairs was the goalkeeper and Docherty had by then regularly captained the club. This was also the first occasion when a club in Britain had won a championship final with a team totally comprising local-born players, although other clubs had on occasions only one or two players from outwith the immediate locale.

St Patricks role of honour was impressive. Championship winners three times, league winners once and runners-up seven times; four times O'Fiaich Cup (Autumn Cup) winners, and British Provincial Championship semi-finalists in 1987 and 1996. In 1988 and 1993, Dumbarton District Council elected St Patricks as its team of the year. St Patricks players also represented the Glasgow and Scotland County Boards on numerous occasions. This particularly so in the case of minor football, an area where the club pursued an active policy. For a period the club also had the best council-owned G.A.A. facility in Scotland, at Posties Park, Dumbarton. St Patricks played its last game against Sands MacSwineys at the beginning of season 2003 but failed to field after that, in the main due to a dwindling player base as well as an ageing panel of participants.

In their time St Patricks made regular visits to Ireland to play football. Donegal, Dublin, Kildare, Louth, Meath, Galway and Mayo have all formed part of the St Patricks itinerary over the years. St

Patricks also hosted clubs from Kildare, Louth, Dublin, Donegal, Leeds, Huddersfield, Leicester and Luton.

Saint Vincents, Glasgow (2006-2006)
St Vincents was a short-lived club that arose after a split between members of Tir Conail Harps in Glasgow. The young side, led mainly by Jimmy Joe Patton (Tir Conail) and Danny Hurley (Mulroy Gaels), played two matches in early 2006 only to be heavily beaten in both.

Sands MacSwineys, Coatbridge (1986)
Founded by Joe Bradley whose roots lie in the Irish midlands and west Ulster, and assisted by Joe Reilly whose people immigrated to Glenboig in Lanarkshire from County Westmeath and Baltinglass in County Wicklow, Sands developed from Pearse Harps in Glasgow. As the numbers of Coatbridge players began to increase with the Glasgow-based club some believed they could give birth to a local-based team in an area previously renowned for its Gaelic sports activities.

Sands MacSwineys first full season was marked with success in reaching the 1986 final of the Glasgow Championship only to lose to St Patricks. By 1988 Sands won its first major trophy winning the O'Fiaich Cup beating Beltane Shamrocks at Pearse Park: the same trophy was won in 1996 and 1998. Sands won three league titles in a row between 1998 and 2000. The Coatbridge team won the Championship in 1990, 1991 and 1999, were runners-up in 1986, 1989, 1996 and 2000, and also won the Pearse Cup in 1990 and 1998. Sands have been regular contributors to the County team and initiated its own minor set-up in the early 1990s. The club also initiated a successful local schools tournament during 1996 and 1997 and this involved approximately one hundred and fifty boys and girls from local primary schools. By the new millennium the Coatbridge side had once again became involved in the wider community sending coaches into local schools and providing coaching for hundreds of youngsters.

Sands MacSwineys have been frequent visitors to Ireland over the years. Since jointly visiting Maghera County Derry, Crossmaglen County Armagh, Letterkenny County Donegal and Belfast County Antrim with Pearse Harps in 1986, Sands have visited clubs in Gortin, County Tyrone, Killarney, County Kerry, Nobber, County Meath, Ballybay, County Monaghan, Ardoyne and Falls Road, Belfast. Sands have also been frequent visitors to Watty Grahams Glen, Maghera, County Derry, who have also reciprocated with visits to Coatbridge. The club has also hosted a number of teams from Mayo, Derry, Monaghan and Leeds as well as the County Sligo senior squad as part of the County Board of Scotland's centenary celebrations in 1997. In 1994, Micky Moran, coach of 1993 All-Ireland football winners

Derry, brought the Sam Maguire trophy to Coatbridge to display to local football enthusiasts. The club celebrated its existence as the longest established team in Scotland since 1984 with a dinner dance at St Patrick's Church Hall Coatbridge in May 2006.

Shotts Gaels (1996-1999)
The village of Shotts in west Lanarkshire was introduced to Gaelic sports during the period 1994/95. Martin McCulloch and Thomas Larkin, formerly footballers with Beltane Shamrocks, inaugurated children's football, camogie and a senior football club that finally made its debut in April 1997.

Supported by a few local businessmen as well as North Lanarkshire Council, Shotts Gaels were able to make headway due in the main to the aid of the local Catholic parish priest and council at Saint Patrick's Church. During the summer of 1996, several club members attended a summer camp organised by St Peter's G.A.A Club of Dunboyne, County Meath. Around the same time the Club was guest of the Dublin County Board, while it also hosted a camogie/shinty tournament involving the local club, Tir Conail Harps, Oban Shinty Club as well as Lochgilphead Shinty Club.

Tir Conail Harps, Glasgow (1994)
Tir Conail was formed in 1994. Other gaels in Scotland admire the efforts, organisation and resources of this club that has strong links with Donegal. The involvement of Tommy Main with the Gaelic scene in the mid to late 1980s proved a boon to the G.A.A. Increasingly drawn towards Pearse Harps in Glasgow, and recognising that youth would provide the future of Gaelic sports in the west of Scotland, Main began to recruit young members to form a number of youth sides in the Pearse Harps set-up. However, with a lack of organisation and little to show for their efforts with Pearse, Main, along with some interested individuals, decided to form their own club.

Drawing mainly on the South side of Glasgow, recruitment by the Tir Conail Club invariably tapped an area rich in recent Donegal immigration, thus the name of the new club. Beginning with a variety of under-age teams, by 1997 Tir Conail contained under-10, 12, 14 and 16 squads as well a young side who entered the senior grade for the first time: overall around twelve teams. By 1997 the club operated with membership numbers of between 150 and 200. This also included a camogie side that played regular matches against Lochgilphead Ladies Shinty Club in Argyll, as well as an aspiring ladies Gaelic football team. In November 1997, Tir Conail won its first trophy, the B League in a final against Paisley Gaels.

Few Gaelic clubs travel to other counties to compete in Gaelic competitions in a similar fashion to Tir Conail. In 1995 its dominant youth side travelled to England to win the under-12 British Provincial

Championship. The Glasgow club set a British Provincial record in the same year having teams in three provincial finals. As a result, the club was awarded a prestigious Irish Post Club of the Year Award in 1997. In 1998 the club achieved a similar feat at under-16 level.

The club has also competed in matches all over Britain and Ireland. In Britain the club won the St Brendans seven a side tournament in Manchester in 1996. Visits to Ireland have included Ballycroy County Mayo, Ballycastle County Antrim and Falcarragh County Donegal. At McHale Park, Castlebar in 1996, the Glasgow players were defeated by Dicksboro of Kilkenny in the final of the prestigious annual 'Peil na nOg' competition in Ireland. Tir Conail has also hosted a number of clubs from both Ireland and Britain.

Much of the success of the Tir Conail club is due to the efforts of some of their members to draw on as wide a local population as possible, although many players remain young Irish-born migrants working in Glasgow or at university there. As a result, since the mid 1990s numerous schools in Glasgow have become accustomed to members coaching their pupils, among them St Fillan's, St Jude's, St Ann's, St Bridget's, St Teresa and St Cuthbert's, St Patrick's, St Bride's, Holy Cross, Annette St and Victoria primary schools.

In the late 1990s and into the new millennium the club set out a development plan which enabled it to purchase a minibus and secure an office base at St.Patrick's Primary school in Anderston, Glasgow. During this period the club also became a registered charity. Towards the end of the plan an extensive fund-raising drive and funding from the Irish government (DION) enabled the club to appoint Tommy Main as full time Development and Health Promotion Officer. In the new millennium the club has won the senior Scotland football Championship (2001), the League (2001, 2002), has been awarded Glasgow City Council Community Club of the Year (2001) and witnessed some of its members receive special awards including the Youth Sports Coach Award Sports Council for Glasgow 2005.

Appendix 3

THE GAELIC ATHLETIC ASSOCIATION IN THE REST OF BRITAIN

The G.A.A. in England has also recognised that its games cannot exist without the involvement of members of the Irish diaspora there. In presenting the London County Board (the largest individual unit outside of Ireland) with a special award to mark its centenary of 1996, the Irish Post believed:

> the formation of the London Minor Board has proved to be a remarkable success, and has ensured that the board can look ahead to another 100 years of promoting our native games.

London has played a significant role in G.A.A. history and Michael Collins, Liam MacCarthy and Sam Maguire, figures involved in the struggle for Irish independence in the early part of the twentieth century, all played Gaelic sports in London. The London championship winning teams participate in the national league competitions held in Ireland every year from October to April.

In recognition of the existence of the London Board for one hundred years, the G.A.A. held its annual convention there in 1996. London Chair, John Lacey, stressed his view that the holding of this major event in centenary celebrating London was 'a manifestation of the policy to embrace all Gaels and an effort to enable all exiles to be part of the movement initiated in Thurles in 1884'. Nevertheless, despite an ongoing emphasis on youth development, and primarily as a result of a significant decline in Irish emigration, ten years after this convention Gaelic sports had declined in London: the county containing ten hurling and twenty four football clubs, a drop of around 40% in ten years.

Gaelic games have developed not only in London but in other parts of England. Previously organised as a division of the London County, in 1960 the Herefordshire County Board was formed by a small group under the leadership of its first founder chairman, Father Jerome O'Hanlon, a native of Lombard in Cork. The first board had nine clubs in affiliation. In 1995 Herefordshire's junior hurlers won their first All-Ireland title beating Tyrone in the final played at Luton. By 2006 Hertfordshire had ten functioning G.A.A. clubs as well as a minor policy.

Gloucestershire formed its first Gaelic hurling club 'The Emmetts' in 1928. Although it was the early 1950s before it began to make a mark, the first county board was founded in the area in 1949. Experiencing many years of struggle to survive, like a number of other counties, Gloucestershire turned its attentions towards youth development as the number of young Irish immigrants arriving in Britain began to fall, although by 2006 this policy was once more experiencing decline. Gloucestershire had four clubs by this time.

St Annes of Keighley, who had previously played its matches in Lancashire due to a lack of local competition, was one of the original Gaelic clubs in Yorkshire that in 1949 formed the first County Board spearheaded by Father Donal Stritch. In the same year famous Yorkshire Gaelic clubs like Hugh O'Neills and St Brendans of Leeds were also founded. Struggling to survive as Irish immigration to Yorkshire began to diminish in 1977, the County gave birth to a minor board that proved to be a key to endurance. By the new millennium the county sustained six football clubs while the G.A.A. in Yorkshire remains a focus for local Irish identity.

Since the 1990s in the English midlands Gaelic sports people have also been active. Ex-patriot communities throughout Birmingham, Coventry, Wolverhampton, Leicester, Derby, Nottingham, Northampton and Corby have traditionally supported football and hurling clubs there. The 1920s saw the birth of Gaelic games in this county whilst the oldest surviving club has been John Mitchell's of Birmingham, founded in

1940. The Warwickshire County Board was formed in 1944. By 2006 Warwickshire contained thirteen football clubs, one hurling club and two others that played both codes.

In Lancashire the first club was founded in 1895 under the auspices of the Liverpool County Board that subsequently became Lancashire. Activity to promote under age Gaelic games during the 1970s in Lancashire meant that by early in the new millennium, the county was sustaining eight Gaelic clubs including one hurling side.

Although many clubs in Britain struggle, many others are centres of vibrancy and are a significant focus for Irish social and cultural identities. By the new millennium the G.A.A. in Britain remained the largest Irish community organisation in the country.

Appendix 4

UNIVERSITY GAELIC GAMES IN SCOTLAND

Most of the initial efforts to establish Gaelic football in Scotland took place at Dundee University as the number of students from Ireland began to increase during the 1980s and 1990s. However, the efforts of Peter Mossey from Gortin in Tyrone were hampered due to a lack of opposition. Barry Grimes, Ian Hannon (Armagh) and Declan Curran (Tyrone), faced a similar problem when they managed to start a team in 1990 but again there was no university opposition and Dundee operated mainly as a club team within the local county scene in Scotland.

Nevertheless, in the 1992/1993 academic year Dundee University students were invited to a tournament held on the Newcastle League University Campus. In one sense, this was the start of university football in Scotland. Importantly, this contact also reflected the fact that there were other students from Ireland trying to do similar things for Gaelic football in other parts of Britain. Such contact was to prove crucial in the development of university Gaelic sport in Britain. On the occasion of Dundee's visit to Newcastle, they were beaten by St Mary's Strawberry Hill in the competition final.

The University of Dundee were also the only representatives from Scotland at the first Birmingham finals held at Pairc Na hÉireann in March 1993 when they were beaten in the semi finals. On their return to Birmingham in March 1994 however Dundee University and Heriott Watt both travelled from Scotland and met in the semi finals, which

Dundee won by a point: subsequently Dundee went on to win the 1994 British University Football Championship.

By the1993/1994 academic year a Scottish Universities League was underway though only four teams competed: Dundee emerged as league champions. The 1994/1995 league campaign included five teams, which included the agricultural college at Auchincruive in Ayrshire: again Dundee proved successful.

In February 1995 at Dawson Park Dundee, the first Scottish Universities Gaelic Football Championship was held with three competing teams; Dundee, Heriot Watt and Paisley Universities: Heriot Watt emerging victorious. The following year the tables were turned with Heriot Watt winning the league and Dundee winning the 1996 Championship. In 1996/1997 both Aberdeen and Robert Gordon's University joined the league along with the University of Glasgow. With the University of Abertay gaining university status there was a nine team league for the first time.

In the following year, when the University of St Andrews applied for affiliation, it was agreed to split into two leagues, east and west. In that year, University of Abertay had a large increase in the number of students from Ireland and consequently contained a stronger team, subsequently winning both the league and championship. There was strong rivalry in Dundee from 1996 through to 2003 during which time University of Abertay contested three British University football finals, eventually winning the trophy in 2001. However, they failed to secure the Scottish Championship loosing to Dundee in the final.

As with Gaelic sports activities generally in the diaspora, the strength of university Gaelic football teams has varied with the intake of students from Ireland which in turn has depended on courses and degrees offered. Traditionally civil engineering has attracted students from Ireland and the discontinuation of this course at University of Abertay and a simultaneous uptake of this course on the part of Napier University has seen a corresponding change in the fortunes of these two institutions with regard to both football and hurling in in the new millennium.

University Gaelic football in Scotland is predominantly played by students from Ireland for all or part of their tertiary education. However, over the years there have been instances of second, third and fourth generation Irish as well as Scots, English and other nationalities playing Gaelic games: Andrew Smith of Robert Gordons University became a British All Stars Football goalkeeper and John Barr (Robert Gordons), a native Scot and Shinty player, won a 2006 University All Star award in Hurling.

In the new millennium hurling has acquired a minor foothold in British Universities, the main initiative coming from the Scottish Universities. Hurling activity is limited to two competitions per year, a seven aside and a fifteen a-side championship, the latter dedicated to the memory of a former Glasgow University student Michael O'Leary from Callan, County Kilkenny. The initiation of hurling at the Scottish Universities was mainly through Shinty when Father Eugene O'Sullivan encouraged University of Abertay to join the Universities Shinty League in the 2001/2002 academic year. Remarkably the Abertay team won both the Universities Shinty League and the Littlejohn Cup (championship) in that academic year with a team of Irish hurlers. Since then Scottish teams have dominated the British Universities hurling scene, only broken by University of Glamorgan who won the Michael O'Leary Trophy in 2005.

Appendix 5

BRITISH UNIVERSITIES GAELIC ATHLETIC ASSOCIATION

The first attempt to initiate a British colleges Gaelic Football tournament was in 1989 only for it to lapse the following year. It was again revived in 1991 by the University of Crewe and Alsager who hosted and won a five team competition. A trophy for the competition was donated by Crewe in memory of Kevin Fallon, a deceased student who played for Crewe and who was also a member of the 1991 organising committee. In 1992 Newcastle/Sunderland Universities jointly organised and hosted a competition that attracted ten teams and was played on two adjoining converted rugby pitches at Newcastle. The winner of the tournament was St Mary's, Strawberryhill from London who beat Scotland's University of Dundee in the final.

The competition was played at Pairc na hÉireann Birmingham for the first time in 1993: Swansea winning this twelve team competition. The Paul Montague trophy was introduced to British University football at that competition and was awarded to the tournament's best player. Paul Montague from Beragh Co. Tyrone joined Aston University in Birmingham in September 1992. Hhaving set up the Aston University Gaelic Football team he did not have the opportunity to see the fruits of his labours as he died of meningitis during his first year at University.

In 1994 the tournament returned to Pairc Na hÉireann where sixteen teams participated: the victors this time being the University of Dundee. The competition was cancelled in 1995 due to an unfortunate and uncharacteristic heavy fall of snow on the Thursday night before the weekend of the competition rendering the pitches unplayable. Consensus on a later date in 1995 could not be achieved. There was a review of the competition after this incident and because of the number of teams expressing an interest in participation and the dependence on one 'all or nothing' annual competition, it was agreed that the competition ought to be regionalised.

In liaison with Paddy Johnson, Uachtaràn of the British Provincial Council, the regional system was introduced in 1996 and two qualifiers from each of four regions contested that years Championship: this tournament was won by Liverpool John Moores while St Mary's Strawberryhill won the trophy in 1997 and 1998. Around this time negotiations took place to have the University games in Britain recognised by Comhairle Ardoideachais and admit a British Universities team to an Irish-based Universities tournament.

In 1999 at Birmingham St Mary's Strawberry Hill were beaten in the semi-final by Liverpool John Moores who went on to beat University of Abertay in the final. The University of Abertay gained revenge on Liverpool in the 2000 semi-final, but lost to St Mary's Strawberryhill in the final. As British University Champions, St Marys subsequently took the 2000 Trench Cup semi-final to extra time. In 2001, Abertay University were British Champions, but were unfortunate in that the Trench Cup was cancelled due to the 'Foot and Mouth' crisis in Britain and Ireland. St Mary's regained the title again in 2002 and retained it in 2003: on both occasions at the expense of Liverpool John Moores. The historic breakthrough came in 2004 when St Marys won the British Universities title and the Trench Cup in Ireland, the first non-Irish-based university Gaelic football team to win a significant G.A.A university trophy on Irish soil. In 2005 they defended the British title, but lost the Trench semi-final. In 2006, Liverpool John Moores gained their third British Universities title.

Appendix 6

GAELIC ATHLETIC CLUBS IN SCOTLAND 1897- 2007

Ayrshire Gaels (Saltcoats)

Beltane Shamrocks (Wishaw)

Brian Boru (Blantyre)

Cavan Slashers (Glasgow)

Clan na hÉireann (Glasgow)

Clan na Gael (Hamilton)

Clan na Gael (Glasgow)

Clan na Ghaeldhilge (Springburn, Glasgow)

Coatbridge (Hurling club)

Coatbridge Gaels (Coatbridge)

Cuchulains (Glasgow)

Cuchulains (Dumbarton)

Cuchulains (Glasgow)

Dalcassians (Carfin)

Derryvale (Glasgow)

Desmonds (Wishaw)

Dr Crokes (Dumbarton)

Dundee Dalriada (Dundee)

Dunedin Connollys (Edinburgh)

Eire Og (Gorbals, Glasgow)

Eire Og (Port Glasgow)

Eire Og (Coatbridge)

Emmets (Hamilton)

Eugene O'Growneys (Glasgow)

Fag an Bealagh (Carfin)

Falkirk (Gaelic football and hurling club)

Faughs Hurling Club (Glasgow)

Fianna Éireann (Glasgow)

Finn MacCumhails (Glasgow)

Fintan Lalors (Govan, Glasgow)

Fitxgeralds (Glasgow)

Glasgow (Camogie Club)

Glaschu Gaels (Glasgow)

Glencovitt Rovers (Clydebank)

Granuailes (Glasgow)

Hibernians (Glasgow)

Lambh Dearg (Cleland)

Lambh Dearg (Kinning Park, Glasgow)

Lord Edwards (Motherwell)

McCurtain Gaels (Springburn, Glasgow)

Mulroy Gaels (Glasgow)

O'Tooles (Kinning Park, Glasgow),

Owen Roe O'Neill (Coatbridge)

Paisley Gaels (Paisley, 1940s & 1950s)

Paisley Gaels (Paisley, 1990s)

Patrick Sarsfields (Coatbridge)

Padraic Pearses (south-east Glasgow)

Pearse Harps (Glasgow, 1920s),

Pearse Harps (Glasgow, 1980s)

Raparees (Glasgow)

Red Hugh O'Neills (Glasgow)

Roger Casements (Paisley)

Rosses Rovers (Glasgow)

Round Towers (Scotstoun, Glasgow)

Rovers (Cambuslang, Glasgow)

Sands MacSwineys (Coatbridge)

Sarsfields (Greenock)

Shotts Gaels (Shotts, Lanarkshire)

South O'Hanlons (Glasgow)

St Brendans (Glasgow)

St Colmcilles (Edinburgh)

St Eunans (Clydebank)

St Francis (Falkirk)

St Malachys (Chapelhall & Calderbank)

St Margarets (Airdrie)

St Marks (Carntyne, Glasgow)

St Patricks (Dumbarton)

St Patricks (Greenock)

St Patricks (Wishaw)

St Vincents (Glasgow)

Taras (Gourock)

Tara Harps (Bridgeton, Glasgow)

Thomas Davis (Motherwell)

Tir Conail Harps (Glasgow)

Wishaw Shamrocks (Wishaw).

Note: Apart from university and school teams mainly found in Glasgow and Coatbridge since the early 1990s, seventy-five Gaelic Football and/or Hurling Clubs have existed in Scotland since 1897: the vast majority, thirty-seven, have originated in the metropolitan area of the city of Glasgow. Smaller towns and villages that have contained Gaelic clubs include Coatbridge with six, Wishaw four and Dumbarton three. Since 1897 other cities, towns and villages in Scotland have given rise to one or two clubs.

Appendix 7

Contacts

Gaelic Athletic Association Coiste Albain

Billy Nugent (Solicitor to the GAA in Scotland)

Telephone 0141 554 1016. E-Mail wnugent@alexjt.co.uk

Fr Eamon Sweeney

Telephone 01236 606808 E-Mail stpatcoat@blueyonder.co.uk

Newspapers referred to

Airdrie and Coatbridge Advertiser
Cork Free Press
Daily Record
Daily Mail (Scotland)
Derry People
Donegal Democrat
Fermanagh Herald
Glasgow Examiner
Glasgow Observer and Catholic Herald
Glasgow Star and Examiner
Guardian
Herald

Irish News
Irish Post
Irish Weekly (Scotland)
Kilkenny Journal
Mirror (Eire)
Observer (Sunday)
Scottish Catholic Observer
Scotland on Sunday
Scotsman
Star (Eire)
Sun
Sunday Mail
Sunday Scot
Sunday Times

G.A.A. PUBLICATIONS USED

Doire: A History of the G.A.A. in Derry, 1984.

G.A.A. Official Guide, 1994.

Gaelic Athletic Association: a century of service, 1984-1994, Published by the G.A.A., Dublin, 1984.

Hogan Stand.

John Mitchells Gaelic football club: The story of the G.A.A. in Liverpool. Centenary Year 1984-1984, Cumann Luthchleas Gael. Printed by Merchant Stationers Ltd, Liverpool, 1984.

The Sam Maguire Cup: Cumann Luthcleas Gael, Dublin, 1986.

Gaelsport G.A.A. Youth Annual: Gaelic Athletic Association, 1984.

Cead: A celebration of the London G.A.A., 1896-1996. Published by the London County Board in association with the Irish Post, Middlesex, 1996.

Also referred to

Cumann Luit Cleas Gaodeal, Ard Comairle Miontuirisci (Minutes of Central Council G.A.A.).

Bibliography

Adams G: *The Politics of Irish Freedom*, Brandon Books, Kerry, 1986.

Adams G: *Before the Dawn: An Autobiography*, London, Heinemann, 1996.

Allison L: *The Politics of Sport*, Manchester University Press, 1986.

Anderson B: *Imagined Communities: Reflections on the Origins and Spread of Nationalisms*, Verso, London 1991.

Audrey S: *Multiculturalism in Practice: Irish, Jewish, Italian and Pakistani migration to Scotland*, Ashgate, Aldershot, 2000.

Bairner A: Sport, *Nationalism and Globalisation: European and North American Perspectives*, State University of New York press, New York, 2001.

Bairner A (Ed): *Sport and the Irish: histories, identities, issues*, University College Dublin Press, Dublin, 2005.

Beresford D: *Ten Men Dead*, Grafton Books, London, 1987.

Boyle R and Haynes R: 'The Grand old game': football, media and identity in Scotland, in, *Media, Culture and Society*, vol 18, no 4, pp.549-564, 1996.

Boyle R and Lynch P (Edts): *Out of the Ghetto: The Catholic Community in Modern Scotland*, John Donald, Edinburgh, 1998.

Boyle R. and Haynes R: *Power Play: Sport, the Media and Popular Culture*, London, Longman 2000.

Bradley J M: *Ethnic and Religious Identity in Modern Scotland*: Avebury, 1995.

Bradley J M: Intermarriage, Education, and Discrimination, in T M Devine, edt, *St Mary's Hamilton: A Social History 1846-1996*, John Donald, Edinburgh, pp. 83-94, 1995.

Bradley J M: Profile of a Roman Catholic Parish in Scotland, in *Scottish Affairs*, No 14, Winter, pp. 123-139, 1996.

Bradley J M: Identity, Politics and Culture: Orangeism in Scotland, in *Scottish Affairs*, No 16, Summer, pp. 104-128, 1996.

Bradley J M: Facets of the Irish Diaspora: 'Irishness' in twentieth Century Scotland, in, *Irish Journal of Sociology*, vol 6, 1996.

Bradley J M: British and Irish Sport: The Garrison Game And The G.A.A. In Scotland, *The Sports Historian*, 19, 1, pp.81-96, 1999.

Bradley J M: The Irish Parading Tradition: Following the Drum in T G Fraser, edt, *Wearing the green: a history of nationalist demonstrations among the diaspora in Scotland*, pp.111-128. Macmillan Press, 2000.

Bradley J.M: The Patriot Game: Football's Famous Tartan Army, *International Review for the Sociology of Sport*, 37, 2, pp.177-197, 2002.

Bradley J M: Unrecognised Middle-Class Revolutionary?: Michael Cusack, Sport and Cultural Change in Nineteenth-Century Ireland,' *The European Sports History Review*, vol 4, pp.58-72, 2002

Bradley J.M., Maguire J., Jarvie, Mansfield L: *Sport Worlds: A sociological perspective*, Human Kinetics, USA 2002.

Bradley J M: Images of Scottishness and Otherness in International Football, *Social Identities: Journal for the Study of Race, Nation and Culture*, 9, 1, pp.7-23 2003.

Bradley J M: *Celtic Minded: essays on religion, politics, society, identity and football*, Argyll Publishing, Argyll Scotland, 2004.

Bradley J M: *Celtic Minded 2: essays on Celtic Football Culture and identity*, Argyll Publishing, Argyll Scotland, 2006.

Brah A., Hickman M.J. & Mac an Ghaill M: *Thinking Identities: Ethnicity, Racism and Culture*, London, MacMillan Press 1999

Brown S J: Outside the Covenant: The Scottish Presbyterian Churches and Irish Immigration, 1922-1938, in *The Innes Review*, Volume XL11, No 1, Spring, pp. 19-45, 1991.

Campbell B, McKeown L & O'Hagan F (edts): *Nor Meekly Serve my Time: The H Block Struggle 1976-1981*, Beyond the Pale Publications, Belfast, 1994.

Campbell T and Woods P: *The Glory and The Dream, The History of Celtic FC, 1887-1986*: Mainstream Publishing, 1986.

Canning Rev B J: *Padraig H Pearse and Scotland*. Published by Padraig Pearse Centenary Commemoration Committee, Glasgow, 1979.

Carey T: *Croke Park: A History*, The Collins Press, Cork, 2004.

Cassidy L: Faded Pictures from Irish Town, in *Causeway*, pp. 34-38, Autumn, 1996.

Conroy J: '"Yet I Live Here. . ." A Reply to Bruce on Catholic Education in Scotland, *Oxford Review of Education,* Vol.29, No.3, Sept pp.403-412, 2003.

Celt: Sporting Nationalism: A look at the political origins of the G.A.A., *IRIS*, no 4, Nov, pp. 25-26, 1982.

Celt: Changing the Rules: A look at the political origins of the G.A.A., *IRIS*, no 5, March, pp. 30-31, 1983.

Coakley J J: *Sport in Society: Issues and Controversies*, Mosby, Colerado, 1990.

Coakley, J J: *Sport in Society: Issues and Controversies*, USA, Irwin, McGraw-Hill, 1998.

Cooney J: *Scotland and the Papacy*, Paul Harris, Edinburgh, 1982.

Cronin M: Defenders of the Nation? The Gaelic Athletic Association and Irish Nationalist Identity, in *Irish Political Studies*, 11, pp. 1-19, 1996.

Cronin, M: The Nationalist History of the Gaelic Athletic Association and the English influence on Irish Sport, in *The International Journal of the History of Sport*, Vol 15, No 3, pp. 36-56, 1998.

Curtice J and Gallagher: in Jowell R, Witherspoon S, Brook L, edts: *British Social Attitudes; the 7th report*: Social and Community Planning Research, Gower Publishing, pp. 183-216, 1990.

Curtis L: Ireland *The Propaganda War*: Pluto Press, 1984.

Curtis L: *Nothing But The Same Old Story: The roots of Anti-Irish Racism*: Published by Information on Ireland, 5th edition, 1988.

Darby P: Gaelic games and the Irish immigrant experience in Boston, in *Sport and the Irish: histories, identities, issues*, Ed A Bairner, University College Dublin Press, Dublin, pp.85-101, 2005.

Davis G: *The Irish In Britain 1815-1914*: Gill and Macmillan, 1991.

De Burca: *The G.A.A: A History of the Gaelic Athletic Association*, Cumann Luthchleas Gael, Dublin, 1980.

De Burca M: *The Story of the G.A.A*, Wolfhound Press, Dublin, 1990.

Devine T M, (edt): *Irish Immigrants and Scottish Society in the Nineteenth and Twentieth Centuries; Proceedings of the Scottish Historical Studies Seminar*: University of Strathclyde, 1989/90, John Donald Publishers Ltd, 1991.

Devine T M (edt): *St Mary's Hamilton: A Social History, 1846-1996*, John Donald, Edinburgh, 1995.

Devine T.M: (Edt) *Scotlands Shame: Bigotry and Sectarianism in Modern Scotland*, Edinburgh: Mainstream 2000.

Dunning, E: *Sport Matters: sociological studies of sport, violence and civilization*, London, Routledge, 1999.

Feehan J M: *Bobby Sands and the Tragedy of Northern Ireland*, Mercier Press, Dublin and Cork, 1984.

Feeney S: *Conradh na Gaelige (Gaelic League) in Scotland, 1895-1995: A centenary celebration* (published by the author) 1995.

Finley R J: Nationalism, Race, Religion And The Irish Question In Inter-War Scotland, in, *The Innes Review*, Vol. XLII, No 1, Spring, pp. 46-67, 1991.

Finn G P T: Racism, Religion and Social Prejudice: Irish Catholic Clubs, Soccer and Scottish Society – 1 The Historical Roots of Prejudice in *The International Journal of the History of Sport*, 8, 1, pp. 72-95, 1991.

Finn G P T: Racism, Religion and Social Prejudice: Irish Catholic Clubs, Soccer and Scottish Society – 11 Social Identities and Conspiracy Theories, in *The International Journal of the History of Sport*, 8, 3, pp. 370-397, 1991.

Finn G P T: Faith, Hope and Bigotry: Case Studies of Anti-Catholic Prejudice in Scottish Soccer and Society; in *Scottish Sport in the Making of the Nation: Ninety-Minute Patriots*, Leicester University Press, 1994.

Finn G P T: Sporting Symbols, Sporting Identities: Soccer and Intergroup Conflict in Scotland and Northern Ireland, pp. 33-55, in, *Scotland and Ulster*, Edt by I S Wood, Mercat Press, Edinburgh, 1994.

Finn G P T: Series of papers lodged with Jordanhill Library, Strathclyde University on the role of conspiracy in anti-Catholicism in Scotland and Northern Ireland, 1990-1994.

Flanagan C: *Sport in a Divided Society: the Role of the G.A.A. in Northern Ireland*, Unpublished post-graduate thesis, Faculty of Humanities, University of Ulster, 1991.

Gallagher C: *The Gaelic Athletic Association in London*. Research project held by the Irish Studies Centre, University of North London, 1993.

Gallagher T: *Glasgow The Uneasy Peace*: Manchester University Press, 1987.

Gallagher T: *The Catholic Irish in Scotland: In Search of Identity* in T M Devine (edt) Irish Immigrants and Scottish Society in the Nineteenth and Twentieth Centuries; John Donald Publishers Limited, 1991.

Giulianotti R: Built by the Two Varelas: The Rise and Fall of Football Culture and National Identity in Uruguay, in Finn G P T & Giulianotti R, *Football Culture: Local Contests, Global Visions*, Frank Cass, London (originally from Galeano E, (1997). Football: in Sun and Shadow, London, 2000.

Gilley S & Swift R, edts: *The Irish in the Victorian City*: Croom Helm, London, 1985.

Greely, A & McCready M: Does Ethnicity Matter, in *Ethnicity*, Vol 1, No 1, April, pp91-108, 1974.

Gruneau R. & Whitson D: *Hockey Night in Canada*, Toronto, Canada, Garamond Press 1993.

Handley J E: *The Irish in Scotland*: John S Burns & Sons, Glasgow. (this book incorporates both The Irish in Scotland 1798-1845 and The Irish in Modern Scotland. 1943 & 1947. Cork University Press), 1964.

Handley J E: *The Celtic Story*: Stanley Paul, London, 1960.

Hargreaves J, (edt): *Sport, Culture and Ideology*, Routledge, 1982.

Hassan D: Still Hibernia Irredenta? The Gaelic Athletic association, Northern Nationalists and Modern Ireland, *Culture, Sport and Society*, 6, 1, Spring, pp.92-110. 2003.

Hayes M: Myths and Matches, in *Causeway, cultural traditions journal*, Summer, 1997.

Healy P: *Irish Nationalism and the Origins of the Gaelic Athletic Association*. Unpublished Dissertation, History B.A. degree, University of North London, 1994.

Hickman M: *A study of the incorporation of the Irish in Britain with special reference to Catholic state education: involving a comparison of the attitudes of pupils and teachers in selected Catholic schools in London and Liverpool*, unpublished PhD, University of London, 1990.

Hickman M: *Religion, Class and Identity. The State, the Catholic Church and the Education of the Irish in Britain*, Avebury, Aldershot, 1995.

Hickman M: Reconstructing deconstructing 'race': British political discourses about the Irish in Britain, *Ethnic and Racial Studies*, Vol.21, No.2, pp.289-305, 1998.

Hoberman J: *Sport and Political Ideology*, Heinemann, London, 1984.

Holmes M: Symbols of National Identity: The Case of the Irish National Football Team, in *Irish Political Studies*, 9, pp. 81-98, 1994.

Holt R: *Sport and the British. A Modern History*, Oxford, 1986.

Holt R: Sport and History: The State of the Subject in Britain, in *Twentieth Century British History*, vol 7, No 2, pp. 231-252, 1996.

Horne J, Tomlinson, A, Whannel, G: *Understanding Sport*, London, E & F N Spon, 1999.

Hughson J: The Croatian Community, in *Sporting Immigrants*, Edts Philip A Mosely, R Cashman, J O Hara and Weatherburn, Walla Walla Press, Australia, pp.50-62, 1997.

Humphries T: *Green Fields: Gaelic sport In Ireland*, Weidenfield and Nicolson, London, 1996.

Hutchinson R: *Camanachd: The Story of Shinty*, Mainstream Publishing, Edinburgh, 1989.

Inglis J: The Irish In Britain: A Question Of Identity, in *Irish Studies in Britain* No 3, Spring/Summer 1982.

Isajiw W. W: Definitions of Ethnicity, in, *Ethnicity*, vol 1, no 2, July, pp 111-124, 1974.

Jacobs S L: Language death and revival after cultural destruction: reflections on a little discussed aspect of genocide, *Journal of Genocide Research*, 7, 3, pp423-430, 2005.

Jarvie G, Walker G (edts): *Scottish Sport in the Making of the Nation; Ninety Minute Patriots*, Leicester University Press, 1994.

Jenkins R: *The thistle and the grail*, MacDonald and Co, Glasgow, 1983.

Jones R and Moore P: 'He only has eyes for the Poms: Soccer, Ethnicity and Locality in Perth, WA', *Ethnicity and Soccer in Australia*, O'Hara J (ed), ASSH, no 10, pp.16-32, 1994.

Jones R L: The Black Experience within English Semi-professional Soccer, *Journal of Sport and Social Issues*, vol 26, no 1, pp47-65, 2002.

Kee R: *The Most Distressful Country*, volume one of the Green Flag, Quartet Books, London, 1976.

Kendrick S: Scotland, Social Change and Politics, in, *The Making of Scotland: Nation, Culture and Social Change*, D McCrone, D Kendrick and P Straw (edts), Edinburgh University Press, 1989.

Kircaldy J: Irish Jokes: No Cause For Laughter, *Irish Studies in Britain*, No 2, Autumn/Winter 1981.

Kinealy C: *This Great Calamity: The Irish Famine 1845-52*, Gill and Macmillan Ltd, 1994.

King, J. E: Dysconscious Racism: Ideology, Identity, and Miseducation in R. Delgado and J. Stefancic (eds) *Critical White Studies: Looking Behind the Mirror*, Philadelphia, Temple University Press, pp.128-132, 1997.

Longley E: Paths to the academy, *Fortnight*, p. 26, December 1996.

Logue P (ed): *Being Irish: Personal reflections of being Irish today*, Oak Tree Press, Dublin 2000.

Mandela N: *Long Walk to Freedom: the Autobiography of Nelson Mandela*, Little, Brown & Company, London, 1994.

Mandle W F: The Irish Republican Brotherhood and the beginnings of the Gaelic Athletic Association, *Irish Historical Studies*, xx, 80, pp. 418-38, 1977.

Mandle W F: *The G.A.A. and Irish Nationalist Politics*, Helm, Gill and MacMillan, Dublin, 1987.

Maver I. The Catholic Community in Scotland in the Twentieth Century in T.M. Devine & R.J. Finley (eds), *Scotland in the twentieth Century*, Edinburgh University Press, Edinburgh, pp.269-284, 1996.

Miller D: (ed) *Rethinking Northern Ireland, Culture, Ideology and Colonialism*, Addison Wesley Longman, Essex 1998.

Mitchell J: Religion And Politics In Scotland, Unpublished paper presented to *Seminar on Religion and Scottish Politics*, University of Edinburgh 1992.

Mitchell M.J: *The Irish in the West of Scotland 1797-1848: Trade unions, strikes and political movements*, John Donald Ltd 1998.

Muirhead, Rev. I. A: Catholic Emancipation: Scottish Reactions in 1829 *Innes Review,* 24, 1, Spring, 1973.

Muirhead, Rev. I. A: 'Catholic Emancipation in Scotland: the debate and the aftermath,' *Innes Review*, 24, 2, Autumn, 1973.

Mullan M: Opposition, Social Closure, and Sport: The Gaelic Athletic Association in the nineteenth Century, *Sociology of Sport Journal*, 12, pp. 268-289, 1995.

Murray B. *The Old Firm: Sectarianism, sport and society in Scotland* John Donald, Edinburgh 1984.

Murray B. *Glasgow's Giants: 100 years of the Old Firm* Mainstream, Edinburgh 1988.

Murray B. *Bhoys, Bears and Bigotry: The Old Firm in the New Age* Mainstream, Edinburgh 2003.

Murray R: *The SAS in Ireland*, The Mercier Press, Cork, 1990.

McPherson, B D, Curtis, J E, & Loy J W: *The Social Significance of Sport*, Human Kinetics, Illinois, 1989.

Mac an Ghaill M: British Critical Theorists: The Production of the Conceptual Invisibility of the Irish Diaspora, *Social Identities*, vol 7, no 2, pp.179-201, 2001.

Mac an Ghaill M. & Haywood C: Young (male) Irelanders: postcolonial ethnicities expanding the nation and Irishness, *European Journal of Cultural Studies*, Vol 6, 3, pp.386-403, 2003.

McCaffrey J. Roman Catholics in Scotland in the nineteenth and twentieth centuries, in *Records of the Scottish Church History Society*, 21, 2, 1983 MacLennan H D: *Shinty: 100 Years of the Camanachd Association*, Balnain Books, Nairn, 1993.

MacLua, B: *The Steadfast Rule: a history of the G.A.A. ban*, Press Cuchulainn Ltd, Dublin, 1967.

MacSwiney T: *Principles of Freedom*, Buffalo, 1975.

McFarland E W: *Protestants First: Orangeism in nineteenth Century Scotland*, Edinburgh University Press, 1990.

Nixon H.L. & Frey J.H. *A Sociology of Sport* London, Wadsworth 1996.

O'Ceallaigh S: *Story of the G.A.A.*, Published by Gaelic Athletic Publications, Limerick, 1977.

O'Conner K: *The Irish in Britain*, Torc, Dublin, 1970.

O'Connor U: *Skylark Sing Your Lonely Song: an anthology of the writings of Bobby Sands*, Mercier Press, Dublin & Cork, 1982.

O'Farrell P: *Ireland's English Question*, New York, 1972.

O'Hearn D: *Bobby Sands: Nothing but an unfinished song*, Pluto Press, London, 2006.

O'Hehir M: *The G.A.A. 100 Years*, Gill and MacMillan, Dublin, 1984.

O'Malley E: *On Another Man's Wound*, Anvil Books Ltd, Dublin, 1979.

O'Malley P: *Biting at the Grave: The Irish Hunger Strikes and the Politics of Despair*, The Blackstaff Press, Belfast, 1990.

O'Tuathaigh M A G: The Irish in Nineteenth Century Britain: Problems of Integration, pp. 13-36, in Gilley and Swift, *The Irish in the Victorian City*, 1985.

Parkes P: Indigenous Polo and the Politics of Regional Identity in Northern Pakistan, pp43-67, in Clancy, J. *Sport, Identity and Ethnicity*, Berg, Oxford, 1996.

Phiney J S, Horenczyk G, Liebkind K, Vedder P, Ethnic Identity, Immigration, and Well-Being: An Interactional Perspective, *Journal of Social Issues*, Vol 57, no 3, pp493-510, 2001.

Phoenix E: 'G.A.A.'s Era of Turmoil in Northern Ireland', *Fortnight*, pp.8-9, 17 December 1984.

Puirseal P: *The G.A.A. in its time*, Published by the Purcell Family, Carrigeen, Dublin, 1982.

Quinn J: *Ulster Football and Hurling: The Path of Champions*, Wolfhound Press, Dublin, 1993.

Reid I: Nationalism, Sport and Scotland's Culture, in, *Scottish Centre Research Papers in Sport, Leisure and Society*, vol 2, 1997.

Reid I A: *Shinty, nationalism and cultural identity, 1835-1939: a critical analysis*, unpublished PhD thesis, 2000.

Rowan P: *The Team That Jack Built*, Mainstream, Edinburgh, 1994.

Rouse P: The Politics of Culture and Sport in Ireland: A History of the GAA Ban on Foreign Games 1884-1971. Part One: 1884-1921, in, *The International Journal of the History of Sport*, vol 10, no 3, pp. 333-360, 1993.

Rowe D and Wood N (edts): Editorial of *Media, Culture and Society*, vol 18, no 4, 1996.

Ryall T: *Kilkenny: The G.A.A. Story*, Published by The Kilkenny People, Kilkenny, 1984.

Sands B: *One Day in My Life*, Mercier Press, Dublin, 1983.

Schermerhorn, R A: *Comparative Ethnic Relations: A Framework for Theory and Research*, Random House, New York, 1970.

Schlesinger P: Media, the Political Order and National Identity, in *Media, Culture and Society*, vol 13, no 3, pp. 297-308, 1991.

Short C: *The Ulster G.A.A. Story*, Published by Comhairle Uladh CLG, printed by R&S Printers, Monaghan, 1984.

Smith A & Porter D: *Sport and National Identity in the Post-War World*, Routledge, London, 2004.

Sugden J and Bairner A: 'Northern Ireland; Sport in a Divided Society', in, Allison L, *The Politics Of Sport*, pp. 90-117, Manchester University Press, 1986.

Sugden J. and Bairner A: *Sport, Sectarianism and Society in a Divided Ireland*, Leicester University Press, Leicester, 1993.

Walker G and Gallagher T, (edts): *Sermons and Battle Hymns; Protestant Popular Culture in Modern Scotland*, Edinburgh University Press, 1990.

Walter B., Morgan S., Hickman M.J. & Bradley J.M: Family Stories, public silence: Irish identity construction amongst the second-generation Irish in England, *Scottish Geographical Journal*, Special Edition on 'The Fate of 'Nations' in a Globalised World', Vol.118, No.3, pp.201-218, 2002.

Walls P. & Williams R: Sectarianism at work: Accounts of employment discrimination against Irish Catholics in Scotland, *Ethnic and Racial Studies*, Vol.26, No.4, pp.632-662, 2003.

Walter B, S Morgan, M J Hickman and J M Bradley, Family Stories, public silence: Irish identity construction amongst the second-generation Irish in England, *Scottish Geographical Journal*, Special Edition on 'The Fate of 'Nations' in a Globalised World', Vol 118, No 3, pp.201-218, 2002.

Walvin J: *The People's Game: The History of Football Revisited*, Edinburgh, Mainstream. 1994.

Werbner P. Our Blood is Green: Cricket, Identity and Social Empowerment among British Pakistanis, *Sport, Identity and Ethnicity*, Ed by J Clancy, Berg, 1996, pp.87-112, 1996.

Wilson B: Celtic, *A Century with Honour*, Willow Books, William Collins Publications, Glasgow, 1988.

Wilson D: Changed Utterly, *Fortnight*, pp. 5-6, October 1981.

Wilson J: *Politics and Leisure*, Unwin Hyman, Boston, 1988.

Whelan K: The Geography of Hurling, *History Ireland*, pp. 27-31, Vol 1, No 1, 1993.

Index